Trails of Historic New Mexico

"Arrival of the Caravan at Santa Fe" from Josiah Gregg's
Commerce of the Prairies, published in 1844 (Library of Congress).

Trails of Historic New Mexico

Routes Used by Indian, Spanish and American Travelers through 1886

HUNT JANIN *and*
URSULA CARLSON

McFarland & Company, Inc., Publishers
Jefferson, North Carolina, and London

McFarland has published eight books by Hunt Janin, including *Claiming the American Wilderness: International Rivalry in the Trans-Mississippi West, 1528–1803* (2006) and *Fort Bridger, Wyoming: Trading Post for Indians, Mountain Men and Westward Migrants* (2001; paperback 2006).

The maps in this book were drawn by Hunt Janin, Ursula Carlson and Daria Tavoularis.

LIBRARY OF CONGRESS CATALOGUING-IN-PUBLICATION DATA

Janin, Hunt, 1940–
    Trails of historic New Mexico : routes used by Indian, Spanish and American travelers through 1886 / Hunt Janin and Ursula Carlson.
    p.   cm.
    Includes bibliographical references and index.

    ISBN 978-0-7864-4010-8
    softcover : 50# alkaline paper ∞

    1. Trails — New Mexico — History. 2. Trade routes — New Mexico — History. 3. New Mexico — History, Local.
I. Carlson, Ursula, 1943– II. Title.
F796.J33 2010
978.9'01—dc22
                                          2009040833

British Library cataloguing data are available

©2010 Hunt Janin and Ursula Carlson. All rights reserved

No part of this book may be reproduced or transmitted in any form or by any means, electronic or mechanical, including photocopying or recording, or by any information storage and retrieval system, without permission in writing from the publisher.

Front cover: Pecos Pueblo ©2010 Shutterstock

Manufactured in the United States of America

McFarland & Company, Inc., Publishers
  Box 611, Jefferson, North Carolina 28640
    www.mcfarlandpub.com

To the memory of
Señora Doña María Gertrudis Barceló
(c. 1800–1852)

*At a time and place when Hispanic women played
virtually no role in public life, she rose from
abject poverty to riches and high social status
during the 1830s and 1840s as the proprietor of
a well-known gambling hall in Santa Fe.*

Acknowledgments

We could not have written this book by ourselves. Here we would like to extend our thanks to the scholars and friends who have so kindly given us advice and encouragement. They include Kim Bevins, Nancy Coggeshall, David Dary, Patricia Etter, Harlan Hague, Jarom McDonald, Reid Miller, Frank Norris, Randy Truelove Pedro, Marc Simmons, Samuel Truett, and Thomas Windes.

We also want to extend special thanks to the staff of the Dini Library at Western Nevada College, especially to Ken Sullivan, Valerie Andersen, Danna Sturm, and Larry Calkins.

Any errors, omissions, or misjudgments in this book are, of course, the responsibility of the authors alone.

Table of Contents

Acknowledgments vi
Preface 1
Introduction 5

I. Prehistoric Indian Trails and Trade   17

II. Highlights of Spanish Exploration, Settlement, and Inspection in the Southwest   22

III. The Royal Road: El Camino Real de Tierra Adentro   61

IV. The Old Spanish Trail   71

V. The Santa Fe Trail   89

VI. Military and Cultural Perspectives on the Mexican-American War   113

VII. The Butterfield Overland Mail Route   121

VIII. The Civil War in New Mexico   127

IX. The Long Walk of the Navajos   132

X. The Goodnight-Loving Trail   141

XI. Steel Trails for the Iron Horse   149

XII. The Southern Trails   163

XIII. Historic Trails, Trade, and Travels Today   176

Appendix 1. The Oñate Expedition: Excerpts from *Historia de la Nueva México* by Gaspar Pérez de Villagrá   185

Appendix 2. "$100,000 Worth of New Goods!" Arrive in Santa Fe   186

Appendix 3. "From Fort Smith, Arkansas, to Santa Fe and Albuquerque, New Mexico"   188

Appendix 4. The Unique Jargon of the Mountain Men   191

Appendix 5. A Fred Harvey Dinner Menu   193

Appendix 6. Excerpts from Geronimo's Autobiography, *My Life*   193

Chronology   197
Chapter Notes   201
Bibliography   211
Index   221

Preface

This is a survey of some of the old and very old trails of New Mexico. It is also an introduction to some of the men and women who traveled along them. These trails were used by Indians, prospectors, soldiers, buffalo hunters, immigrants, and cattle and sheep drovers. The region that became the state of New Mexico has a long, varied, and distinctive history.

Our story begins with the Anasazi Indians, who between about 850 CE and 1250 CE built a prehistoric culture centered in the Four Corners area, where New Mexico, Colorado, Utah, and Arizona come together. Just as we begin with the Indians, we will end with them — with the final surrender, in 1886, of Geronimo, the famous Apache warrior who led the last and most significant guerrilla warfare raids ever conducted in the United States. He was a master of trails and travels in New Mexico, Arizona, and northern Mexico.

Written for the educated general reader, this book focuses chiefly on New Mexico; but it also touches on events in other parts of the Southwest, in California, and in northern Mexico. It tries to fill a gap in the scholarly literature of the American West: To the best of our knowledge, no other single work has previously covered all the trails, trade, and travels addressed here. This opinion is shared by Marc Simmons, considered by many to be the preeminent historian of New Mexico.[1]

The present work tries to focus single-mindedly on the topic at hand in a given chapter. For this reason, a topic which has a long history and which is quite complex will deserve — and get — a much longer examination than its less demanding counterparts. A concluding chapter examines historic trails, trade, and travels as they are preserved today and offers some thoughts on their enduring significance. When an important region, event or person is mentioned for the first time, we often state that a discussion will follow later. We have done so in the conviction that it is better to be too thorough than not thorough enough.

A vast amount has already been published about the Oregon and California trails but *the network of southwestern trails* has been largely ignored. This is a shame because the southwestern trails, being chiefly based on reciprocal trade patterns rather than on one-way migrations, demanded constant travel back and forth. The best case in point here is the Santa Fe Trail, over which people, goods, and livestock moved in two directions: Missouri traders headed west to Santa Fe and Hispanic traders headed east to Missouri.

New Mexico has a long and stormy past which is worth highlighting here. It was initially controlled by a fragmented assortment of Indian tribes, later by Spain, then by Mexico, and, finally, by the United States. Western New Mexico came into being thanks to the Treaty of Guadalupe Hidalgo, which ended the Mexican-American War of 1846–1848. This treaty between the United States and Mexico was extremely important because it gave the U.S. undisputed control of Texas; established the U.S.–Mexican border at the Rio Grande River; and ceded to the Americans over 500,000 square miles of territory, including all the future states of California, Nevada, and Utah, almost all of New Mexico and Arizona, and parts of Colorado and Wyoming.

For its part, eastern New Mexico, i.e., from the Rio Grande east to the present New Mexico–Texas border, was a result of the Compromise of 1850 — a series of legislative bills aimed at resolving the territorial and slavery controversies arising from the Mexican-American War. The Territory of New Mexico became an organized territory of the United States in 1850.

The Gadsden Purchase (1854), which will be discussed later, added a small area to the New Mexico Territory, namely, the southernmost strip of Arizona and New Mexico. The Texan cession of 1850 (in which Texas ceded to the Federal government many of its western claims) and the Gadsden Purchase had already expanded the New Mexico Territory, but it was the redrawing of boundaries — due to the establishment of the Colorado Territory in 1861 and the creation of the Arizona Territory west of the 109th meridian in 1863 — that produced New Mexico as we know it today.[2] (The 109th meridian demarcates the present border between New Mexico and Arizona on the one hand and between Colorado and Utah on the other.)

Chapter notes have been used extensively in this book but generally for attribution rather than for comments on substantive matters, which are usually covered in the text itself. Accents are used on Spanish words, e.g., Río Conchos, but not on words of Spanish origin adopted by long usage into English, e.g., Rio Grande. In some cases, an important event or an important personality (the Mexican-American War and Kit Carson are excellent examples here) will be discussed several times as the spotlight shines on different trails.

The generic term "Indians" is used in this book without apology. Technically speaking, there were no such people in the New World as "Indians." There were instead hundreds of different tribes of indigenous people *who were called Indians by people other than themselves*. These indigenous people often defined themselves in terms which were consciously designed to be exclusive: a classic example is "The Real People" or "The People, Preeminently." Today, however, because there is no demonstrably better term for us to use, we will either refer to them as "Indians" or, where possible, we will use their tribal names — most of which, ironically, are not indigenous but were bestowed on them by other tribes or by Europeans or Americans.[3]

New Spain was one of the four viceroyalties created by the Spanish to govern the lands they had conquered in the New World. Established in 1535, its boundaries were not delineated precisely but were held to embrace all or parts of Mexico, Central America north of Panama, Florida, California, Arizona, Nevada, Utah, Colorado, New Mexico, and Texas. This vast region was never fully settled or fully controlled by Spain. The geographically more limited concept of the *frontera septentrional* (the northern frontier of New Spain) has an enticing vagueness about it and is also impossible to define precisely. For our purposes here, this northern frontier will be taken to mean, very roughly and using modern terminology, (1) that portion of Mexico lying north of Mexico City and (2) much of the American Southwest. References to well-known modern cities or locales are sometimes provided, giving readers easy geographical context when we are discussing historical places or events.

In the few places where it seems helpful to do so, two conventional abbreviations are used to pinpoint dates: BCE (Before the Common Era) and CE (Common Era). The Common Era begins with year 1 of the Gregorian calendar.

Events in our historical narrative are generally presented in chronological order but this rule has been ignored when there are good reasons to do so. Some Spanish conquistadors (explorers), for example, need to be discussed in more than one chapter because there is a chronological overlap.[4] Since this book covers such a big sweep of history, i.e., from about 850 CE to the present day, a selected chronology is included to keep the most important dates and historical sequences in their proper order.

We have sketched out, sometimes at length, the achievements and personalities of a few of the many memorable characters who played direct or indirect roles in the historic travels of the Southwest. The most detailed portrait painted here is that of the celebrated frontiersman Kit Carson. Readers who want more background on him and on the other men and women mentioned in this book will find useful sources listed in the chapter notes and in the bibliography.

In the interest of simplicity and clarity, only a few of the most important historic trails are mapped in this book. Many others can be found in the references cited in the bibliography. The seven outline maps used here are taken from a variety of reliable sources but they must be considered to be only *illustrative*, not definitive. The course of a given trail could easily move with the seasons, with weather conditions, and in response to external forces, e.g., hostile Indians, changes in commercial priorities, or shifts in domestic and international politics. In the case of the Gila (Gila is pronounced "Hee-la") River Trail, moreover, there was never *one single trail*, but rather many parallel tracks. It must be remembered, too, that, taken in its entirety, the trans–Mississippi West was well laced with trails, old and new: the ones discussed in this book are only a tiny sample of the whole.

It has been our pleasure — indeed, our *delight* — to include in this book a large number of "I-was-there" accounts of historic trails, trade, and travels. We have quoted from some of these quite extensively, especially in the appendices. It would have been easy enough to paraphrase them but they appear here in their present form for one very good reason: they convey the flavor of the times much better than any other version possibly can. Indeed, because they are in most cases the actual words of contemporary travelers themselves, they are arguably the most important parts of this book. As such, we think that they will interest the scholar as well as the educated general reader. To avoid confronting the reader with solid blocks of text, some of the longer quotations have been broken down into shorter paragraphs for ease of reading.

To borrow a phrase traditionally used to describe the work of the French painter Georges Seurat (1859–1891), we have experimented in this book with what might be called "literary pointillism." Pointillism is a technique of painting in which a large number of tiny dots of color are combined to form a picture. We hope that, when read as a whole, our carefully chosen dots of historical fact will combine to form a vibrant portrait of trails, trade, and travels in New Mexico and elsewhere in the Southwest.

Introduction

Pecos, New Mexico: A Microcosm of the Old Southwest

New Mexico itself has traditionally — and correctly — been described as a crossroads and fusion point of three very different cultures: Indian, Spanish (defined here as including Mexicans and Hispanics), and Anglo-American. This diversity has played a key role in the region's historic trails, trade, and travels. We have chosen Pecos Pueblo — pueblo means "village" in Spanish — as a cross-cultural peg on which to hang our story. Herbert E. Bolton (1870–1953), one of the most prominent scholars of Spanish-American history, gives some good reasons why we should do so:

> [Pecos] has occupied a distinctive position in all the major developments of the region. It was the gateway for Pueblo Indians when they went buffalo hunting on the Plains; a two-way pass for barter and war between Pueblos and Plains tribes; a portal through the mountains for Spanish explorers, traders, and buffalo hunters; for the St. Louis caravan traders with Santa Fe; for pioneer Anglo-American settlers; for Spanish and [Anglo-]Saxon Indian fighters; for Civil War armies; and for a transcontinental railroad passing through the Southwest.[1]

Pecos is about 25 miles southeast of Santa Fe, but it has a longer and more singular history than Santa Fe. Today Pecos is only a ruin set on a remote, high-altitude mesa, but in the past it was vibrantly alive. It served the very different needs of, first, the Indians; then the Spaniards and Mexicans; and, finally, the English-speaking newcomers. Used here in its literal sense of being "a little world," *microcosm* is surely the best one-word description of Pecos.

When the Spanish first visited this four-story pueblo in 1540 they called it "Cicúye," a name borrowed from the Tiwa-speaking Indians of the Rio Grande. (The Pueblo Indians of New Mexico constitute different ethnic groups and speak different languages. The languages of these peoples are Tiwa, Towa, Tewa, Keres, and Zuni.[2]) The name "Pecos" was derived from "Paequiu," the native name for the pueblo.³ By world standards, Pecos itself was never very big and never played a decisive role in southwestern history. Nevertheless, for a thousand years — from the ninth century, when pit-houses (dugouts) were built there, to after 1821, when the Santa Fe Trail opened — this little world served Indians, Spaniards, Mexicans, and Anglo-Americans alike as a crossroads where their social, economic, religious, and military paths could profitably intersect. By looking briefly at some of the events in and near Pecos, we can get a much better understanding of the region as a whole and of the changing times.⁴

Archeological studies show that Indians were living in small adobe and rock villages in the upper Pecos Valley as early as the 1100s. Larger one-story adobe buildings were built in the 1200s, sometimes with kivas contiguous to the rooms. A kiva is an underground chamber entered through a hole in the roof. Pueblo peoples believed that kivas were a special "halfway house" between the underworld (where tribal myths held that the first human beings, i.e., the Indians, had been created) on the one hand, and their own world above ground on the other. Pueblo Indians used kivas as ritual gathering places for ceremonies and social events. By the 1300s circular kivas, detached from dwellings, were being constructed. It was not until about 1450, however, that the Indians built a large, multistoried, rectangular pueblo on the Pecos mesa itself. It enclosed a plaza which contained circular kivas.⁵

Regrettably, there is no authoritative written account of the earliest history of the Pecos pueblo. The little we know about what it was like at that time comes either from archeology or from infrequent references in official Spanish documents. Today by far the best way to get a feel for Pecos is to visit it, as we ourselves did while researching this book. Standing in its ruins, it is easy enough to see (in the mind's eye) the pueblo as scholars tell us it existed at its heyday in about 1450 — as a busy, prosperous, well organized adobe and stone fortress standing five stories high which was home to more than 2,000 residents and was able to field some 500 warriors. Although the Pecoseños (the Indians who lived in Pecos) themselves seemed to be quite peaceful, the Spanish realized soon enough that they could be doughty warriors when and if the need arose.

Geographically, Pecos occupied a very favorable position. On the west, the southern foothills of the Sangre de Cristo Mountains separated it from the settled and relatively prosperous agricultural pueblos of the Rio Grande Valley. On the east, the Tecolote Mountains kept it apart, but not too far, from the nomadic buffalo hunters of the High Plains of eastern New Mexico.⁶ A narrow trail through Glorieta Pass (which is about 7,500 feet high and is located six miles west of Pecos) provided access from Pecos to both of these very different economic-cultural regions.

Consequently, Pecos was ideally located for the trade fairs to which Apaches and other Plains tribes brought such diverse items as buffalo products; artifacts made from alibates flint, a multicolored stone found in the Texas Panhandle which, when chipped, will hold a very sharp edge; tubular clay pipes for smoking tobacco and herbs; shells; and Indian slaves, this last to be discussed below.

Trade continued well into the days of Spanish and then Mexican control of Pecos. In 1705, for example, Governor Francisco Cuervo y Valdes issued a proclamation (*bando*) to the effect that no one could trade without a license from him. If a trader was caught doing so, stiff penalties were imposed: forfeiture of the goods traded or received, plus a fine. Cuervo y Valdes also prohibited cheating. When illegal trading continued nevertheless, a later governor, Juan Ignacio Flores Mogollon, published a new *bando* in 1712. He ordered that Spanish settlers and Pueblo Indians, who were using fraudulent practices in their trading with Apaches and Utes, must stop doing this because it was jeopardizing the security of New Mexico. Mogollon also ordered a jail term of several months for any traders violating his proclamation.[7]

The modern scholar James F. Brooks finds that there is "strong evidence for an early Plainswide trade in slaves and for the role of Pueblo Indians as their captors or purchasers."[8] The Spanish reported that trade in slaves was well established in the Southwest. For example, Fray (Friar) Domínguez, who will be discussed later, describes a trade fair at Taos in about 1776 (the phrasing used here follows a translation of the original document): "The Comanches usually sell to our people [i.e., to the Spaniards] at this rate: ... an Indian slave, according to the individual, because if it is an Indian girl from twelve to twenty years old, [the price is] two good horses and some trifles in addition, such as a short cloak, a horse cloth, [or] a red lapel...; or a she-mule and a scarlet cover, or other things are given for her...."[9] (In the Southwest, for reasons that will be discussed in chapter two, mules were often more valuable than horses.)

At Pecos the Plains Indians bartered their own goods for items made by the Indians of the Rio Grande Valley, e.g., matte and glaze paint pottery, corn and crops, textiles, and turquoise ornaments. Thanks to their pivotal geographic position, the Pecos Indians were excellent middlemen and traders. They exchanged local and imported products with Indians living further south and west, receiving from them in return parrot feathers, unworked turquoise, and other exotic and useful items.

Pecos would thus become one of the six primary interlocking Indian trade centers identified by the Smithsonian Institution in its definitive *Handbook of North American Indians*. These centers were permanently inhabited. They produced agricultural or other surpluses which were in considerable demand and which could therefore easily be traded. (The six primary trade centers were Pecos; the Zuni trade center in western New Mexico; the Corazones trade center in northwestern Mexico; the Dales trade center in central Oregon; the Mandan-Hidatsa trade center in central North Dakota; the Arikara trade center in northern South Dakota.)[10]

The Pecos Indians were not only skilled traders but they were also good farmers. They raised the Southwest's usual trinity of crops — corn, beans, and squash — along local waterways, e.g., Glorieta Creek and the Pecos River. (The 926-mile-long Pecos River is one of the major tributaries of the Rio Grande. It rises on the western slopes of the Santa Fe mountain range; flows southward through New Mexico; enters Texas near the Carlsbad Caverns National Park; continues southeast across Texas; and, finally, joins the Rio Grande near Del Rio, Texas.)

Harvests could be impressive. When the Spanish explorer Francisco Vásquez de Coronado visited the Pecos Indians in 1541, he found that their storerooms were piled high with what was said to be a three-year supply of corn. Coronado had already been approached by the Pecos Indians a year before this visit. The Spaniards had only recently arrived in New Mexico but their fame (or infamy) had preceded them. This was no wonder: Coronado's forces were frighteningly and overwhelmingly powerful. He had at his disposal 336 well-armed Spanish soldiers (250 of whom were mounted) and hundreds of lightly armed Indian allies. The Pecoseños immediately understood how important it would be to win his military support in their own conflicts with other tribes.

For this reason, delegates from Pecos Pueblo had previously visited Coronado at Zuni. A Pecos war captain, whom the Spanish nicknamed "Bigotes" ("mustaches") because of his long mustaches, which were unusual among the Indians, later led the Spaniards back to Pecos, then the largest of the pueblos. Coronado's men, approaching Pecos from the west, immediately perceived that Glorieta Pass offered an excellent passageway to the Great Plains. They did not, however, treat the inhabitants of Pecos with any courtesy. In fact, at one point during a heated dispute about some nonexistent gold bracelets, the Spanish temporarily arrested both Bigotes and the chief of the pueblo, hoping to extract from them the source of the alleged gold.[11]

The Spanish wanted to understand the Pecos region but they could not learn very much about its history. In his invaluable and well written *Narrative of the Expedition to Cíbola*, Pedro de Castañeda de Nájera, Coronado's chief chronicler, had only this to say about the many abandoned pueblos the Spanish found in the vicinity of Pecos: "All that we could find out about them was that some sixteen years before some people called Teyas had come to that land and had destroyed those pueblos."[12]

The Teyas, who lived in the eastern part of the Texas Panhandle and the adjoining part of Oklahoma, were buffalo hunters like the Plains Apache. The Spaniards learned that the Teyas had also attacked Pecos itself but it was so well defended that in the end they decided instead to make peace. (Archeological evidence indicates that there was, indeed, a flurry of warfare at Pecos during this time.) The Spanish also learned that Teyas later returned to Pecos each winter to engage in peaceful trade, being forced to camp *outside the pueblo*, however, because the Pecoseños did not trust them inside.

Other early Spanish explorers included Antonio de Espejo, whose expedition stopped briefly at Pecos in 1583. He extorted provisions from the Indians by threatening to burn the pueblo to the ground if *pinole* (a gruel made from ground corn) was not provided. After the *pinole* was grudgingly surrendered to them, the Spanish then seized two men of Pecos as guides to lead them to the buffalo herds on the eastern plains.[13] One man escaped; the other was taken to Mexico so that Spanish linguists could learn his language and teach a little of it to future explorers.

In 1584 Baltazar de Obregón, a Spanish visitor, was favorably impressed by Pecos. He tells us that it was set on a "high and narrow hill, enclosed on both sides by two streams and many trees. The hill itself is cleared of trees.... It has the greatest and best buildings of these provinces and is most thickly settled.... [The Indians] possess quantities of maize [corn], cotton, beans, and squash. [The pueblo] is enclosed and protected by a wall and large houses, and by tiers of walkways which look out on the countryside. On these they keep their offensive and defensive arms: bows and arrows, shields, spears, and war clubs."[14]

The most detailed contemporary description of Pecos is the journal of the Spanish explorer Gaspar Castaño de Sosa, who in 1590–1591 led an *entrada* into New Spain and whose story will be discussed later. (*Entradas*—literally "entrances" or "openings"—were official Spanish penetrations into, and explorations of, unknown and potentially hostile lands.) Led by a young Indian he named Miguel, Castaño set out from the silver mining center of Santa Bárbara in Chihuahua, Mexico, on what was essentially a prospecting enterprise. He was accompanied by 170 prospective settlers and by a cumbersome wagon train which creaked forward slowly under a heavy load of equipment and supplies. This was the first Spanish expedition in the region to make use of two-wheeled carts.

To get an invaluable description (in English) of these carts, we must jump ahead to the New Mexico of 1846–1847. The carts had not changed at all by that time. One of the U.S. Army officers who accompanied General Stephen Watts Kearny on his expedition to conquer New Mexico was Colonel James W. Abert, an officer of the Corps of Topographical Engineers. This is what Abert heard and saw during his travels in New Mexico:

> We suddenly heard the most horrible screechings and groans, as if one was approaching the portals of Erebus ["Erebus" was often used as a synonym for Hades, the Greek god of the underworld]; and all these horrid sounds proceeded from the never greased wheels of some Spanish "carretas" [carts]. These curious structures are formed of pine, chiefly; the axle is of pine, and the wheels of cotton-wood; they are made thus:
>
> A rectangular piece of wood, about four feet long, two and a half feet wide, and one foot thick, is procured; this is diminished in thickness, so as to leave a projection on each side, which forms the hub, and its extremities are rounded. The remaining arcs of a circle, of four feet, are fastened to the first piece, with large wooden pins, so as to complete the circumference of the wheel. A large hole is pierced in the vicinity of the centre, to receive the spindle of a huge pine axle; a body like a hay crate [the body of the cart was usually about 30 inches wide, 7 feet long, and from 4 to 5 feet high], and a tongue, complete the "carreta." The oxen are attached by the means of a bar of wood, that is lashed to their horns.[15]

Thus equipped with primitive carts, Castaño moved slowly north to the Rio Grande River and then headed for the Pecos River. There he was frustrated by precipitous canyons that his horses could not traverse, by terrain too rough for the carts, and by lack of water. He finally managed to get down to the river itself and eventually reached Pecos Pueblo in 1590. As Antonio de Espejo had done seven years before, Castaño obtained corn from the Pecos Indians. However, because the Spanish authorities had not given him official permission to launch his exploration, these same authorities had him pursued, arrested, and carried back to Mexico City in chains.

Spain eventually decided to colonize New Mexico, basing this decision on the three classic and alliterative goals that guided all their explorations in the Southwest:

- *Gold*, i.e., the ceaseless hunt for the mineral wealth the Spanish confidently expected to find in the region.
- *God*, i.e., the Spaniards' deeply held belief that it was their duty to convert the pagan Indians to Christianity.
- *Glory*, i.e., the hope of personal profit and, as a consequence, rapid advancement up Spain's semi-medieval, highly stratified, and rank-conscious social ladder.

For all these reasons, the first officially approved Spanish migration began in 1598 when Juan de Oñate, whom we will discuss again later at greater length, led settlers to New Mexico. Under the energetic leadership of Fray Andrés Juárez, the pueblo began to serve as a base for missionary activities while at the same time continuing its earlier role as a trading center. By 1617 Pecos had become a well-established stop for itinerant Spanish traders who wanted to barter their wares with the Plains Apaches.

Trade and economic growth, however, did not mean that the Spanish missionaries were delinquent in their religious duties. Visually, the most impressive part of Pecos was always the mission church. The first church at Pecos, known as the "lost" church, was built off the mesa in about 1617 but was never entirely finished. The Spanish built a bigger church on top of the mesa, beginning in 1720. It was damaged during the Pueblo Revolt of 1680 (discussed later) but some of its beams were salvaged and were used to build kivas. In its original form, the ruined church that stands in Pecos today was smaller than the 1720 church. The ruined church was remodeled in about 1780 after the Pueblo revolt. Some of its old beams would find new homes in new places, e.g., on the East Coast of the United States in the 1850s and 1860s, thanks to the Civil War; in anthropologists' houses in Santa Fe in the late 1800s and early 1900s; and in homes in the village of Pecos today.[16]

Trade with the Indians was not conducted only by itinerant traders. Trying hard to make his own fortune from the Apache trade, between 1637 and 1641 Governor Luis de Rosas ordered that knives and other metal goods be stored with his frontier agents at Pecos and neighboring pueblos. He hoped that Plains Indians would want these goods so badly that they would bring in more and more hides for trade. These hides the governor planned to send to Mexico, where they could be sold for his own profit.

During the great Pueblo Revolt of 1680 the people of Pecos joined other pueblos in a coordinated attack on Santa Fe, the capital of Spanish rule. This rebellion, unique in the annals of Indian-European relations in North America, finally forced the Spanish out of New Mexico for 12 years. When at length they returned (in 1692), they were indeed fortunate in having as their leader a very capable officer — Governor Diego de Vargas — who is still remembered today for directing Spain's relatively peaceful reconquest of the Pueblo world. In this process Diego de Vargas received invaluable help from Juan de Ye, the leader of the Pecos Indians, who would be assassinated by other Indians in 1694 while he was trying to negotiate a peaceful settlement with the rebellious inhabitants of Taos Pueblo.

Most of the Pueblo Indians revolted again against the Spanish in 1696, though on a lesser scale. Pecos was one of the five pueblos which maintained allegiance to Spain. Even there, however, the population was split into anti–Spanish and pro–Spanish factions. Although Governor Don Felipe hanged, jailed, or beheaded the most recalcitrant anti–Spanish elements in Pecos, after 1700 the pueblo remained divided in its loyalties.

Beginning in the early 1700s the people of Pecos suffered increasing attacks from mounted Comanches. At the same time, their Apache customers were forced by the Comanches to flee from the plains and to seek refuge in the distant mountains. Since the Apaches could no longer safely attend trade fairs in Pecos or other pueblos, they themselves resorted to raiding to get the goods they needed. In 1715 about 30 Pecoseños, together with other Pueblo Indians, launched a punitive expedition against the Faraon Apaches, who had formerly been their allies. Remarkably, the Apache force included Pecoseños who had fled from the pueblo during the Spanish reconquest.

These fugitives from Pecos often revisited the pueblo during the periodic "ransoming of captives," i.e., the trade fairs, known as *rescates*, which were attended chiefly by the *indios bárbaros* (the tribes who refused to submit to Spanish rule). At these fairs, Indian captives were traded or were ransomed by bartering. The Indian children ransomed by the Spaniards were baptized and raised as Catholics; they would then be employed as domestic servants by settlers and by Franciscan missionaries. The Plains Indians generally kept other captives as their own slaves but, after ransoming their own kinsmen, returned them to their original tribe.[17] After such fairs, however, the former Pecoseños proved themselves to be most untrustworthy and unwelcome guests: they sometimes robbed and killed their own hosts.[18]

In 1751 more than 300 Comanches attacked Pecos but were driven back by Pecos warriors, reinforced by 10 Spanish soldiers. Governor Vélez Cachupín, following through on his promise to retaliate for any attack on Pecos, soon mounted a counterattack from his headquarters in Santa Fe. He scored a significant victory over the Comanches when his soldiers trapped them in a box canyon with a deep pond at its head. (A box canyon is a canyon whose entrance is also its only exit, not counting any climbable walls.) The Comanches had only two choices: either to drown in the pond, or to turn around and face the volleys being fired at them at close range by the *escopetas* of the Spanish soldiers. As later described by a Texas Ranger, an escopeta was "a short bell-mouthed, bull-doggish looking musket, carrying a very heavy ball, which is 'death by law' when it hits..." [i.e., being hit by one of these bullets was equivalent to receiving a death sentence from a court of law].[19]

During this combat, many Comanches were drowned or were killed by gunfire; the wounded and the others surrendered.[20] Comanche hostility, however, was not broken by this defeat and by 1775 Pecos was enduring renewed Comanche attacks. These so terrified the inhabitants that they were afraid to leave the pueblo to work in the irrigated fields. By 1776 the population stood at only 100 families comprising only 269 men, women, and children. The Spanish finally decided to make peace with the Comanches and did so at Pecos in 1786. The attacks continued, however. Coupled with smallpox epidemics, migration, and drought, these reduced the population of Pecos to such a low level that in the late 1700s the pueblo could not even support one resident friar.

By the early 1800s, some of the Pecoseños who had learned wood carving and other trades from the Spanish decided to leave the pueblo for good and to move into the new settlements built in the Pecos Valley. Pecos itself was thus nearly a ghost town when trade along the Santa Fe Trail began to flow past it in 1821, though, as the last stop before Santa Fe, it would become a popular rest stop for travelers on the trail. The final baptism in Pecos was held in 1828. Ten years later, when the population had fallen to only 17 souls, the pueblo was abandoned entirely.

During the last days of Pecos, the famous Santa Fe Trail trader Josiah Gregg (1806–1850) described the desolation he found there. Gregg was a sickly intellectual who had hoped that traveling the Santa Fe Trail would restore his health. It did indeed: between 1831 and 1843 he made nearly a dozen trips over the trail. His definitive work was based on these trips and was entitled *Commerce of the Prairies*. First published in two volumes in 1844, it was an immediate and lasting success, being factual, accurate, and very well written — all in all, an invaluable guidebook for travelers along the Santa Fe Trail. *Commerce of the Prairies* appeared in six editions over the years and was translated into French and German. Because it is still the bedrock for all later studies of the Santa Fe Trail, we shall quote from it frequently in this book.

Having passed Pecos many times during his travels along the Santa Fe Trail, Gregg recalled that "The traveller would oftentimes perceive but a solitary Indian, a woman, or a child, standing here and there like so many statues upon the roofs of their houses, with their eyes fixed on the eastern horizon, or leaning against a wall or a fence, listlessly gazing at the passing stranger while at other times not a soul was to be seen in any direction, and the sepulchral silence of the place was only disturbed by the occasional barking of a dog, or the cackling of hens."[21]

The few remaining occupants of Pecos eventually joined their Towa-speaking relatives at Jémez Pueblo, 80 miles to the west. Their descendants still live there today. Subsequently, Pecos itself rapidly fell into total decay, a process speeded up by the Mexican soldiers who used structural wood from the pueblo to make their campfires and by others who made off with some of the beams of the old church. When the 18-year-old Santa Fe Trail traveler Susan Shelby Magoffin (1827–1855), who will be discussed later in some detail, visited Pecos in 1846, she noted the following in her diary:

> I have visited this morning the ruins of an ancient pueblo, or village, now desolate and a home for the wild beast and bird of the forest.... The only part now standing is the [shell of the] church. We got off our horses and went in, and I was truly awed. I should think it was sixty feet by thirty. As is the custom

among the present inhabitants of Mexico, this pueblo is built of unburnt bricks and stones. The ceiling is very high and doleful in appearance....

All around the church at different distances are ruins; the side of one house remains perfect still, and 'tis plain to see a three storied building once was there. The upper rooms were entered by a ladder from the outside — and in case of an enemy's coming these ladders were drawn up, and no communication being afforded below they were perfectly secure to cast stones or any other missile at their not so well protected enemy.

Mi alma [literally "my soul," i.e., Susan's affectionate nickname for her husband] pointed out to me the door of a room in which he had once slept all night in some of his trips across the plains, and while some of the inhabitants still remained. It was in the second story of a house, which is now entirely fallen in, and the doors are so entirely closed by rubbish (except this room) that it had nothing of the appearance of being a house.[22]

In 1849 John Robert Forsyth, one of the many fortune seekers spurred into travel along the Santa Fe Trail by the California gold rush, visited Pecos Pueblo and made this entry in his diary: "At night a few of the men explored the ruins with torches & dug up a part of the floor [of the church] which was found full of Human bones. One of the Mummys was in perfect state of preservation. Money was the object of the digging but none was found."[23]

Even though Pecos itself had been abandoned, a perceptive visitor could still find scenes of interest there. Chronicling his travels in 1846 and 1847, Colonel Abert had this to say:

Our road now lay by the foot of a high bluff that raised its crest 600 feet above the valley. Its sides were clothed with groves of cedar and pinon. The groves on each side of the road were full of stelar [*sic*] jays ... red shafted flickers, and robins; the woods were vocal with the varied notes of these lively birds.

As we journeyed along we were continually seeing most motly [*sic*] groups of human beings; sometimes we met long trains of men and women mounted on mules; the senoras with their heads enveloped in their "rebosas" ["robozos" are cotton or wool shawls worn by women], the men with their pantaloons open at the side from their hip down, thus displaying their ample drawers of white linen, and with their heels armed with immense jingling spurs. Sometimes we met single couples mounted on the same mule. Most of these men were armed with naked swords that lay close against the saddle. At one time we passed a group of Indians; they had pack mules laden with buffalo robes and meat. Their jet black hair was tied up in short stumpy queues with some light colored ribbons. They told me that they were "Teguas" Indians; that they had been far out on the prairies trading with the Camanches [*sic*], and were now going to sell their robes in Santa Fe.[24]

By about 1858 the roof of the church had collapsed entirely. Pecos was subsequently ignored by the outside world until 1902, when a private firm

(Gross, Kelley, and Company) acquired the pueblo and the surrounding land. In 1920 the ruins of the pueblo and mission were deeded to the Archdiocese of Santa Fe, which in turn donated them to the School of American Research in Santa Fe. The long, slow process of saving the remains of the pueblo had at last begun.

Harvard archeologist Alfred K. Kidder excavated Pecos at intervals between 1915 and 1927. He believed that no other Southwest ruin "seems to have been lived in continuously for so long a period."[25] To test his theory of stratigraphy, i.e., that in an archeological site the oldest deposition is on the bottom and the youngest is on top, Kidder trenched into the great midden (refuse heap) on the east side of the pueblo. Initially, it looked like it was only a natural part of ridgeline; but when examined closely it proved to be a time capsule containing hundreds of years of discards, laid down in precise chronological order. It was thus, the National Park Service tells us, "a treasure trove of scientific data."[26]

From it, Kidder worked out a chronology for the ancient Southwest. Now much modified and known as the Pecos Classification, it is still in use today. It showed that there have been no fewer than six successive settlements at Pecos, one literally laid down on top of the other, beginning with buffalo hunters in about 9000 BCE and ending with the Spanish occupation of the 1540s.[27] Pecos was declared a New Mexico state monument in 1935. After New Mexico donated it to the U.S. government, Pecos was designated as a national monument in 1965 and since then has been administered by the National Park Service. New lands were added to the park in 1990 and its official name was changed to Pecos National Historical Park.

CHAPTER I

Prehistoric Indian Trails and Trade

The American Southwest, especially New Mexico, is the home of some of the oldest Indian cultures in the United States. Indian trails and, indeed, Indian roads can still be found throughout New Mexico, e.g., in Chaco Canyon, Zuni, Acoma, Taos, Picuries, Gran Quivira, Jemez Springs, and Frijoles Canyon, to name just a few sites. As used here, the difference between *trails* and *roads* is that the former came into being basically through use; the latter were *built* in some way, e.g., by being dug into the ground. One of the most interesting of these early Indian cultures is that of the Anasazi, who are now officially known as the Ancient Pueblo People or as the Ancestral Puebloans. These formal names are preferred by their descendants today because "Anasazi" is a Navajo word variously meaning "ancient enemy," "old-time stranger," "outsider," "alien," or "foreigner."

The Anasazi lived in the Four Corners area. Moccasined feet usually do not make lasting scars on the landscape, so it can be difficult to see Anasazi trails today. Anasazi roads, however, are another matter entirely. They were often cut deep into the tuffa (soft volcanic rock) of the region and are still clearly visible there. A focal point of Anasazi culture was Chaco Canyon, a high desert region located about 120 miles northwest of Santa Fe. There the Anasazi grew surpluses of corn; turned the surrounding piñon/juniper woodland into timber for construction; and, when this resource was exhausted, ventured 50 miles into the surrounding mountains to cut heavy ponderosa pine, spruce, and fir beams for buildings. In the process, they also created a vigorous center for trade and tribal rituals.

From about 850 to 1250, Chaco Canyon was a major urban center of Anasazi life. Modern estimates of its population vary widely, from a low of 2,500–3,000 people to a high of about 15,000.[1] The biggest single structure was Pueblo Bonito ("Beautiful Village"), which once stood five stories high and had between 600 and 800 small rooms. To build it, thousands of ponderosa pine logs (some of them 16 feet long and weighing 700 pounds) and up to one million pounds of stone veneer were moved and used in construction.[2] Dams, ditches, canals, and storage ponds collected water for agriculture.

The Chacoan way of life was so well organized that some modern scholars believe that by the early twelfth century as many as 70 outlying communities were associated with Chaco, perhaps through a trade network involving a minimum of 130 miles of carefully constructed unpaved roads.[3] These roads are quite remarkable, given the fact that the Chaco culture possessed neither livestock nor wheeled vehicles. Far from being only narrow trails worn into the soil by centuries of travel, they are up to 39 feet wide and sometimes have edging stones, masonry walls, ramps, and even staircases cut into the rock. The most elaborate road construction is located near the biggest ceremonial houses: double and quadruple road segments can be found there.[4]

Coupled with the enormous amount of time and effort needed to build such roads, this fact suggests that for the men and women of Chaco culture they almost certainly had considerable *religious and symbolic importance* as well as practical importance. Indeed, tribal lore passed on by Pueblo Indians today still remembers Chaco as a hallowed communal meeting place, where different peoples and clans could meet in safety to share their rituals and their knowledge.[5] It must be added, however, that archeologists today are still unsure about all the uses of these roads. As the archeologist Brian Fagan put it in 2005, "From the moment of their rediscovery, Chaco's roads were an enigma…. The Chaco roads are deeply intriguing because they provide unequivocal evidence that the canyon was the hub of a much larger world, but they defy interpretation because many of them seem to lead nowhere…. Interpretations have ranged over the entire gamut, from sophisticated economic networks to pilgrimage roads."[6]

One reasonable guess is that Chacoan traders may have relied on these roads as pathways to use when bartering turquoise for such exotic items as seashells from California; copper bells; brightly colored macaw feathers from central Mexico; and minerals and ores from the Rockies. Archeologists have unearthed an Anasazi cache of 2,969 assorted beads, pendants, and inlay pieces. This cache was buried in a pottery jar and may have been the stock in trade of some early Indian businessman. Moreover, an excavation of the Great Kiva in Chaco Canyon has disclosed over 17,000 shell and stone beads, strung together in strands up to 17 feet long.[7]

Chaco's roads were clearly built to last. They have a depth of between 4 and 20 inches and, where necessary, were cut down into the topsoil to reach a solid substratum.[8] To construct such a road, the Chaco builders first dug and then compacted a broad trench, piling the remains along the downhill side of the road. The roadbed itself was surfaced with sandstone, which had to be carried by hand to the building site for this purpose. Hills, mesas, and canyons were surmounted by using steps, ramps, curbs, berms, and roadcuts. This was construction work on a grand scale: there are 45 staircases cut into the stone of Chaco Canyon alone.[9]

The earliest map of the region was produced by Don Bernarado de Miera y Pacheco in 1774. It identified the Chaco Canyon area as "Chaca." This term may have been a Spanish translation of Navajo words meaning "rock-cut," "canyon," or "white string of rocks" (this latter phrase perhaps referring to the white sandstone on top of the mesa).[10] Modern cartographers think that eight roads may have radiated out from what is called the Chaco "core." The most extensive of these is about 60 miles long and heads due north, leading towards the prehistoric communities of Salmon and Aztec. Other roads of varying lengths depart from the core toward other points of the compass. All in all, about 400 miles of prehistoric roadway have been identified.

At first glance, it would make sense to assume that the timber used to build the dwellings of Pueblo Bonito must also have been transported along these well-constructed roads, but this does not appear to have been the case. The construction of Pueblo Bonito alone is thought to have required over 50,000 pieces of timber.[11] Yet only a small number of stone axes have been found in Chaco itself. This suggests that logs must have been shaped into beams where the trees were felled. With roads up to 39 feet wide, heavy logs could have been rolled along them, no matter how slowly and laboriously, by human muscle power, perhaps aided occasionally by wooden levers.

The weakness of this theory is that the beams in Chaco houses bear no telltale scars from being rolled, dragged, or pried. Instead, they appear to have been *carried by hand*, e.g., presumably by organized teams of strong young men, probably supervised by experienced foresters. Hundreds of people each year may have been involved in these communal undertakings.[12]

However, times change. Eventually the bustle and hum of human activity in Chaco Canyon died away into the lonely silence of the high desert: at some point between 1150 and 1200, the canyon was abandoned entirely. The reasons for this remarkable collapse are not known with certainty but very probably involved the combined pressures of severe drought, which made irrigation and thus corn production impossible; gradual deforestation, which made it difficult to repair old buildings and erect new ones; tribal warfare, including evidence of cannibalism; overpopulation; and, possibly, the failure of outlying villages to support the bustling capital by shipping food to it along those fine roads.[13]

In the end, the remaining Chacoans almost certainly migrated to other locations where life was easier. Perhaps some of them walked about 200 miles southeast — to the less densely populated and better-watered pueblos strung out along the Rio Grande. If so, they must have integrated, imperceptibly, into the tribes already living there. What is certain is that they disappeared entirely from Chaco Canyon itself, which would remain unoccupied until Navajo shepherds eventually began to settle there in about 1800.

Although the mystery of Chaco roads may never be solved, one of their prime uses must surely have been intertribal trade. Such trade was not, of course, confined to Chaco Canyon alone and it did not end with the disappearance of the Anasazi. A thumbnail sketch of intertribal trade in the Southwest may therefore serve as a fitting conclusion to this brief account of prehistoric Indian trails, trade, and travels.

When the Spanish first came to the Southwest in the sixteenth century, they were impressed by how much trade was going on and by how far Indian traders walked before the horse came into widespread use in Indian life. Indeed, a modern map of traditional trade routes in the Southwest reveals a dense network of trails. Centered on the Santa Fe region, they extended northwest into Colorado, Utah, and Wyoming; south into Mexico; east into the Great Plains; and west to the coast of southern California.[14]

The following lists give us some idea of what one particular southwestern tribe — the Hopis, who lived in mesa-top pueblos in northeastern Arizona — offered in trade to their fellow Indians, and what goods they got in exchange[15]:

- *What the Hopi people offered in trade:* corn, other foodstuffs (e.g. peaches), rabbit skin robes, skin pouches, spoons, pottery, coiled baskets, wicker baskets, salt, cooking pots, bottles, yucca sieves, shell beads, buckskin, mantas (cotton blankets), kilts and belts, leggings and yarn, blankets, buffalo hides, turquoise, silver, livestock, red ocher, iron tools, tinklers (little bronze or brass bells), ceremonial items.

- *What the Hopi people got in exchange* (The names of the tribes providing these trade items are shown in brackets.): silver [Eastern Pueblo Indians, Navajo, Zuni];, turquoise [Zuni, Keresans, Jemez, Sandia]; shell beads [Zuni, Acoma, Eastern Keresans, Jemez]; salt [Zuni]; buckskin [Zuni, Havasupai, Walapai, Northern and Southern Tonto]; buffalo skins [Zuni, Eastern Pueblo Indians]; quivers made from mountain lion skin (used to carry arrows) [Navajo, Paiute, Northern Tonto]; firewood [Navajo, Paiute]; vigas (heavy wood rafters), sheep, mutton, blankets, antelope skins, water [Navajo]; horses [Navajo, Paiute, Havasupai]; bows and arrows [Havasupai, Paiute]; mescal (a liquor distilled from cactus) [Havasupai, Walapai]; piñon nuts [Havasupai, Walapai]; baskets, leather clothing, horn ladles, sea shells, abalone, stones containing copper, tobacco, grass, willows, cottonwood roots, yellow pigment, skins of mountain sheep [Havasupai]; green (unseasoned) bows, arrows, moccasins [White Mountain Apache]; cotton [Pima, Zuni]; macaw feathers [Pima, Havasupai]; deer meat [Paiute, Jemez]; piñon gum [Paiute]; corn [Isleta, Santo Domingo, San Felipe]; tools [Eastern Pueblo Indians]; feather caps [Southern Tonto].

No commodity in intertribal trade was used as money but, in the modern period at least, long and short strings of shell beads, known as *hishi*, could be converted into other goods at any time. Some items were so universally wanted that exchange rates have been worked out for them. Scholarly accounts published between 1928 and 1948, for example, show that the following items were considered by Indian traders and customers in the Southwest to be of equal value and thus were interchangeable: a large buckskin, a good-sized blanket, a buffalo skin or a buffalo robe, a horse, a large basket of shelled corn, a gun.[16] To the modern reader, the idea that a horse could be of equal value to a large basket of shelled corn may seem incongruous, but these examples demonstrate more than anything else the harsh environment these Indians had to endure in the Southwest. Not to possess even one of these items might well have led to suffering for an Indian and his family.

CHAPTER II

Highlights of Spanish Exploration, Settlement, and Inspection in the Southwest

The routes, achievements, failures, and memorable characters of the Spanish *entradas* are of considerable interest today because the Spanish impact on New Mexico was so deep and so persistent. Although many of these *entradas* penetrated other areas of the Southwest as well, their imprints on the local population of New Mexico itself were monumental. While it is not politically correct today to admire the Spaniards' single-minded pursuit of gold, God, and glory in the Indian lands they conquered and exploited, one still cannot fail to be impressed by their courage, their endurance, and their pathfinding abilities. Not all of the explorers mentioned in this chapter were active in New Mexico, yet collectively they illustrate both Spain's dominion in the Southwest and the broad, unrelenting nature of its quests.

An important legal characteristic of *entradas* was the *Requerimiento* ("Requirement" or "Requisition"), which the leader of an expedition was required to read aloud, in Spanish, to the Indians of the New World. Interpreters would try to translate its main points into the local language as best they could. Whether the Indians actually understood the *Requerimiento* or not, its underlying message would very soon become painfully clear to them: that, on pain of slavery or death, they were required to submit completely to Spanish rule.[1]

Exploring the Gulf Coast by Sea: Álvarez Alonso de Pineda

This Spanish navigator did not lead an overland *entrada* but in 1519 he became the first person to explore the Gulf Coast by sea; he set off from the

Florida Keys and ended near Veracruz, Mexico. Regrettably, no narrative of this expedition has survived. The only contemporary source which sheds any light on his adventure is a reference in a royal *cédula* (decree) of 1521, granting to Francisco de Garay, Spanish governor of Jamaica, the lands which Álvarez Alonso de Pineda had already explored in his name.[2] What is clear is that Álvarez Alonso de Pineda was the first European to record the strong outflow of the Mississippi River into the Gulf of Mexico, which he detected off the Mississippi River Delta. He christened this powerful stream Río del Espíritu Santo (River of the Holy Spirit) because he crossed it on or about the Christian holy day of Pentecost. He did not go ashore on the American portion of the Gulf Coast but instead spent 40 days ashore in eastern Mexico, overhauling his ships on the banks of the Río Pánuco near Tampico.[3]

Afoot in the Deserts: Cabeza de Vaca

The first and most unique of the overland *entradas* into the trans-Mississippi West is also one of the greatest survival stories in the history of North American exploration. It began in 1527–1528 as a Spanish plan to install Pánfilo de Narváez as *adelantado* (a governor-like military office) of Spanish Florida. It ended in 1536, after "four ragged castaways," as their leader Ávar Núñez Cabeza de Vaca accurately described himself and his three surviving men, had endured shipwreck and eight years of wandering on foot through the deserts of the Southwest. These four men were saved only because they finally encountered, in northern Mexico, a party of Spaniards who were trying to enslave the local Indians.

The "butcher's bill" (an archaic but still useful British naval expression, which refers to the number of killed and wounded) of the Pánfilo de Narváez expedition was staggering. Of the approximately 300 men who initially set out by land from near Tampa Bay, Florida, on this *entrada*, only four survived. The rest were killed by drowning, disease, starvation, exposure to the elements, or Indian arrows. The four survivors were Cabeza de Vaca himself; Alonso del Castillo Maldonado; Andrés Dorantes de Carranza; and a North African Negro slave, Estevánico, who was also known as Estevan and who remains one of the most engaging historical figures of the Southwest. Over a period of eight years, Cabeza de Vaca and his little band slowly wandered, by fits and starts, from the site of their shipwreck (Galveston Island, on the eastern coastline of Texas) all the way to Culiacán, the northernmost Spanish settlement on the frontier, which was located near the east coast of the Gulf of California.

During his eight years in the deserts, Cabeza de Vaca survived by his wits alone, since he had no firearms, no sword, no armor, and almost no clothing of any kind. Indeed, he describes himself as figuratively and literally *desnudo* (naked). "I wandered through many very strange lands, lost and naked," he writes.[4] Everything of any value or use had been lost in the shipwreck. With a strong gift of endurance and survival, however, he learned Indian languages and mastered the art of trading local produce and artifacts with different groups of Indians. Most remarkably, he also became a successful and highly popular faith healer. This is how he healed the sick: "The way we treated the sick was to make the sign of the cross over them while breathing on them, recite a Pater Noster and Ave Maria, and pray to God, our Lord, as well as we could to give them good health and inspire them to treat us well. Thanks to his will and the mercy he had upon us, as soon as we made the cross over them, all those for whom we prayed told the others they were cured and felt well again."[5]

De Vaca met with considerable success in his faith healing. Referring to the eight months he spent with a Texas tribe he calls the Avavares, Cabeza de Vaca tells us:

> During that time people came to us from far and wide and said that we were truly children of the sun. Until then Dorantes and the Negro had not cured anyone, but we found ourselves so pressed by the Indians coming from all sides that all of us had to become medicine men.... We never treated anyone that did not afterward say he was well, and they had such confidence in our skill that they believed that none of them would die as long as we were among them.... Among all these people it was believed that we came from Heaven.[6]

Cabeza de Vaca describes this faith healing and his other adventures in his *Chronicle of the Narváez Expedition*, written in 1542 and known in Spanish as *La relacíon* (*The Report*). While it still makes excellent reading today, the accuracy of some of his statements has long been open to serious question. In particular, the route he took has been the subject of a long-running and intense historical controversy. Regrettably, Cabeza de Vaca is often so vague and imprecise where travel is concerned that today no one can chart with certainty the course he followed on any given part of his journey.[7]

Educated guesses abound, however. We cannot do justice here to all the scholarly research on this point but as a broad generalization we can hazard the guess that, after the shipwreck, Cabeza de Vaca began his wanderings by heading west along the Texas shoreline, beginning from Galveston Island. Gradually and circuitously, he made his way across Texas and up the Rio Grande River. He may then have crossed the Mimbres Mountains and Big Burro Mountains (both in the Gila National Forest in southwestern New Mexico) and followed the Gila River into southern Arizona.[8]

II. Highlights of Spanish Exploration, Settlement, and Inspection

The Gila River, a tributary of the Colorado River, rises in western New Mexico and flows westward into Arizona and along the southern slope of the Gila Mountains. It passes near Phoenix and then flows southwestward to join the Colorado near Yuma, Arizona. By turning south at the Gila River, Cabeza de Vaca put himself, albeit unknowingly, directly on a course to intersect the Spanish slavers who were hunting for Indians near Culiacán.

For our purposes, what is most noteworthy about Cabeza de Vaca is not the precise route he followed but that in his extensive travels he was often guided by the local Indians along their trails. These trails were not marked; local Indians simply "knew" where to go, perhaps occasionally indicating the way at confusing trail intersections by leaving little piles of rocks. The Spaniards themselves had absolutely no knowledge of this region: Pánfilo de Narváez had confidently set off from Florida in the mistaken belief that his destination — the Spanish settlement on the Pánuco River, near Tampico, Mexico — was not very far away. In fact, the distance is about 1,200 miles as the crow flies and much further if one has to hug the Gulf coast. The Spaniards themselves were often totally lost but the Indians had a perfect understanding of their own homelands and could move through them at will. Without Indian guides, Cabeza and all his men would surely have perished.

Some tribes treated Cabeza de Vaca very harshly, even enslaving him temporarily, but others were quite helpful and willingly served as guides. For example, at one point during his travels Cabeza de Vaca was warmly received by a certain Indian village:

> When we were about to leave, a few women from the Indians living further on arrived and, finding out the location of their homes, we left, although the Indians entreated us to remain a day longer, since our destination was very far away and there was no trail to it. They pointed out how tired the women who had just arrived were, but that if they rested until the next day, they could accompany and guide us. We left, nevertheless, and soon the women followed with others of the village. There being no trails in that country, we soon lost our way. At the end of four leagues [a Spanish league was the equivalent of about 2.6 U.S. statute miles] we reached a spring where we met the women who had followed us, and who told us of all the trouble they had to find us. We went on, taking them as guides.[9]

By the same token, in later stages of his journey we also learn from Cabeza de Vaca that "when traveling with [another band of friendly Indians], we crossed a big river that came from the north, and crossing about thirty leagues of plains, met a number of people that came from afar to meet us on the trail.... They guided us for more than fifty leagues through a desert of very rugged mountains, so arid that there was no game.... The same Indians led us to a plain beyond the chain of mountains, where people from far away came to meet us."[10] It is thus clear from Cabeza de Vaca's account that he was rarely, if ever, traveling in a wilderness entirely devoid of human beings and their trails. There were many local trails — faint, perhaps, but easily visible to the Indians. He wrote that he and his companions decided "not to follow the road to the cows [i.e., a trail leading to the buffalo herds], since the latter carried us to the north, which meant a very great circuit, and since we were always sure that by going towards sunset we would reach our desired goal [i.e., the Spanish settlements of northern Mexico]. So we went on our way and crossed the whole country to the South Sea [the Gulf of California]."[11]

Spain's earlier conquests of Mexico and Peru had produced such a torrent of gold and silver that finding similar riches in the Southwest was one of the motivating forces behind the Spanish *entradas*. No comparable treasure trove had been found thus far in North America but the conquistadors were always hopeful and were always on the lookout for Indian wealth. Prospects in this regard seemed suddenly more favorable for Cabeza de Vaca toward the end of his travels:

> [W]e traveled more than a hundred leagues, always coming upon permanent houses and a great stock of corn and beans, and [the Indians] gave us many deer hides and cotton blankets better than those of New Spain. They also gave us plenty of beads made of the coral found in the South Sea and good turquoises, which they get from the north. In the end, they gave us everything they owned. They presented Dorantes with five emeralds shaped like arrow points, the arrows of which they use in their feasts and dances. Because they seemed to be of very good quality, I asked where they got them, and they said they came from some very high mountains toward the north, where they traded feather brushes and parrot plumes for them. They also said there were villages with many people and big houses there. [This was an accurate description of the pueblos of the upper Rio Grande.][12]

The "emeralds" were probably only bits of green turquoise or pieces of malachite (a green carbonate of copper) but they never made it back to Mexico City for closer inspection. When Cabeza de Vaca and his men finally came across the Spanish slavers, he reports that they "had many and bitter quarrels with the Christians [i.e., the slavers], for they wanted to make slaves of our Indians [a large throng of Indians had been following Cabeza de Vaca on this last stage of his travels], and we grew so angry at it that at our departure we forgot to take along many bows, pouches, and arrows, as well as the five emeralds, so they were left and lost to us."[13] Nevertheless, as we shall see in our account of the next *entrada*, many Spaniards would take Cabeza de Vaca's report of "emeralds" as convincing proof that untold riches did indeed await them somewhere in Mexico's unexplored northern frontier.

Sun-Dazzled Eyes: Fray Marcos de Niza

Marcos de Niza was a Franciscan friar assigned by Viceroy Antonio de Mendoza, in 1538, to search for the fabulously wealthy golden "Seven Cities of Cíbola," which were believed to be located somewhere in Spain's unexplored northern frontier in North America. The concept of these mythical cities arose from an eighth-century Portuguese legend which claimed that seven Christian bishops, laden with gold and other treasures, had fled from the conquering Moors and found safe refuge in a land across the Atlantic Ocean known as "Antilia."[14] This fantasy would become the source of the place name "Antilles" in the Caribbean islands, but of course the golden cities were not to be found there. Obligingly, however, this elusive concept simply migrated further westward, always remaining just beyond the breaking wave of European exploration. By Fray Marcos' time it had come to rest somewhere in Spain's northern frontier in the New World.

Fray Marcos' account of his own travels—his *Relación (Report)*—gives us wonderful glimpses into his journey and some clues about his possible route, but it leaves many important questions unanswered. Preceded by the North African Negro slave Estevánico—who, thanks to his years of wandering with Cabeza de Vaca, was fluent in several Indian languages and was thus, in a land without maps, an invaluable pathfinder—Fray Marcos set off from Culiacán in 1539.

His exact route is not known to us today but he almost certainly began by following Indian trails which paralleled the Gulf of California coastline along the mainland of Mexico. He was the first to record the trade in buffalo hides from the Great Plains to northwest Sonora in Mexico. Led by relays of Indian guides, at some point he turned north and eventually crossed into eastern Arizona. Later, he must have headed northeast, probably following the Zuni River and finally reaching his destination: Cíbola. This pueblo was located in western New Mexico, close to the Arizona border and 12 miles south of the modern town of Zuni, New Mexico. Cíbola was supposed to be the first of the seven golden cities but it turned out be an enormous disappointment, being only a sun-baked pueblo known to the local Zunis as Háwikuh. It was nothing more than the typical and very modest adobe village of those parts.

Because he had set off earlier than Fray Marcos, Estevánico reached the pueblo well before the friar and boldly entered it. He sent back word to Fray Marcos that besides the Seven Cities there were also other rich territories called Marata, Acus, and Totonteac. He said that Acus was an independent kingdom and described its people as *encaconados*, meaning that they had turquoise hanging from their noses and ears.

Alas, Estevánico was murdered in Cíbola by the Zunis. They feared that he was a spy for the Spaniards and was the advance guard of a planned Spanish invasion. It is also possible that, banking on the enthusiastic reception as a faith healer he had received from other Indians during his earlier travels with Cabeza de Vaca, Estevánico may have bragged to the Zunis that "he came from Heaven," i.e., that he was a god. The chronicler Pedro de Castañeda reports:

> After the said friars [Fray Marcos was initially accompanied by Fray Daniel and Fray Antonio de Santa Maria] and the negro Estevan set out, it seems that the negro fell from the good graces of the friars because he took along the women that were given to him, and collected turquoises, and accumulated everything....[15] I say, then, that when the Negro Estevan reached Cíbola, he arrived there laden with a large number of turquoises and some pretty women, which the natives had given him. The gifts were carried by Indians who accompanied and followed him through every settlement he crossed, believing that, by going under his protection, they could traverse the whole country without any danger. [The oldest and wisest Indians, however] thought it was nonsense for him to say that the people in the land whence he came were white, when he was black, and that he had been sent by them. So they went to him, and because, after some talk, he asked them for turquoises and women, they considered this an affront and determined to kill him. So they did, without killing any one of those who came with him.[16]

By the time Fray Marcos learned of Estevánico's death, he himself was not far from the pueblo. This is how he describes Cíbola in his *Relación*:

> With [three local chiefs] and my own Indians and interpreters, I continued my journey until I came within sight of Cíbola. It is situated on a level stretch of the brow of a roundish hill. It appears to be a very beautiful city, the best that I have seen in these parts; the houses are of the type that the Indians had described to me, all of stone with their storeys and terraces, as it appeared to me from a hill whence I could see it. The town is bigger than Mexico [i.e., Mexico City]. At times I was tempted to go to it, because I knew that I risked nothing but my life, which I had offered to God the day I commenced the journey; finally I feared to go, considering my danger and that if I died, I would not be able to give an account of this country, which seems to me to be the greatest and best of the discoveries. When I said to the chiefs who were with me how beautiful Cíbola appeared to me, they told me that it was the least of the seven cities, and that Totonteac is much bigger and better than all the seven, and that it has so many houses and people that there is no end to it.[17]

Scholars have long wondered how Fray Marcos, who had a good reputation with his superiors and had been handpicked for this assignment, could have been so impressed by what was in reality a very drab pueblo. Indeed, some have even doubted whether he saw it at all, but instead relied only on what he could learn — however imperfectly, given problems of translation — from

Indians who may have heard something about it. A better and more charitable guess is two-fold.

First, Fray Marcos himself *very much wanted to believe* that this was indeed a golden city; he also knew that his superiors and other readers would have expected nothing less. Second, the gloriously clear sunlight and cloudless skies of New Mexico, which today still draw artists and photographers to the state in their tens of thousands, may have lit up tiny chips of mica embedded in the adobe walls. If so, this may have created some kind of optical illusion which, to Fray Marcos's sun-dazzled eyes, turned these earthen walls into gold.

Even if we give Fray Marcos the benefit of the doubt on this issue, however, it is nevertheless very clear that he let his imagination run away with him. In another section of the *Relación* he assures us:

> When I showed the natives the sample of gold I had, they said there were vessels of it among their people. They wore ornaments of it hanging from their noses and ears, and also they have blades of gold to scrape the sweat from their bodies. Many of the people I saw wore silk clothing down to their feet. Of the richness of that country I cannot write, because it is so great that it does not seem possible. They have temples of metal covered with precious stones — emeralds, I think. They use vessels of gold and silver for they have no other metal.[18]

A Great Expedition Results in a Great Failure: Francisco Vásquez de Coronado

Fray Marcos' stories seemed to credulous officials in Mexico City to confirm the existence of Cabeza de Vaca's "emeralds" and other untold riches in the north of New Spain. As a result, a massive follow-up *entrada* was sent out in 1540 under the leadership of Francisco Vásquez de Coronado for the conquest of Cíbola. This expedition, initially launched from the west coast of Mexico, blazed a trail as far east as Kansas, where Cíbola was thought to be located. Much of its path would later become the east-west path of historic Route 66 and, later on, part of today's Interstate 40.

Approved by Viceroy Antonio de Mendoza, who was inspired by the promises of untold wealth held out by Fray Marcos, this formidable *entrada* consisted of more than 1,000 men (about 300 Spaniards, some 800 Indians, and six Franciscan friars); 1,500 horses and mules; and herds of sheep, pigs, and cattle to feed the hungry travelers.[19] (The horses and mules could be eaten during "starvin' times"— an apt phrase coined by the beaver trappers of a later era.) Moreover, two Spanish ships under the command of Captain Hernando de Alarcón sailed up the Gulf of California to support the Coronado expedition by sea.

Like his fellow explorers, Alarcón believed that Cíbola was located so close to the head of the Gulf of California that maritime support would indeed be feasible. In fact, as the crow flies, Cíbola lay about 325 miles northeast of the head of the Gulf. Nevertheless, Alarcón did his very best. By ordering his crewmen to sail and row the two ships' boats up the Colorado River, he got as far as its junction with the Gila River near Yuma but turned back when he learned that Coronado's expedition had already gone much farther inland.

Setting out from Compostela (on the west coast of Mexico) in February 1540, Coronado's great *entrada* had traveled along old Indian trails and followed river valleys during the long march north. These valleys included those of the Río Sonora in Mexico; the San Pedro River in Arizona, where Coronado's presumed line of march through southeastern Arizona is now commemorated by the Coronado National Memorial, which will be discussed in our last chapter; and the Gila River in New Mexico. The expedition finally reached Háwikuh (the fabled Cíbola) in July 1540. This Zuni pueblo strenuously resisted Coronado's advance; as a result it was quickly attacked and captured by Spanish soldiers. Háwikuh and other neighboring pueblos proved to be so devoid of wealth, however, that Coronado had to send a negative report to Viceroy Mendoza. It read in part:

> It now remains for me to tell you about the city and kingdom and province of which [Fray Marcos] gave Your Lordship an account. In brief, I can assure you that in reality he has not told the truth in a single thing he said, but everything is the reverse of what he said except the name of the city and the large stone houses.... The Seven Cities are seven little villages.... They are all within a radius of 5 leagues. They are all called the kingdom of Cevola [i.e., Cíbola], and each has its own name and no single one is called Cevola, but all together are called Cevola.... The people of the towns seem to me to be of ordinary size and intelligence, although I do not think they have the judgment and intelligence they ought to have to build these houses in the way in which they have, for most of them are entirely naked except [for] the covering of their privy parts.[20]

Fray Marcos himself was sent back to Mexico in utter disgrace.

Although bitterly disappointed by Cíbola, Coronado's expedition nevertheless reported accurately on all the lands it crossed and all the villages it visited. For example, Pedro de Castañeda, Coronado's chronicler, found himself quite impressed by Pecos:

> [It was] a pueblo of as many as five hundred warriors. It is feared throughout the land. In plan it is square, founded on a rock. In the center is a great patio or plaza with its kivas. The houses are all alike, of four stories. One can walk above over the entire pueblo without there being any street to prevent it. At two levels it is completely rimmed by corridors on which one can walk over the entire pueblo. They are like balconies which project out, and beneath them one can take shelter.

The houses have no doors at ground level. To climb the corridors inside the pueblo they use ladders which can be drawn up; in this way they have access to the rooms. Since the doors of the houses open on the corridor on that floor the corridor serves as street. The houses facing open country are back to back with those inside the patio, and in time of war they are entered through the inside ones. The pueblo is surrounded by a low stone wall. [Scholars now believe that this wall was too low for defensive purposes. It may have delineated the area where intertribal trade could be conducted.] Inside there is a spring from which they can draw water.

The people of this pueblo pride themselves that no one has been able to subdue them, while they subdue what pueblos they will.[21]

After spending the winter of 1540–1541 at Tiguex (a cluster of 12 Southern Tiwa pueblos between Albuquerque and Bernalillo), Coronado began searching the plains of Kansas for the legendary city of Quivira. His Plains Indian guide, nicknamed El Turco ("the Turk") by the Spanish because they thought he looked like an Ottoman Turk (possibly because his cloth headpiece resembled a turban), had described Quivira as a fabulously rich city to the east, located on an endless plain full of buffalo. The Spaniards were only too ready to believe El Turco's farfetched story, which follows:

> [I]n his land there was a river, flowing through plains, which was two leagues wide, with fish as large as horses and a great number of very large canoes with sails, carrying more than twenty oarsmen on each side. The nobles, he said, traveled in the stern, seated under canopies, and at the prow there was a large golden eagle. He further stated that the lord of that land took his siesta under a large tree from which hung numerous golden jingle bells, and he was pleased as they played in the wind. He added that the common table service of all was generally wrought silver, and that the pitchers, dishes and bowls were made of gold. He called gold *acochis*. At first he was believed on account of the directness with which had told his story and also because, when [the Spaniards] showed him jewels made of tin, he smelled them and said that it was not gold, that he knew gold and silver very well, and that he cared little for other metals.[22]

Pursuing the chimera of enormous wealth to be had for the taking, by the spring of 1541 Coronado, guided by El Turco, ventured out onto the Great Plains, probably getting as far east as Lyons, Kansas. The local Indians always wanted him to move out of their own territory and so frequently assured him that the riches he sought were "only a little bit further on." Coronado's exact route is not known today but these endless expanses of featureless flat land truly unsettled the Spaniards. Indeed, Pedro de Castañeda tells us:

> The land is in the shape of a ball, for wherever a man stands he is surrounded by the sky at the distance of a crossbow shot [that is to say, at a great distance]. There are no trees except along the rivers which there are in some barrancas

[deep gulches]. These rivers [more accurately, these are the escarpment canyons through which the rivers run] are so concealed that one does not see them until he is at their edge. They are of dead earth [i.e., they consist of ancient soils exposed by eons of wind and weather], with approaches made by [the buffalo] in order to reach the water.

Who could believe that although one thousand horses, five hundred of our cattle, more than five thousand rams and sheep, and more than fifteen hundred persons, including allies and servants, marched over these plains, they left no more traces when they got through them than if no one had passed over them, so that it became necessary to stack up piles of bones and dung of the cattle at various distances in order that the rear guard could follow the army and not get lost. Although the grass was short, when it was trampled, it stood up again as clean and as straight as before.[23]

Like the Pueblo lands, this vast prairie region, which was supposed to be the site of golden Quivira and thus bring fame and fortune to the *entrada*, held absolutely nothing of value for the Spaniards. Coronado was so furious with El Turco that he had him interrogated to learn his real purpose in leading them so far astray. El Turco finally confessed his plan, telling the Spaniards:

[H]is country was in that region, that the people of Cicúye [Pecos] had asked him to take the Spaniards out there and lead them astray on the plains. Thus, through lack of provisions, their horses would die and they themselves would become so feeble that, upon their return, the people of Cicúye could kill them easily, and so obtain revenge for what the Spaniards had done to them. [In Pecos, the Spaniards had put chains and collars on three Indians — Cacique, the chief; Bigotes; and El Turco himself— to force them to reveal the source of a rumored bracelet made of gold.] This, the Turk said, was the reason that he had misdirected them, believing that they would not know how to hunt or survive without maize [corn]. As to gold, he declared that he did not know where there was any.[24]

Upon hearing this, Coronado gave orders that El Turco should be garroted — the traditional Spanish punishment for treachery. After the execution was carried out, Spaniards buried El Turco's body at night, broke camp, and rode westward, back towards the lands of the Pueblo peoples.

Although the Coronado expedition learned a good deal about the geography and the Indian cultures of the Southwest, its signal failure to find any gold or silver marked it as a real disaster in contemporary eyes. Moreover, Coronado himself found the climate to be intolerable. In October 1541 he wrote to the King of Spain:

It would not be possible to establish a [Spanish] settlement here [on the river of Tiguex], for besides being 400 leagues from the North Sea [the Arctic regions] and 200 from the South Sea [the Gulf of California], with which it is impossible to have any sort of communication, the country is so cold, as I have written to Your Majesty, that apparently the winter could not possibly be spent here, because there is no wood, nor cloth with which to protect the men, except the skins which the natives wear and some small amount of cotton cloaks.[25]

In April 1542 Coronado began his return to Mexico, where he faced charges (later dismissed) for attacking two Tiwa pueblos which had refused to provide the food and blankets demanded by the Spaniards and for burning the surviving occupants at the stake.[26] Spanish officials were so disillusioned by Coronado's failure that they would make no further move to explore or develop New Mexico for nearly forty years.[27] Nevertheless, they never lost sight of the tantalizing possibilities for gold, God, and glory held out by Spain's unexplored northern frontier.

Blazing a New Trail to New Mexico: Fray Agustín Rodríguez and Francisco Sánchez Chamuscado

The next expedition into New Mexico was spurred not by gold but by silver. In 1546 the Indians in Zacatecas (central Mexico) had showed Spanish prospectors some chunks of silver ore. These samples turned out to come from a remarkably rich lode of silver, which soon attracted hordes of miners. By the mid–1560s the Spanish mining frontier had extended far north into Chihuahua. Five thousand mines sent huge amounts of silver flowing south to Mexico City. Zacatecas would eventually produce about 20 percent of all the silver mined in Mexico. It would become the third largest city of the colony; indeed, by 1807 its population was estimated at 7,000 souls. Prospects were so good in the region that a new silver mining center, Santa Bárbara, was soon sending out its own expeditions into New Mexico and Texas to enslave Indians, who would be forced to labor in the mines until they died.

Since Santa Bárbara was located on the Río Florido, one of the tributaries of the Río Conchos, which flowed northeast toward the Rio Grande, it soon became a primary Spanish base for the exploration, exploitation, and colonization of New Mexico. The junction of the Río Conchos and the Rio Grande was known as La Junta de los Ríos and had been a settled farming area since 1500. Today La Junta de los Ríos is the location of two communities: Presidio, Texas, on the north bank of the Rio Grande, and Ojinaga, Mexico, on the south bank. In the late 1500s, however, it was home to the La Junta Indians, who had eight villages there, some of them with more than 2,000 inhabitants.[28] (These Indians were also known as Jumanos, but the real Jumanos were nomads who wintered in villages along the Rio Grande and then left to hunt across Texas as far as eastern Texas. The Spanish referred to both tribes as "Jumanos." These Indians had the trait of tattooing or painting stripes on their faces.)[29]

In 1581 a relatively small *entrada* led by Franciscan Fray Agustín Rodríguez and Captain Francisco Sánchez Chamuscado set out from Santa Bárbara, bound for New Mexico.[30] They brought with them eight soldiers, 19 Indian guides and servants; 90 horses; and 600 head of livestock. (Extra horses were needed as replacements for those being ridden; the livestock was for consumption en route.) This expedition had two objectives, to which the Spanish accorded equal weight: to discover new silver mines and to convert the Indians.

The *entrada* followed the Río Florido to the spot where it joined the Río Conchos; it then continued on to the confluence with the Rio Grande. A map of New Mexico, drawn up in about 1746 and reflecting inspection tours conducted by Visitor General Juan Miguel Menchero, clearly shows the importance of these two rivers as the best landmarks to follow to get to northern New Mexico.[31] These rivers not only prevented travelers from getting lost in the arid wastes but also eliminated suffering caused by lack of water. En route, the *entrada* learned from the local Indians that many years earlier yet another band of foreigners — three Spaniards and a Negro — had passed through their lands. The men of the *entrada* surmised, correctly, that this prior group had consisted of Cabeza de Vaca and the three other survivors of his ill-fated expedition.

The *entrada* continued along the west bank of the Rio Grande and eventually reached the pueblos of New Mexico. There, for the first time, the explorers formally took possession of the whole region for the king of Spain. Chamuscado named it San Felipe de Nuevo México, a name that was soon shortened to Nuevo México. En route to the pueblos, the *entrada* went through El Paso del Norte (the Pass of the North), which was a deep chasm separating two mountain ranges looming up out of the desert. It merits a brief discussion here because its history is such an important part of trails, trade, and travels in New Mexico and elsewhere in the Southwest.

Today the oldest structure that survives in the El Paso area is Nuestra Señora de Guadalupe Mission, founded by Fray García de San Francisco in 1659. Later, during the Pueblo Revolt of 1680, many Spanish colonists and Indians fled to El Paso for safety. A presidio (a military post) was built here in 1684. The area became an important trade center on El Camino Real de Tierra Adentro (the Royal Road to the Interior Land, which will be discussed in a chapter of its own). Indeed, it would eventually become the site of two border cities — one in the United States, the other in Mexico.

For many years El Paso was part of New Mexico. The first Mexican constitution (1824) awarded El Paso to Chihuahua because of the dominant influence of the local Chihuahua merchants. El Paso was never considered to be part of Texas until 1848, when the treaty of Guadalupe Hidalgo, which ended the Mexican-American war, made the settlements on the north bank of the Rio Grande part of the United States, thus officially separating them from El Paso del Norte on the south (Mexican) bank. The present-day Texas–New Mexico boundary was drawn up in the Compromise of 1850. In 1888 the Mexican town of El Paso del Norte was renamed Cuidad Juárez. Its counterpart, the little railroad town on the American side of the river, has retained the historic name of El Paso.[32]

To return now to the Rodríguez-Chamuscado expedition: this *entrada* made its way to the Zuni pueblos, where the chronicler Hernán Gallegos was impressed by what he saw: "The valley is the best that has been discovered, since all of it is cultivated and not a grain of corn is lost. All the houses are of stone, which is indeed amazing. There is not a house of two or three stories that does not have eight rooms or more, which surprised us more than anything else, together with the fact that the houses are whitewashed and painted inside and out."[33] The expedition spent the remainder of 1581 traveling in New Mexico and in lands to the east, covering some of the same ground first explored by Coronado. During this time, one member of the expedition, Fray Juan de Santa María, ignored warnings from his colleagues and set out with two Indian servants to report to the viceroy in Mexico. He wanted to complain about the greed and insubordination the secular Spaniards were demonstrating. He also wanted to bring back more friars. This earnest man, however, was soon killed by the Indians, who murdered him the same way they got rid of witches — by dropping a heavy rock on him while he slept. The Indians feared that if they did not kill him but let him continue on his trip, he would certainly return with more Spaniards, who would not fail to occupy their lands.[34]

Early in 1582 the remainder of the expedition decided to return to Santa Bárbara and submit its own report. However, Fray Rodríguez and another missionary (Fray Francisco López) vowed — over Chamuscado's strongest warnings and protests — not to return but to stay at Puaray, a Tiwa pueblo near Bernalillo north of Albuquerque, and to establish a mission there. (Both clerics would be killed by the Tiwas of Puaray shortly after Chamuscado and his soldiers began their return journey to Santa Bárbara in January 1582.) On the way back, Chamuscado himself fell ill. No one in his party had a lancet so, "as soldiers do in time of need,"[35] a soldier used a dirty horseshoe nail to bleed him. Not surprisingly, infection set in and Chamuscado died on route.

In summary, this *entrada* deserves a mixed report card. Although the soldiers claimed they had seen 11 different places where there might be silver, no new mines were opened as a result of this trip. Few if any Indians were converted. Four members of the expedition met their deaths. Nevertheless, the expedition had blazed a new and relatively easily followed route to New Mexico and had further stoked Spanish dreams of unlimited wealth there. These factors, plus mounting concern for the welfare of the two friars who had been left behind, prompted another expedition that same year.

Seeking Redemption and Enrichment: Antonio de Espejo

Antonio de Espejo, a former functionary in the Spanish Inquisition's enforcement branch in Mexico, had been charged with complicity in the murder of one Indian cowboy and the wounding of another. He received only nominal punishment (a fine, which he seems not to have paid) but decided to move north to be beyond the clutches of the law and to start a new life at Santa Bárbara. His objectives there were twofold: to redeem his tarnished reputation and to enrich himself by finding gold or silver. Toward these ends, he offered to finance an expedition from Santa Bárbara to rescue Fray Rodríguez, having no way of knowing then that the friar was already dead.

In November 1582, accompanied by Fray Bernaldino Beltrán (the nominal leader of the expedition), 14 soldiers, Indian guides and servants, and 115 horses and mules, Espejo set out from San Bartolomé, a mining outpost north of Santa Bárbara, en route to Texas and New Mexico. He followed the same route used by Chamuscado the year before. One month into its journey, the expedition reached El Paso. They then followed the Rio Grande upstream, passing through a "mountain chain on each side of it, both of which were without timber."[36] This was what the Spaniards termed El Paso del Norte, the natural gateway lying between today's cities of Cuidad Juárez in Chihuahua and El Paso in Texas.

By January 1583, the *entrada* had made its way from Texas into New Mexico and had reached the numerous pueblos dotting the course of the Rio Grande River near Albuquerque. The explorers found that many thousands of Indians were living in these pueblos, raising turkeys and growing corn, beans, gourds, melons, and peppers. The Spanish friars remarked that the religious shrines and grottoes of the Indians reminded them of similar Roman Catholic shrines.[37]

Espejo and his party then followed the Jemez River northwest to the Acoma pueblo, located about 50 miles west of Albuquerque and built on a mesa 357 feet above the plateau. (Today Acoma is known as the "Sky City" and is the oldest continuously inhabited city in the United States.) Espejo spent three days there in 1582 and took notice of the vibrant intertribal trade that was being conducted, e.g., Indians who lived in the mountains, thought to be of Apache stock, would come down to the settlements near Acoma and trade for corn, salt, deer, rabbits, and tanned deerskins. Probably trying to lure Espejo away from Acoma, the Indians regaled him with wonderful tales of a "lake of gold," located even further west, i.e., in Arizona. What they probably meant was that metallic ores could be found near this big lake.[38]

Obligingly, Espejo made his way to the Hopi region of Arizona, where the Moqui Indians welcomed him with lavish presents, including hundreds of woven cotton *mantas* (blankets). They, too, pointed him towards the lake of gold but, they said, it lay even further west. Espejo never did find this lake but he did find several places where veins of copper or silver ore could be seen. However, the principal chronicler of the expedition, a soldier named Diego Pérez de Luján, reported that the veins were worthless.[39] He also recorded, in chilling detail, how Espejo had treated the Tiwas of Puaray. Having murdered the two missionaries (Francisco López and Agustín Rodríguez), these Indians now feared Spanish retaliation. Most of them had abandoned the Puaray pueblo when Espejo and his men approached it to ask for provisions. However, about 30 Tiwas remained on the rooftops and hurled insults at the Spaniards. Diego Pérez de Luján tells us what happened next:

> In view of this, the corners of the pueblo were taken [captured] by four [Spaniards], and four others with two servants began to seize those natives who showed themselves. We put them in a kiva. Because the pueblo was large and the majority had hidden themselves in it, we set fire to the great pueblo of Puala [Puaray], where some we thought were burned to death because of the cries they uttered. At once we took out the prisoners, two at a time, and lined them up against some cottonwoods close to the pueblo of Puala where they were garroted and shot many times until they were dead. Sixteen were executed, not counting those who burned to death. Some who did not seem to belong to Puala were set free. This was a remarkable deed for so few people [i.e., so few Spaniards] in the midst of so many enemies.[40]

Indian guides showed Espejo a quicker way back to the pueblos, where he met up with the rest of his comrades. After he made it back to San Bartolomé in September 1583, he wrote to the archbishop of Mexico: "Some twenty-five days ago I arrived at the mines of Santa Bárbara, in this jurisdiction, very worn and tired after traveling for more than a year, in which I covered eight hundred leagues, examining and exploring the provinces of New Mexico."[41] He also assured the viceroy and the king that he had discovered positive and sure signs of mineral wealth in New Mexico and in Arizona. In 1584 Fray Pedro Oroz, Franciscan commissary general for New Spain, wrote to the king urging that Espejo "be pardoned for a certain unfortunate episode."[42] Espejo's own enthusiastic report to the authorities, published in 1586, fanned the Spaniards' interest in the riches and the excellent settlement prospects allegedly offered by this beckoning land. The archbishop of Mexico wrote: "If what they tell me is true, they [Espejo and his men] have indeed discovered ... another new world."[43]

As a result, many Spaniards would compete vigorously for the royal authorization needed to conquer, colonize, and exploit New Mexico. Espejo himself sailed for Spain to petition King Felipe II, in person, for permission to lead a major expedition there but he died en route in Havana, Cuba. By then, however, the king had learned enough from the favorable reports of the Chamuscado and Espejo expeditions to decide that New Mexico should now be colonized by Spain. This prestigious and potentially lucrative assignment would eventually be given to Juan de Oñate in 1595, who will be discussed later.

Pioneering the First Cart-Route into New Mexico: Gaspar Castaño de Sosa

The historical record presents us with two very different views of Castaño de Sosa, who was the lieutenant governor of Nuevo Léon (New Spain's most northeasterly province). At this chronological distance only two things seem certain: that Castaño led an *entrada* into New Mexico without having received formal official permission to do so, and that this turned out to be a fatal mistake for him. Castaño himself was variously painted (by his enemies) as a ruthless adventurer eager to enslave the Indians and amass riches to further his own career, or (by his friends) as an ambitious officer simply doing his best for king and country. Here we will try to cut this Gordian knot by offering a straightforward account of his activities.

The Spanish Crown knew that an illegal slave trade in Pueblo Indians was being conducted on the northern frontier.[44] In fact, the governor of Nuevo Léon, Luis de Carvajal de la Cueva, was one of its key operatives. After Luis de Carvajal was burned alive by the Inquisition for secretly practicing Judaism, this slave trade continued under Lieutenant-Governor Castaño, who led a band of 50 soldiers described by the viceroy as "outlaws, criminals, and murderers — who are rebels against God and king."[45] When a new viceroy (Luis de Velasco) came to power, he moved against Castaño almost immediately, ordering him to stop capturing and selling Indians as slaves and, moreover, explicitly forbidding him to travel without official permission.

Probably fearing that both his lucrative business and his official position were now in grave danger, Castaño decided to ignore this order. He probably calculated that if he could set up the first Spanish colony in New Mexico, the king would graciously overlook any irregularities in the process and would reward him handsomely. In July 1590 Castaño therefore set off for New Mexico from the mining town of Almadén (its name means "mine" in Spanish; today it is the city of Monclova in the Mexican state of Coahuila), leading a long cavalcade. It included 160 to 170 followers; several Indian guides and interpreters; supplies of corn and wheat; beef on the hoof and other animals; and at least 10 heavy two-wheeled wooden carts, laboriously pulled by oxen.[46]

He managed to pioneer, however slowly, the first cart route into New Mexico. The expedition got to the Rio Grande in September 1590, having taken 24 days of actual travel to go 200 miles, and crossed the river near Del Rio, Texas. This route was so well chosen that a Mexican highway now follows it the whole way and a railway line part of the way. After much hard searching and many exertions, the Spaniards managed to find the point where the Pecos River joins the Rio Grande, which is about 30 miles northwest of Del Rio. Because of their heavy carts they needed a place where access to the river and crossing it was easy, so they marched northward along the rocky canyon of the Pecos and tried to find an easy way down to the river itself. A 26 March 1590 entry in Castaño's journal tells us the following: "In order to get down to the river, a descent could not be found except along some great slopes, where much labor was expended in making a road to get down. Some carts were broken in the descent, among which was one which carried the royal treasury, with its royal fifths."[47] [This cart apparently carried the expedition's strongbox with the gold or cash needed for the journey. "Fifths" were royal taxes.] The next day the cart was repaired and was taken down to the river, at a point probably about 15 to 20 miles south of Sheffield, Texas. We are told that in this arduous process the expedition wore out 25 dozen horseshoes and that some of their horses were lame thereafter as a result.

This *entrada* had not been planned very carefully. The explorers did not know they still faced 500 miles of hard travel through a landscape that had little water; was dissected by canyons and ravines; had minimal forage for their livestock; and offered only long sandy stretches, endless winds, and biting cold in wintertime.[48] Moreover, the Spaniards were now running short of food. As a result, Castaño led an advance party northward, always following the Pecos River and finally reaching Pecos Pueblo on the last day of 1590. There the Spaniards came into conflict with the inhabitants, killing some of them, seizing others to act as guides, and helping themselves to the Indians' food supplies. In January 1591 the *entrada* marched west, probably through Glorieta Pass, heading for the pueblos near Santa Fe and the Rio Grande.[49] Castaño established his own headquarters at Santo Domingo (north of Albuquerque).

In the meantime, Viceroy Valasco was furious when he learned that Castaño had left for New Mexico with "all the riffraff left over from the war against the Chichimecas."⁵⁰ ("Chichimecas" meant "savages." It was a highly derogatory term used by the Spanish to describe the seminomadic, warlike peoples of the northern frontier.) Valasco thereupon sent his deputy, Captain Juan Morlete, and a force of 40 men to pursue Castaño. Writing nearly 60 years later (in 1649), a Spanish author claimed that Morlete, "an irascible man and not of good disposition," was jealous of Castaño's success and wanted to take revenge on him because of an earlier falling out between the two men. Morlete therefore informed the High Court of Mexico that Castaño had "gone inland, rebelled, and become a tyrant."⁵¹

Whatever the rights and wrongs of the matter, the upshot is beyond dispute: Castaño was charged with leading an unauthorized expedition. He was therefore arrested at Santo Domingo and, laden with heavy leg irons and a chain, was led by Morlete back to Mexico in total disgrace. On the return route, Morlete seems to have blazed a new trail from El Paso directly to Santa Bárbara, rather than using the well-beaten path along the Río Conchos and the Rio Grande. If so, this may well have been the route used by Oñate (discussed in a later section) in 1598 in his march north to colonize New Mexico.⁵²

In 1593 Castaño was tried, convicted, and sentenced to six years of military service, without pay, in the Philippines for invading the "lands of peaceable Indians." He appealed to the Council of the Indies—more formally known as the *Real y Supremo Consejo de Indias* (Royal and Supreme Council of the Indies), which sat in perpetual session in Madrid. This council was the most important administrative institution of the Spanish Empire, exercising full legislative and executive powers. It eventually established his innocence and repealed the sentence. Unfortunately, the council's pardon came too late to help Castaño: he had already been killed during a mutiny of Chinese galley slaves aboard the ship taking him to the Philippines.

Searching for Mythical Riches: Francisco Leyva de Bonilla and António Gutiérrez de Humaña

The lure of being the first Spaniard to find mineral wealth in New Mexico and to colonize it proved so strong that it soon led to another unauthorized expedition and to more Spanish and Indian deaths. In 1593 Captain Francisco Leyva de Bonilla decided to mount his own *entrada* into New Mexico, ostensibly as a freelance if illegal extension of Viceroy Velasco's campaign to punish Indians who were robbing Spanish cattle ranches east of Santa Bárbara. In fact, however, his real objective was to enrich himself.

Toward this end, he followed the route chosen by Chamuscado and Espejo, namely, down the Río Conchos and up the Rio Grande. Leyva set up his headquarters at San Ildefonso Pueblo (about 25 miles northwest of Santa Fe) before heading out onto the Great Plains. Searching for the mythical riches of Quivira, he seems to have reached the Arkansas River in Kansas and then, after traveling another 12 days north, may have arrived at the Platte River in Nebraska. There Leyva's lieutenant, António Gutiérrez de Humaña, killed Leyva with a butcher's knife during a quarrel and assumed command himself. (The knife was probably a *belduque*, a long broad-bladed hunting knife made entirely of metal and used in the Indian trade. The exchange rate offered by Comanches to Spanish traders was one buffalo hide for one *belduque*.)[53]

Later, Plains Indians attacked the party, killing Gutiérrez de Humaña and most of his companions. Five of the expedition's Indian guides were spared by the attackers; of these, only one Indian, named Jusephe by the Spaniards, managed to get back to New Mexico and tell the tale — after first surviving a year of captivity with the Apaches.[54]

The Last Conquistador: Juan de Oñate

Known as "the last conquistador" because he led the last major Spanish expedition into the American Southwest, Juan de Oñate won the exclusive right to explore and colonize New Mexico because of his political connections and his great wealth.[55] The rich Zacatecas silver mines of north central Mexico had been discovered and developed by Cristóbal Oñate (among others), who was Juan's father and a former governor of Nueva Galicia. (Nueva Galicia, a Spanish colonial administrative region in western Mexico, covered the states of Jalisco and Nayarit and part of Sinaloa.)

The Spaniards' permanent occupation of New Mexico dates from 1598, when Juan de Oñate brought about 560 colonists (including 130 soldiers and 10 Franciscans), 80 wagons and carts, and 7,000 head of livestock into northern New Mexico. We may well ask why these colonists were willing to risk their lives by moving to such a distant, little known, and potentially dangerous region. The answer lies in what the Spanish historian Jaime Vincens Vives called "hidalgo-mania."[56]

By this he meant that after five years of living in New Mexico every male head of household became eligible to receive the title of *hidalgo* (the lowest rung of the Spanish nobility) and the designation of *caballero* (knight). Upon being granted this title, a man would thereupon be entitled to the same rights, honors, and privileges enjoyed by his counterparts in Spain. These aristocratic and, indeed, semi-medieval benefits included the right to use the title *Don* (meaning "of noble origin") before his name, exemption from taxes, immunity from arrest for debt, and freedom from manual labor. Such social and practical advantages had a tremendous appeal to many of the colonists because, as members of the Council of the Indies later complained to the king, New Spain was full of idle, lazy, and undisciplined people.[57]

Oñate led a small detachment up the Rio Grande valley to Ohkay, a Tewa pueblo. He renamed it San Juan de los Cabelleros and initially planned to use it as the capital of his new colony. In 1599 he decided instead to build the capital across the Rio Grande at San Gabriel Pueblo. (In 1608 his successor, Pedro de Peralta, moved the capital to its present location, which was then the site of an abandoned pueblo at the foot of the Sangre de Cristo Mountains.) While waiting for the rest of his expedition to arrive, Oñate embarked on three reconnaissance trips from San Juan Pueblo to explore the lands of the Pueblo Indians and to look for gold or silver. These travels took him, respectively, north to Taos Pueblo; east to Pecos Pueblo; then southwest to the Tano villages of the Galisteo Basin; and, finally, southwest to the Jemez Mountains of the Towa pueblos.

In September 1599 he sent out his nephew Vincente with 60 men to hunt buffalo on the eastern plains and bring in a winter supply of dried buffalo meat. With Jusephe (the sole survivor of the ill-fated Leyva-Gutiérrez de Humaña expedition) as a guide, Vincente ventured east beyond Pecos to the plains, where he met the Apaches. He noted how these Indians used "medium-sized, shaggy dogs" to pull their tents, poles, and belongings. It was "both interesting and amusing," he wrote, "to see them traveling along, one after another, dragging the ends of their [travois] poles, almost all of them with sores under the harness. When the Indian women load these dogs [e.g., when they strapped onto them small packs containing meat or other foodstuffs], they hold their heads between their legs, and in this manner they load them or straighten their loads."[58]

Near the Texas border Oñate's men encountered huge herds of buffalo. Knowing that buffalo meat was excellent and that buffalo robes were warm, they decided to see whether buffalo could be raised like cattle. The first step was to try to corral them. The Spaniards spent three days building a big corral made of cottonwood logs. But the buffalo refused to cooperate: when horsemen tried to drive them into the corral, they simply turned around and stampeded in the other direction. They were also very clever. The Spanish complained that they were "stubborn animals, brave beyond praise, and so cunning that if one runs after them, they run, and if one stops or moves slowly, they stop and roll [i.e., they roll on their backs], just like mules, and after this rest they renew their flight."[59]

The next month Oñate set out to find the sea, where he wanted to build a port for ships to supply the new colony. He headed westward, passing the Acoma and Zuni pueblos, and sent an officer, Marcos Farfán, southwest to find a way to reach the Gulf of California. Farfán returned with the news that the Gulf was 30 days beyond the point where he had stopped and begun to retrace his steps. During his travels, he learned from the Indians that the Gulf had rich beds of pearls. In mid–1600 Oñate sent Vincente on a follow-up mission towards the Gulf. Vincente reached the southwest corner of Arizona and came back to report that the sea was only three days' travel from that point (a modern map puts this distance at about 40 miles). Oñate, however, did not pursue the fantasy of establishing a port on the Gulf. The reason was that the legend of Quivira was still alive and well in Spanish minds.

In 1601, accompanied by 70 soldiers and eight baggage carts, Oñate therefore sallied forth to find the alleged riches promised by this myth. He followed the Canadian River across the Texas panhandle and then headed northeast, crossing the Cimarron River into Kansas, finally reaching the Arkansas River and, at last, Quivira itself. This little village had not changed at all from the days of Coronado: it was still only a modest settlement of round, grass-thatched dwellings, surrounded by cultivated fields.

When he got back to San Gabriel Pueblo, Oñate discovered to his chagrin that most of the settlers had mutinied and gone back to Mexico, where they complained to the authorities about the depressing conditions and his poor leadership. These authorities had no further interest in New Mexico's aridity, food shortages, cold winters, and lack of gold or silver. The Franciscans, for their part, were upset by Oñate's heavy-handed suppression of Indian rebellions at Acoma and Taos, which made it nearly impossible for them to convert the Pueblo peoples.

After another journey toward the Gulf (led by Fray Francisco de Velasco early in 1604), Oñate's expedition crossed central Arizona in late 1604 and reached the Bill Williams River, which led him to the Colorado River. Oñate arrived at the mouth of the Colorado in January 1605 and claimed that it would be a fine harbor. Today this lowest section of the Colorado River forms the border between the Mexican states of Baja California and Sonora. This part of the river contains only a trickle of water: most of the water has been diverted to irrigate California's Imperial Valley. Before the twentieth century, however, the mouth of the Colorado was a biologically rich estuarine marshland and might conceivably have become the site of a small port.

During his travels on this *entrada*, Oñate — using a little literary license — had an inscription carved on a rock at what is now El Morro National Monument in western New Mexico, where it can still be seen today:

Pasó por aquí el Adelantado Don Juan de Oñate al descumbrimiento del Mar del Sur a 16 abril de 1605.

[The translation:] There passed by this way the Adelantado [literally "one who goes before," i.e., a military officer representing the king of Castile] Don Juan de Oñate, from the discovery of the South Sea [the Gulf of California — still known locally as the Sea of Cortez — whose existence had already been established], the 16th of April 1605.[60]

Conditions in the colony continued to slide downhill until Oñate had no choice but to resign. In August 1607 he wrote to the viceroy, stating sadly: "Finding myself helpless in every respect, because I have used up on this expedition my estate and the resources of my relatives and friends, amounting to more than six hundred thousand pesos, and anxious that the fruits of so many expeditions and of more than eleven years of labor should not be lost ... I find no other means ... than to renounce my office, which resignation I am sending to your excellency."[61] The viceroy accepted his resignation without regret and Oñate returned to Mexico City in 1609. The next year the official historian of the expedition, Gaspar Perez de Villagrá, chronicled Oñate's *entrada* by writing the first Euro-American history of New Mexico. This 34-canto epic poem, entitled the *Historia de la Nueva México*, damned Oñate's leadership by revealing the hardships and brutality the expedition had experienced in New Mexico. Excerpts from this work, in English prose, can be found in Appendix 1. They are worth reading because they give the reader an extraordinary and contemporary insight into the less glamorous aspects of the Oñate expedition.

The wheels of justice in New Spain ground very slowly but they never came to a complete halt. In 1613 Oñate was tried for using excessive force against the Acomas (800 of them had died; 600 had been taken prisoner; each captive man was sentenced to have one foot amputated and to serve 20 years of forced labor); for executing Indians, mutineers, and deserters; for adultery with the women of the camp; and for swearing falsely to New Mexico's potential as a Spanish colony. The upshot was that he was fined 6,000 ducats and court costs, stripped of his titles, banished permanently from New Mexico, and exiled from Mexico City itself for four years. In 1621 he sailed to Spain to appeal his case but met with only limited success. He eventually became a mining inspector in Spain and died there in 1626.[62]

In retrospect, it is clear that while Oñate's ambitious *entrada* was a failure in most respects, it did have one lasting result. Oñate was a very good pathfinder: he managed to extend the Camino Real ("royal highway") — which originally ran only between Mexico City and Santa Bárbara — some additional 600 miles, i.e., into northern New Mexico. He also chose the official *parajes* (campsites or stopping places) along this new section of the trail. The Camino Real was to be North America's longest road (2,000 miles) for several hundred years and would become the artery that kept the Spanish colony in New Mexico alive. We will discuss it in more detail in chapter three.

Inspired by a Mysterious "Lady in Blue": Juan de Salas, Diego López, Ascencio de Zárate, and Pedro de Ortega

The Spanish commitment to converting the Indians remained strong. As missionary activity expanded in New Mexico, more and more Franciscans came to the Isleta mission (south of Albuquerque) — at least 53 of them between 1612 and 1629 — to teach the Jumano Indians the rudiments of Christianity.[63] They were very well received there: indeed, about 50 Jumanos even turned up at the mission in 1629 and asked that missionaries be sent to them.

The Jumanos said they had come to the mission at the request of the "Lady in Blue" — a light-skinned woman, dressed in blue, who had appeared to them. They asserted that she seemed to be floating in the air in a kind of haze while she spoke to them in their own language about the Christian faith. It is clear that here the Jumanos were referring to the legend of a Spanish nun, María de Ágreda, who claimed that, while physically remaining in her convent in Spain, she was able to proselytize the Indians of New Mexico by visiting them "in ecstasy." Tried by the Inquisition in 1635, she was acquitted of any heretical beliefs.

It seems more likely that the Jumanos came to the mission not because of any visitation by the Lady in Blue but simply because they wanted to open trade relations with the Spanish and wanted the well-armed Spanish to keep the encroaching Apaches at bay. The Jumanos knew just how vulnerable they themselves were: in fact, they would vanish entirely by about 1700, either because they had voluntarily moved out onto the plains where they traditionally traded or because they were driven out of their homeland by the Apaches.

Two Franciscan missionaries — Juan de Salas and Diego López — and three soldiers (and undoubtedly their Indian guides and servants as well) left Santa Fe in 1629 and made their way toward Jumano territory, which was located along the Concho River, near the Colorado River on the plains of southwestern Texas. During their journey the Franciscans briefly explored the region east of the Pecos River and tried to persuade the nomadic tribes there to settle down in permanent homes and grow crops. After a short stay with the Jumanos, the friars returned to the Isleta mission. Three years later, in 1632, two other Franciscan missionaries — Ascencio de Zárate and Pedro de Ortega — devoted themselves to converting the Jumanos.

Concho Pearls: Hernando Martín and Diego del Castillo

Two captains of the Spanish army — Hernando Martín and Diego del Castillo — were sent out from Santa Fe in 1650 by the governor of New Mexico, together with a few soldiers and Indians, to blaze a new trail across the plains of Texas to the homeland of the Jumano Indians in order to convert them.[64] Spanish explorers were by now so experienced in plains travel that they could safely cross long arid stretches, relying on the knowledge of local Indians to find water holes. These captains traveled about 600 miles to the Jumano territory and stayed with the Jumanos about six months.

This *entrada* was motivated by the usual Spanish preoccupation with gold, God, and glory. The expedition did not discover any riches there but, along the Concho River, it did come across great quantities of shells (*conchos* in Spanish), some of them containing iridescent pink or purple pearls. These were produced by the freshwater Tampico pearly mussel, which thrives in the area's rivers and lakes. Big purple pearls, called "Concho pearls" by the Spaniards, had the highest value.

After leaving the Jumanos, the Martín-Castillo expedition traveled eastward toward Shreveport, Louisiana—the forested and humid lands inhabited by the Tejas Indians (our word "Texas" comes from the name of this tribe)—returning to Santa Fe by a slightly different route. The pearls they brought back with them interested the viceroy so much that he decided to send another expedition to the Jumanos.

A Prudent Retreat: Diego de Guadalajara

Led by Sergeant Major Diego de Guadalajara, this *entrada* of 1654, staffed by 30 soldiers and some 200 Indian guides and servants, followed the route of the Martín-Castillo expedition to the basin of the Conchos River in the plains of southern Texas.[65] A temporary headquarters was set up for some months among the Jumanos, who were recruited to harvest mussels in hopes of finding gem-quality pearls. In the meantime, a detachment under Captain Andrés López explored the surrounding region, looking for the mythical "Kingdom of the Teyas [Tejas]," which was long rumored to be extremely wealthy. However, Guadalajara's force got into a battle with a neighboring tribe (the Cuitaos) and won, capturing 200 prisoners and many deerskins and buffalo hides. Then, fearing an Indian counterattack, Guadalajara decided to quit while he was ahead and prudently ordered the expedition to return to Santa Fe.

Looking for the Kingdom of the Tejas: Juan Domínguez de Mendoza and Fray Nicolás López

As time passed, the Jumanos became increasingly interested in getting Spanish protection from Apache attacks and in establishing trade relations with the Spaniards. In 1683 Jumano delegations invited missionaries to come to their homeland, enticing them with tales of the Caddo-speaking Indians who allegedly ruled the "Kingdom of Tejas." (The word "Tejas" comes from a Caddoan term meaning "friends" or "allies." The "kingdom" consisted only of very modest agricultural settlements, built close to fields of corn, beans, squash, watermelons, and melons.)[66] In any case, the governor of New Mexico sent out Captain Juan Domínguez de Mendoza from El Paso in 1684 to collect pearl samples, study Indian cultures, instill in the Indians a respect for the friars sent among them, and harvest some of the apparently infinite number of buffalo on the plains.

After traveling downstream along the Rio Grande to the Río Conchos, at La Junta de los Ríos (now Presidio, Texas) the captain was joined by Fray Nicolás López, custodian of missions at El Paso, and two other Franciscans. The party then headed north to join up with the Pecos River, followed it southeast, and marched east across the dry plains of Texas. The route they followed is not known precisely but it is now thought they reached the point where three branches of the Conchos River come together, i.e., near San Angelo, Texas.[67] They remained in the region for six weeks, killing large numbers of buffalo and returning to New Mexico with their pack animals heavily laden with dried meat and hides.

Maintaining the Northern Frontier of New Spain: Pedro de Rivera and the Marqués de Rubí

The French and the Spanish, along with other powers, competed vigorously for control of the trans-Mississippi West.[68] A report of an unauthorized French presence could galvanize the Spanish into action. In 1720, for example, Governor Valverde ordered his inexperienced deputy, Pedro de Villasur, to launch a military expedition from Santa Fe, heading for the Pawnee country along the Platte River in Nebraska. In this region, located more than 600 miles northeast of Santa Fe, French trappers and traders were said to be living with — and, feared the Spanish, plotting with—the Pawnee Indians.

Villasur foolishly set up his camp in high grass at the confluence of the Platte and Loup rivers near North Platte, Nebraska. The Pawnees, possibly led or supported by a few Frenchmen, slipped quietly through the grass, surrounded the camp, and at dawn opened a withering fire with muskets and bows and arrows. Out of 42 Spanish soldiers, 30 were killed, including Villasur himself. Many of his 60 Pueblo Indian allies were killed or wounded as well. With such heavy losses, New Mexico's settlements now lay undefended.

Despite the Villasur disaster, the king of Spain, Philip V, still wanted to defend northern New Spain but, at the same time, he wanted to reduce the high costs of doing so. He therefore needed a reliable military officer to study the situation and make recommendations. At the urging of Juan Manuel de Olivan Rebolledo, the royal "auditor of war," and Juan de Acuña y Bejaraño, the new viceroy, this challenging assignment was ultimately given to Brigadier General Pedro de Rivera.

Between 1724 and 1728 Rivera traveled more than 7,000 miles along the frontier and visited more than 300 places, including the 23 presidios which marked the frontiers of settlement, and several important cities. Rivera did not waste any time once he was in the saddle, averaging about 20 miles per day.[69] His inspection trip took him as far west as Sinaloa, as far north as Santa Fe, and as far east as Los Adaes (near Robeline, Louisiana).

His conclusions, later embodied in the Regulations of 1729, gave his superiors a very accurate snapshot of conditions, describing the location of settlements, the customs of the Indians, and the products of the soil.[70] Rivera also made a number of recommendations, for example:

- The Apaches should be suppressed in order to halt or at least reduce their raids on settlements.
- The Jicarilla Indians should be moved to Taos to protect them from attack by the Apaches. This was in lieu of building a new presidio in northeast New Mexico, a plan Rivera rejected on the grounds that, as he put it, "If every proposal for the founding of a presidio were acceded to, the treasury of Midas would not suffice."[71] (The Spanish decision not to build a new presidio had the unintended effect of opening up this region to the Comanches.)
- Spanish defenses should be modified to save money, e.g., the garrison at the presidio at San Antonio, Texas, should be reduced. (This presidio, founded in 1718, was the center of Spanish defenses in western Texas. It and an adjacent town, both known collectively as San Antonio de Béxar, were often referred to by the Spaniards simply as "Béxar" and by the Anglos as "Bexar." These terms will be used interchangeably in this book.)

This third recommendation raised howls of protest from the missionaries and settlers in the region, who believed that the Apaches would attack as soon as they learned of the smaller force. These fears turned out to be unfounded. The Apaches never tried to overrun San Antonio (probably calculating that a frontal attack on a well defended fort would cost them too many casualties) but they did continue to wage guerrilla warfare against the Spaniards during the 1730s and 1740s.[72]

In the years ahead, Spanish rulers, mired knee-deep in the red tape, corruption, and military inefficiency of northern New Spain, would remain unwilling to invest the large sums of money necessary to defend the region.

Trying gamely if belatedly to strengthen Spain's feeble military capabilities there, in 1765 King Charles III appointed the Marqués de Rubí—a loyal, hard-working, competent officer—to make yet another inspection tour. The king hoped that Rubí would be able to do the impossible, namely, to consolidate local defenses, to strengthen the frontier against Indian attacks, to reduce the government's defense expenditures, and to correct the financial abuses then rampant along the frontier.

Rubí began his inspection tour in 1766, spent 23 months in the field, and traveled some 7,600 miles between the Gulf of California and Louisiana. In essence, he recommended that Spain gear back its imperial pretenses in the region because, as the modern scholar Elizabeth John tells us, "With rare exceptions, the northern frontier presidios were military mockeries: crumbling structures, incompetently and corruptly managed; garrisons of untrained soldiers short of basic equipment, skills, and morale.... Each garrison lived braced against a siege that never came because that was not the Indian style of warfare, while Indian raiders plundered settlements and missions, mines and ranches, and for good measure stole most of the presidial horse herd."[73] Rubí wanted the king to reorganize the defenses of the far northern frontier by building a network of presidios, each one about 100 miles apart and each one garrisoned by 50 men. This new defensive line would stretch from the head of the Gulf of California to the mouth of the Guadalupe River, about 85 miles northeast of Corpus Christi, Texas—a line which would roughly parallel today's border between the United States and Mexico.

Two key Spanish settlements—Santa Fe and San Antonio—lay north of this proposed defensive line and were much too important to surrender to the Indians. Under Rubí's plan, each of them would be protected by its own presidio with a detachment of 76 soldiers. As for the other regions lying north of the line, Rubí had a dour recommendation: they "should be given back to Nature and the Indians."[74] There would be, in all, a total of 17 presidios. Rubí also called for a two-pronged policy toward the Indians: a war of extermination against the Apaches, coupled with efforts to improve Spain's relations with the Comanches and Wichitas, who were enemies of the Apaches. Some of his recommendations were promulgated in a royal order of 1772 known as the New Regulations for Presidios. Rubí's long line of presidios, however, was never built because of the great expense involved.[75]

An Outstanding Trailblazer: Juan Bautista de Anza

In 1773 Juan Bautista de Anza, then captain of the small presidio of Tubac[76] (45 miles south of Tucson, Arizona) received permission from Antonio María

Bucareli y Ursúa, viceroy of New Spain, to blaze a 1,200-mile trail from Sonora in Mexico to northern California.[77] For Spain, this expedition had two important goals. The first was to find a way to supply its missions and presidios in California by land: trying to do so by sea had proved to be too risky and unreliable because of storms and fickle winds. The second was to begin colonizing California to ensure Spanish control over San Francisco Bay, which has been described as the greatest harbor in the world, and to ward off threatened encroachments by other great powers, notably England and Russia.[78]

Anza would become the most experienced and most successful officer of the Provincias Internas, or Interior Provinces, of New Spain. (To strengthen its very tenuous control over New Spain, in 1776 the Council of the Indies had created this new bureaucratic entity, which covered northern New Spain in its entirety.) Anza's first *entrada* left Tubac in January 1774 with almost 300 people. He paralleled the Mexico/California border, crossed the Colorado River at the junction with the Gila River at Yuma, and finally reached Mission San Gabriel Arcángel, near what is now Los Angeles, in March 1774. To make this epic journey, Anza had to pioneer a horse and mule train route across deserts and over mountain passes never previously crossed by any non–Indian. He brought with him 140 saddle horses, 35 mules, and five mule drivers.[79]

To get an idea of the daily routine of his travels, we will pause here to dip into Walter Nordhoff's wonderful book, *The Journey of the Flame* (1933), a fictional but historically accurate account of a trip by mule train from the southern tip of Baja California, to San Francisco.[80] Mules were widely used throughout the Southwest because, for a number of reasons, they were superior to horses for travel in the deserts and mountains.[81] According to a British horseman's manual, written in about 1875:

> [T]he mule has long been bred and used successfully in the southern semitropical regions of the United States. It is essentially the animal [of choice] for a country of bad or no roads, coarse and scanty herbage, uncertain supply of water, a mountainous or sandy country, and hot climate. Under certain circumstances the mule will endure privations that would kill a horse, but he requires management by people who understand his peculiarities. The mule is of little use without the mule-driver.... To carry burdens or pack-saddles the mule is, no doubt, from his conformation [physical build] superior to the horse. In war, for drawing [pulling] artillery, he has one disadvantage; it is not every man who will make a muleteer, but every one can lead a horse.[82]

A modern American mule breeder gives some specific reasons for the mule's continuing superiority over horses under the harshest conditions. In his experience, "It is the hybrid vigor that they have, larger lungs, larger pancreas, more sure-footed. Eyes are positioned differently than a horse's, [so that] mules can see their hind hooves. Wonderful endurance animals. Less spooky [than horses], and when it is time to stop for health reasons, they stop. Not stubborn, but great [sense of] self-preservation."[83]

The fictional trip described by Nordhoff was set in 1810 but it captures the flavor of Anza's own journeys very well. Nordhoff writes:

> A small fire served our cook, while around a larger one — for our nights are chilly in winter even on deserts — those who rested lay and talked of days past and those to come. We ate chiefly meat, fresh when it was to be had, or otherwise dried bull's beef, which tests the teeth but fills the belly with sustenance. Fruits when we were in their vicinity, or sugar cane peeled and chewed. Afterwards on our trip, when all else failed, the cook gave us dry, hard, white cheese to be eaten with lumps of *panocha* [small round cakes of hard brown sugar, formed in moulds].... [E]ach man carried a cup slung to his belt [for coffee, when it was available], just as his own knife cut such meat as politeness demanded his teeth should not touch. Not even a savage uses his teeth to sever a string of dried meat from that other portion of which his neighbor must eat.[84]

Promoted to lieutenant-colonel for his successful expedition to California, Anza was then charged by Bucareli with leading settlers there, where they were to build both a presidio and a mission on San Francisco Bay. Setting out from Tubac in October 1775, his expedition must have become quite familiar with the brusque command he gave, bright and early, every morning when all was ready: "¡*Vayan subiendo!*" — "Everyone mount up!" Anza's party finally arrived at the presidio of Monterey, California, in March 1776 and continued on to San Francisco. He did not establish a settlement there himself: this was done later by the colonists, led by Lieutenant José Joaquin Moraga. In April Anza left California for Mexico City, where in 1777 he was appointed governor of the province of New Mexico.

Anza is usually remembered for his California travels: indeed, in 1990 the U.S. Congress honored his memory by establishing the Juan Bautista de Anza National Historic Trail. For our purposes here, however, we must note as well that he was far from idle in his capacity as governor of New Mexico. In 1779 he led a punitive expedition against the Comanches, who had been raiding Taos. With from 500 to 800 Spanish soldiers, supported by the Spaniards' Ute and Apache allies, he moved north along the Rio Grande, then through the San Luis Valley of Colorado, and finally made his way out onto the vast plains to the east.

At Colorado Springs he surprised a small party of Comanches and pursued them south down Fountain Creek, crossing the Arkansas River near Pueblo, Colorado. In that area he came across the main Comanche force, which was returning from a raid on New Mexico and which was led by Cuerno Verde — "Green Horn" in English, so named by the Spaniards because of the green-tinted buffalo horns he wore on his battle headdress. Comanche and Spanish forces fought a series of running clashes during four days in late August and early September 1779. Cuerno Verde, together with his eldest son and 15 other Indian warriors, were killed during one of these fights. With Cuerno Verde's death, Spanish-Comanche hostilities eased in that region because the Comanches shifted their depredations to Oklahoma and Texas.

In late 1779 Anza pioneered a route from Santa Fe to Sonora in Mexico and scored successes against other hostile tribes. In 1783 he led a campaign against the Comanches on the eastern plains of New Mexico; the next year most of them sued for peace. After the remaining chiefs fell into line, a formal peace treaty was concluded in 1786. This would ease the way not only for the established traders but also for the Comancheros, low-income Spaniards who traded with the Comanches. Josiah Gregg gives us a good snapshot of these men:

> These parties of *Comancheros* are usually composed of the indigent and rude classes of the frontier villages, who collect together, several times a year, and launch upon the plains with a few trinkets and trumperies of all kinds, and perhaps a bag of bread and maybe another of *pinole* [a food made from parched ground grain], which they barter away to the savages for horses and mules. The entire stock of an individual trader very seldom exceeds the value of twenty dollars, with which he is content to wander about for several months, and glad to return home with a mule or two, as the proceeds of his traffic.[85]

Anza himself continued to serve as governor of New Mexico until 1787, when he returned to Sonora in Mexico. Appointed in 1788 to be the commander of the presidio at Tucson, he died before taking office there.

Pursuing Elusive Goals: Fray Francisco Anastasio Domínguez and Fray Silvestre Vélez de Escalante

The Spaniards wanted to find a way to resupply their California missions and presidios from New Mexico, but they ruled out blazing a direct trail from Santa Fe west to Monterey because of the Pima and other potentially hostile tribes along the line of travel. Instead, two Franciscan missionary explorers, Fray Domínguez and Fray Escalante, took up the challenge and decided to pioneer a new *northerly* trail from Santa Fe to Monterey. In so doing they had four objectives:

1. Tactically, they wanted to avoid hostilities with the Hopis and Apaches who lived to the west and who did not welcome outsiders.
2. Strategically, their goal was far more ambitious. They wanted to

unravel, once and for all, what the celebrated historian and ethnologist of the American West,[86] Hubert Howe Bancroft (1832–1918), would much later call the "great and perpetual Northern Mystery." By this evocative term Bancroft was referring to the widely held belief that an as-yet-undiscovered navigable waterway cut across western North America and flowed into the Pacific Ocean, perhaps near Puget Sound. This elusive waterway had many different names, among them the Great River of the West; the Strait of Anian; the Mer de l'Ouest (the Western Sea); the Río San Buenaventura; and, more simply, the Passage. As Bancroft put it in his elegant fashion, "There was always a fascination attending this region [the northern reaches of the trans-Mississippi West], with its great and perpetual Northern Mystery; perhaps the Arctic Ocean came down hereabout, or at least an arm of the Anian Strait might be found; nor were forgotten the rivers spoken of by different persons on different occasions as flowing hence into the Pacific."[87]

Other seasoned travelers, including Lewis and Clark during 1803 to 1806, reasoned that, if they could only find it, this Passage would greatly facilitate European and American trade with East Asia, Southeast Asia, and India, and would make their own fortunes as well.[88] There was only one little problem: further explorations would prove conclusively that the Passage did not exist.

3. Fray Domínguez and Fray Escalante also hoped that pioneering a northerly route would put them in touch with a mythical "lost" tribe of Spaniards, who were thought to be the descendents of survivors of sailors shipwrecked on the California coast. Many explorers believed that this tribe, often described by the shorthand phrase "bearded Indians," was living somewhere in the Southwest. These resourceful clever Spanish sailors, it was thought, had not only survived the loss of their ships but had also successfully adapted to the Indian way of life.[89]

4. Finally, the friars yearned to discover the rumored (but nonexistent) Indian pueblos in the north that had not yet been introduced to Christianity.

Their *entrada* left Santa Fe in July 1776. It was a modest undertaking, consisting in the end of some 11 Spaniards (one of them Bernardo Miera y Pacheco, a soldier-cartographer whose important map is described below), two Indians, and beef on the hoof. The Spaniards would become the first non–Indians to explore southwestern Colorado and eastern Utah. This little band rode north into Colorado and crossed into Utah near present-day Dinosaur National Park in northwest Colorado. It then went west toward Spanish Fork on Utah Lake and headed north toward the towns of Springville and Provo.

As chronicler of the expedition, Escalante kept an excellent journal which makes good reading today.⁹⁰ The modern scholar Jarom McDonald has summed up its importance in these words:

> [Escalante's] record of [the Spaniards'] exploration, their observations, and their recommendations was priceless for contemporaneous Spanish colonial settlement and political strategy, as it allowed the governors of New Mexico and California to gain an insight into the nature of the bordering Indian tribes and their lands. It also is invaluable as a historical record today, allowing us to look back at the character of these two Franciscan explorers, their methods of observation and knowledge production, their development of a sense of authorship, and the relationship of the missionary/Indian encounter to the politics of late 18th century Mexico.⁹¹

By the time the expedition reached Utah, it was October and there had already been a heavy snowfall. The men were running short of food and saw that winter was quickly approaching: the mountain passes would soon be blocked. The journal of the Domínguez-Escalante expedition describes the situation:

> Today [8 October 1776] we suffered greatly from the cold because the north wind did not cease blowing all day, and most acutely. Up to here we had kept our intent of reaching the garrison and new establishments of Monterey ... [but it now became clear that] we had many leagues left to us toward the west. Since winter had already set in most severely, for all the sierras [mountains] were covered with snow, the weather very unsettled, we therefore feared that before we got there the passes would be closed to us, so that they would force us to stay two or three months in some sierra [i.e., mountain range] where there might not be any people or the wherewithal for our necessary sustenance. For the provisions we had were very low by now, and we could not expose ourselves to perishing from hunger if not from the cold. We also figured that, even granting that we arrived in Monterey this winter, we could not be in La Villa de Santa Fe until the month of June the following year.... Weighing all this ... [we decided] to continue south for as much as the terrain permitted us as far as El Río Colorado [the Colorado River], and from here point our way toward Cosnina, Moqui, and Zuni [three Indian settlements lying to the south, in Arizona and New Mexico].⁹²

At this point, the pious Spaniards decided to seek divine intervention on whether they should risk pushing on to Monterey, which mapmaker Bernardo Miera y Pacheco and some of the others wanted to do, or abort their journey and return to New Mexico, which was the preference of the friars. Not being able to agree on which course of action to follow, the friars decided to "cast lots." Their journal describes this:

> And so, in order that God's cause stood better justified, and to make [our companions] understand more clearly that we had changed our mind neither out of fear nor by our own despotic will, we decided to lay aside altogether the great weight of the arguments mentioned and, after imploring the divine mercy and

the intercession of our holy patron saints, to search anew God's will by casting lots — putting *Monterey* on one and *Cosnina* on the other — and to follow the route which came out.[93]

It is not clear from the historical record precisely how this was done but the word "Monterey" seems to have been marked on one lot and "Cosnina" on the other. Cosnina was the name of an Indian tribe, now known as the Havasupai, who lived in the Grand Canyon area and whom the explorers wanted to visit. When the lots were cast, Cosnina won. Escalante wrote: "This we all heartily accepted now, thanks be to God, mollified and pleased."[94] Accordingly, they began to make their way back towards Santa Fe, first heading south and, later, east.

They were very lucky on their return journey. At Glen Canyon in southern Utah they managed to get across the Colorado River without any losses. The place where they did so became known as the Crossing of the Fathers and was one of the best places to cross the river. (The Crossing of the Fathers is now submerged about 550 feet beneath the surface of Lake Powell.) The men had to hack steps into the steep sandstone slope to help the horses keep their footing and had to use slings to lower their equipment and livestock down to the river. Fray Escalante writes of it, with a studied calm he may not have felt at the time:

> We got down to the canyon and after going a mile we reached the river and went along it downstream for about as far as two musket shots [about 500 yards], now through the water, now along the edge, until we came to the widest part of its currents where the ford appeared to be. One man waded in and found it all right, not having to swim at any place. We followed him on horseback, entering a little further down, and in its middle two mounts which went ahead missed bottom and swam through a short channel. We held back, though in some peril, until the first one who crossed on foot came back from the other side to lead us, and we successfully passed over without the horses on which we were crossing having to swim.[95]

The *entrada* made its way back toward Santa Fe without any further mishaps, finally reaching the city early in January 1777. The route pioneered by the friars did not lead them to California but it did introduce them to many of the cultural and geographic highlights of southwestern Colorado, eastern Utah, northern Arizona, and western New Mexico. Their epic journey, which took 159 days and covered more than 1,700 miles, paid good dividends, listed below:

1. It increased Spanish understanding of the geography and Indian cultures of a largely unexplored part of the Southwest.
2. In 1777 mapmaker Bernardo Miera y Pacheco produced the best map

of the western interior drawn up thus far and the first to depict the Great Basin on the basis of firsthand experience. This map is entitled *Plano Géographico, de la tierra descubrierta, nuevamente, á los Rumbos Norte Noroeste y Oeste, del Nuevo Mexico* (*Map of the newly discovered land in the North, Northwest, and West regions of New Mexico*).[96] Six manuscript copies of it are known to exist today. What the mapmaker saw himself is recorded accurately. What he had learned only by hearsay is sometimes in error; for example, he guessed that the Great Salt Lake, which the explorers had heard about but did not visit, and Utah Lake were a single body of water.[97]

3. Later travelers would profit considerably from the expedition's efforts: traders from Santa Fe would filter into the region and one section of the Domínguez-Escalante route would become the eastern leg of the Old Spanish Trail.[98]

4. This *entrada* proved conclusively how impractical it would be to try to supply the Spanish holdings in California via a northerly route from Santa Fe.

Last of the Great Spanish Explorers of the Southwest: Pedro Vial

Born in France in the middle decades of the eighteenth century, Pedro (or Pierre) Vial entered the service of Spain and became one of its most remarkable, accomplished, and untiring explorers in the Spanish Southwest. Indeed, he was the last of the early explorers of this region. His major pathfinding explorations linked Santa Fe to far-flung cities like San Antonio, Texas; Natchitoches, Louisiana; and St. Louis, Missouri. Even a very condensed account of Vial's achievements is impressive.[99]

Vial first came to the notice of Spanish authorities in Natchitoches and New Orleans in 1779, thanks to his formidable knowledge of the Indian lands and cultures along the Missouri River. It is likely that he had learned all this from being a fur trader there. He came to San Antonio in 1784 after living for a time with the Taovaya Indians, supporting himself as a gunsmith and trader. The Taovayas carried on an extensive trade with the Comanches, providing corn, beans, melons, gourds, and tobacco in return for horses and slaves. This tribe was one of the "Nations of the North" that gave the Spanish a great deal of trouble in the eighteenth century.

The Spanish quickly saw Vial's great value and hired him as a trailblazer, agent, and interpreter. The governor of Texas, Domingo Cabello y Robles, asked him to gather information about the Comanches, who were closely associated with the Taovayas. Vial was a loner who liked to travel by himself or with only one Spanish companion. He passed the summer months of 1785 in the Comanchería. A huge region spreading across the plains, beginning east of Santa Fe, the Comanchería was, as its name implies, dominated by the Comanches. It was the site of numerous Kiowa, Apache, and Comanche raiding trails and of Comanchero cattle trails.

Spanish officials were especially interested in anything Vial could do to reduce the menace posed by the Comanches. Vial understood that their decentralized lifestyle was itself the greatest obstacle to peace negotiations. He knew them well and in 1785 told his Spanish employers:

> The Comanche Nation has no fixed villages because they have many horses, because of which it is necessary to find places to pasture them, and which have buffalo and deer, for that is their food and clothing, and with which they make the tents which they make from buffalo hides, and [which are] very strong, useful, and durable. Their *Rancherias* [temporary Indian settlements] are organized by the captains, who, each endeavoring to have his own, they do not have a fixed number of subjects [i.e., inhabitants], but only those who can adjust to the spirit of the captain.[100]

The Spaniards could do nothing to resolve this fundamental problem but with Vial's help they managed to hammer out treaties with the Comanches of Texas in 1785 and with those of New Mexico the following year. Vial wisely recommended a conciliatory course of action: "From what we have learned when among this nation, theirs should be a lasting peace as long as they are treated fondly and warmly when they come to visit this Presidio and care is taken to make an annual gift to the captains and principals of the nation, without neglecting the youths; and to maintain a trader for them, and have [other Indians] urge them to keep good relations."[101]

In 1786 the governor assigned Vial the task of finding the most direct route between San Antonio and Santa Fe, a line-of-sight distance of only about 625 miles. The governor also directed him to keep a diary and record the distances traveled, the groups of Indians he met, and the size of their camps. En route, however, Vial became ill. Seeking a cure, he consulted an Indian medicine man by taking a very roundabout route via the Indian villages near today's Waco, Texas — even though the governor had made it quite clear that Vial should not tarry at all en route. When he was in good health again, Vial continued on to the Red River, where he lived for some further time with the Taovayas. He told them when he left, "Now I am going to open this road to Santa Fe in order that the Spaniards of San Antonio may cross through Comanche country and that those from Santa Fe may pass from there to San Antonio, since they are all friends. And if on my return I see that you Taovayas are quiet, I will take you to San Antonio before the Spanish captain, and you will see that he is a kind-hearted man to you as soon as you promise him not to do harm."[102] From the Taovaya villages, Vial followed the Red and Canadian rivers westward, finally reaching Santa Fe in 1787. In traveling such a leisurely, circuitous route he had covered approximately 1,000 miles of hard country.

In 1788 he left Santa Fe for Natchitoches, traveling by way of the Texas Panhandle and the Red River. From Natchitoches he went to San Antonio and then made a second journey to Santa Fe, traveling an estimated 2,377 miles in fourteen months. From 1792 to 1793 (in successive summers) he traveled over what would later become the Santa Fe Trail, making a round trip estimated at 2,279 miles between Santa Fe and St. Louis. His route closely resembled one that Santa Fe traders would follow during the next century and proved that the distance between the Louisiana Territory and New Mexico was not insurmountable. Indeed, he claimed that he could have made the trip from St. Louis to Santa Fe in only 25 days if hostile Indians had not captured him.[103] After these exploits, in 1798 he left the Spanish to live among the Comanches but returned to Santa Fe in 1803, where he died in 1814.

"Encumbered" by a Comanche Band: José Mares

The governor of New Mexico, Fernando de la Concha, became increasingly concerned about his geographical isolation from the northern provinces of Mexico when he learned that French traders had already established five posts between the Taovaya villages on the Red River and New Mexico itself. Fearing an unwanted growth of French influence, Concha decided to find a shorter and more direct route for Spanish travelers and soldiers to get from Santa Fe to Bexar (San Antonio). He therefore commissioned José Mares, a recently retired corporal, to blaze such a trail.[104]

Mares discharged his duties in a workmanlike manner. In the process he left us an excellent "I-was-there" journal, which he called his "journal of discovery," covering his travels in 1787 and 1788. He was initially accompanied by Cristóbal de Los Santos, who had made a trail-breaking trip with Pedro Vial, and by an Indian interpreter named Alejandro Martín. Setting out from Pecos, Mares first traveled southeast to the Taovaya villages, then swung south to Bexar, and finally turned northwest back toward Santa Fe. His journeys totaled about 1,815 miles.

The first leg of his trip, i.e., from Pecos to Bexar, proved to be very difficult. The reason was (as his superiors in Bexar later informed the viceroy) that by the time Mares reached Bexar, he had acquired a motley band of 81 Comanche fellow travelers, namely, four chiefs, 10 sub-chiefs, 38 braves, 23 women, and 6 boys. The official report to the viceroy explained that while the agreed objective of Mares' trip had been to open "the most convenient and most direct road" to Bexar, "because the Comanches encumbered him excessively and guided him between the east and southeast in order to fall upon [i.e., to visit] the important establishments of the Taovayas, the work that he especially undertook resulted in a failure [because the Taovaya villages lie far to the east of a straight line drawn between Pecos and Bexar]."[105]

Nevertheless, despite this official wrist-slapping, Mares proved himself to have been a successful pathfinder between New Mexico and Spanish Texas. He showed that while travel between Santa Fe and Bexar was time-consuming, it was not impossibly difficult. In fairness to his memory we must add that, in the southwestern wilderness of his time, getting rid of a band of 81 "helpful" Comanches might have proved to be a fatal undertaking. The Indians probably considered themselves to have been "hired" as guides. As such, they would have expected a substantial reward once they got to Bexar. If Mares had tried to discharge them en route, his own life might have been in peril.

High Praise for Successful Leadership: Francisco Amangual

Between March and December 1808, Francisco Amangual, a Spanish army officer, led an expedition of 200 men southeast from El Paso to San Antonio; from there northwest to Santa Fe; and, finally, south from Santa Fe back to El Paso. This campaign seems to have been a belated effort by Spain to strengthen its communications with distant Santa Fe and to set up some kind of defense against the threat of American expansion. It did not deter the Americans but it did leave us a thorough and complete diary of Amangual's travels. This diary gives us the true flavor of trail life in eastern Texas and western New Mexico at the beginning of the nineteenth century and, since it is not well known, deserves to be quoted at some length. Here are four excerpts from it:

> This day [2 April 1808] dawned with a furious storm, accompanied by terrible thunder and lightning and constant rains, very cold.... [T]he *cavallada* [horse band] of the New Kingdom of León and veterans stampeded [these were military units under Amangual's command]; 87 animals were lost, and a party of 10 men and a corporal went out to look for them, and returned with them at 4 o'clock without one missing. It continued to rain and the weather stayed cold. Night fell with no other unusual incident....[106]
>
> Upon our arrival [at an Indian village on 8 May 1808], the big chief and the other chiefs of the tribe came out to meet us. They were very well dressed, but they wore very unusual clothes [i.e., they were wearing unusual combinations of Spanish, English, and Indian clothing]: long red coats with blue collars and

cuffs, white buttons, yellow (imitation gold) galloons [a galloon is a narrow trimming, e.g., of braid with metallic threads, with both edges scalloped]; one was dressed in ancient Spanish style: a short red coat, blue trousers, white stockings, English spurs, an ordinary cornered hat worn cocked, a cane with a silver handle shaped like a hyssop [an aromatic plant]. Others wore red neckties; they wore sashes made out of otterskin, adorned with beads and shells; their hair was nicely braided and trailing on the ground; they were painted with chalk and red ochre....[107]

[A] heavy rain began to fall [on 13 June 1808], and it was necessary for us to move our camp because of the flood that came down the river. We had hardly moved out when it became almost impossible for the vehicles to get out.... [This entry proves that Amangual's expedition included either two-wheeled or four-wheeled carts. Indeed, his men sometimes had to use pickaxes and crowbars to clear a way for them up or down steep riverbanks.][108]

We set out [on 14 October 1808] ... to follow the trail of the Indians to the north northwest [Amangual was tracking the Indians because they had attacked a Spanish settlement and had kidnapped a Spanish boy].... I ordered the men to dismount, and, leaving 14 men to guard the *cavallada*, I went up [a] hill with the remaining 74 men. The Indians ran away, but I pursued them as far as I could, but these Indians, forewarned, waited for us behind rocks, and began to rain bullets and arrows upon the men. The great difficulty encountered by our men at every step because of our unfamiliarity with the terrain, and the great advantage the Indians had — who even threw rocks down upon us from the top of the *sierra* [hill] — obstructed our troops in such a manner that, after attacking them for three hours, I ordered a retreat....[109]

Amangual deserves praise for his successful leadership of this expedition. He took good care of his men and his livestock during his extensive travels over wilderness terrain in all kinds of weather. It has been estimated that — accompanied by 200 men, 800 animals, and some wheeled vehicles — he traveled for a total of 121 days, covered 2,255 miles, and averaged 18.8 miles a day.[110] He retired with the rank of captain and died in 1812.

CHAPTER III

The Royal Road: El Camino Real de Tierra Adentro

El Camino Real de Tierra Adentro (the Royal Road to the Interior Land) ultimately extended more than 1,500 miles, running between Mexico City itself and the Tewa pueblo of Ohkay, which, as mentioned earlier, the Spanish renamed San Juan de los Caballeros. It was located in the Española Valley north of what would later become Santa Fe. This famous trail began to stretch north from Mexico City not long after the Spanish conquered the Aztec metropolis in 1521. Its growth was in large part due to Spain's intensive efforts to find new silver mines.

Heading north, the trail passed successively through a large number of little towns and small cities in Mexico. The founding dates of some of them are given below in parentheses. They included San Juan del Río and Querétaro (both 1531), Celaya (1570), Silao (1553), León (1576), San Juan de los Lagos (1563), Aguas Calientes (1575), Zacatecas (1546), Fresnillo (1554), Sombrerete (1555), Nombre de Dios (1563), Durango (1563), and, finally, Santa Bárbara (1563). This last city was located in the district known as the Valle de San Bartolomé, where the trail halted for about 20 years because of the desert beyond it. After this brief pause, the trail would later stretch to Chihuahua, El Paso, Albuquerque, and Santa Fe.[1]

By 1580 the frontier line stretched some 850 miles north of Mexico City—all the way to the settlements in the Valle de San Bartolomé (now known as Villa Allende, Chihuahua).[2] The 550-mile segment of the trail north of Chihuahua would become known as the Chihuahua Trail and would link the mines of Nueva Viscaya and the towns and missions of New Mexico.

Today almost all of the trail—which actually resembled a *braid* of different routes trending in the same general direction rather than a single well-worn pathway—has long been incorporated into the modern rail and highway system of Mexico and New Mexico. The general course of the trail, however,

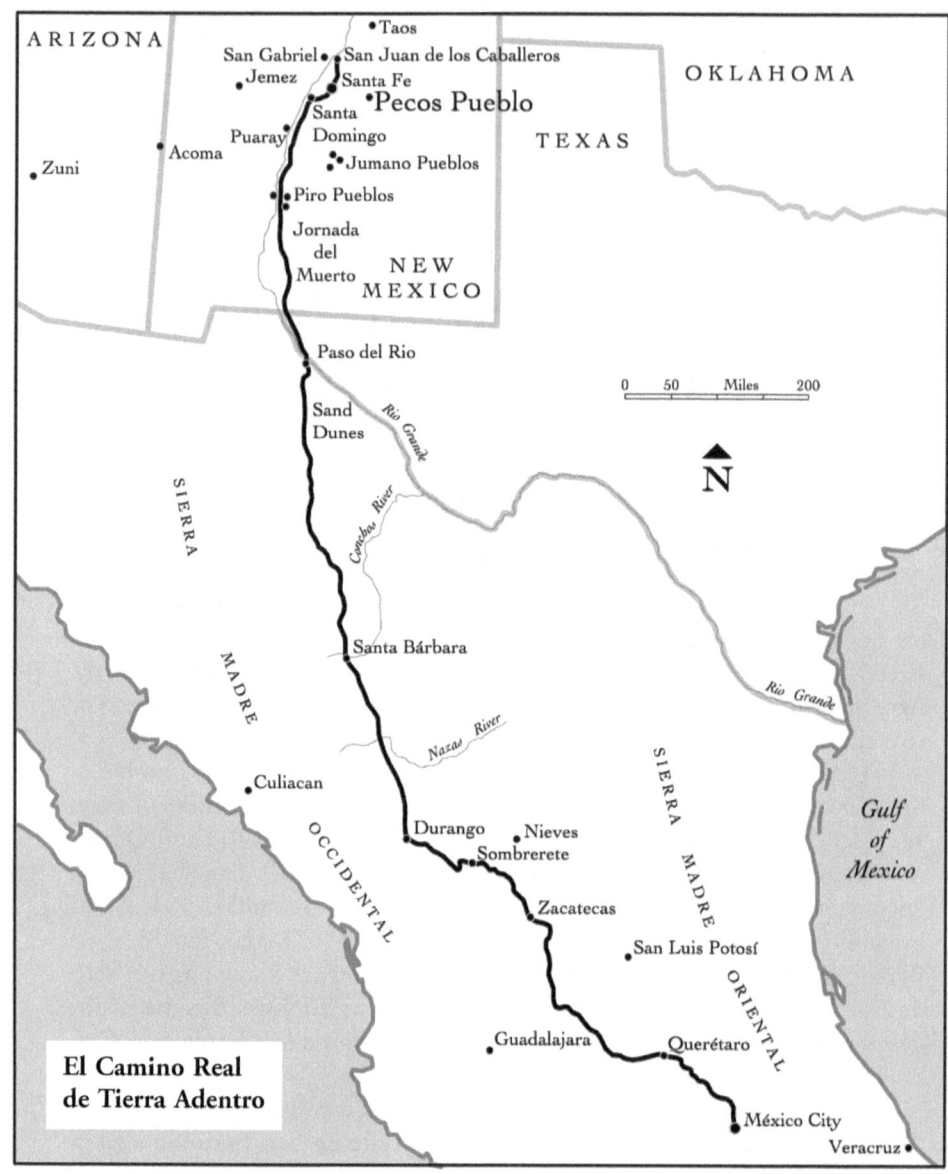

can still be traced today, thanks to the directions in Hal Jackson's *Following the Royal Road: A Guide to the Historic Camino Real de Tierra Adentro* (Albuquerque: University of New Mexico Press, 2006).

In January 1598, as mentioned earlier, the "last conquistador," Juan de Oñate, set out for New Mexico, beginning at San Gerónimo (near Santa Bárbara).[3] The men of Oñate's extensive entourage, which stretched out for three miles along the trail, had three main assignments: (1) to conquer New Mexico for Spain — a campaign which, if successful, would bring honor and glory to Oñate and his men; (2) to convert the Indians to Christianity; and (3) to find a mother lode of silver, i.e., a principal vein or zone of veins of silver ore. While the conquistadors genuinely believed in the importance of the first two goals, the great silver strike in Zacatecas (1546) had aroused in them the keenest expectations of untold wealth in New Mexico. If only it could be found, they reasoned, a mother lode would not only enrich them personally but would also ensure lasting prosperity for their extended families.

Once he arrived there, Oñate did not plan to leave New Mexico any time soon. As the modern scholar John L. Kessell puts it:

> Although Oñate called it an army, this was a migration.... Settlement had eclipsed exploration. Now [the colonists] drove not only reserve war horses but breeding mares, not only pack animals but wheeled vehicles freighting heavy crates of building tools and mining equipment. The ratio of female helpmates and squealing children to men was far higher. The numerous Mexican Indians among them, neither segregated nor arrayed for battle, came as servants, not as a military force. In boxes and bundles, the Franciscans had brought not only tools to erect crosses but also the liturgical furnishings for churches. This time, the invaders had come to stay.[4]

The colonists also expected to conduct a profitable business in New Mexico. Oñate's wagons and carts were filled with a veritable cornucopia of trade items chosen to seduce Indian customers. They included about 80,000 glass beads of various kinds and colors, rosaries, religious images made of tin, amulets, medals, clay whistles, knives, mirrors, needles, thread, thimbles, rings, glass earrings, and hawks bells[5] [little bells designed to be attached to the feet of sparrow-hawks].

Oñate sent his nephew, Vincente de Zaldívar, on ahead to pioneer a more direct route to the Rio Grande by crossing the Chihuahua Desert west of the Río Conchos. Vincente's assignment was to blaze a new trail from Chihuahua north to the Rio Grande, reaching it about 40 miles below El Paso. This new trail would replace the much longer but well-watered and therefore safer traditional route north from Chihuahua following the river systems. The old route ran northeast from Santa Bárbara, down the Río de Parral to its confluence with the Río Florido, down the Florido to the Río Conchos, and down the Conchos to the Rio Grande at what is now Ojinaga (opposite Presidio, Texas).[6] Vincente succeeded in this ambitious attempt and the whole *entrada* finally creaked and groaned its way into Santo Domingo Pueblo (about 26 miles southwest of Santa Fe) in May 1598. After Santa Fe itself was founded by Governor Pedro de Peralta in 1610, the new capital would become the northern terminus of El Camino Real de Tierra Adentro.

During the seventeenth century this trail would be virtually the only means for the Spanish in Mexico to communicate with their settlements in

New Mexico and to supply the missions there. A scheduled supply caravan financed by the royal treasury was supposed to travel from Mexico City to Santa Fe every three years.[7] In practice, however, this service was very irregular. Friar Alonso de Benavides, who traveled with a supply caravan in 1625, commented on how the infrequent caravan arrivals made life very difficult for the missionaries when their supplies ran out.

None of the travelers on this trail in the early days has left us detailed descriptions of the wagon trains themselves but by studying official shipping contracts, modern scholars have been able to piece together how this supply service worked. The following information comes from a contract of April 30, 1631.[8] A wagon train consisted of about 32 wagons, split into two sections, each of which was led by a *mayordomo* (wagon master). The lead wagon of each section flew the royal banner. A company of 12 to 14 soldiers, led by a captain, protected the wagon train, which also included beef on the hoof and spare draft animals.

The wagons themselves are of interest to us because they were a far cry from the normal two-wheeled oxcarts used by the Spanish. They were specially built heavy duty wagons with four iron-tired wheels. Each wagon was drawn by a team of eight mules and could carry about 4,000 pounds of supplies. The contents of each wagon were protected by arched hoods and covers made from 40 yards of coarse woolen cloth. The wagons were built to survive very hard service on the trail and were well equipped for emergencies. Every wagon was supplied with an extra team of eight mules; 32 extra mules were also available for the caravan as a whole. Each set of eight wagons was required to carry the following repair kit: 16 extra axles; 150 extra spokes; 24 reserve iron tires, each one weighing 27 pounds; 500 pounds of tallow for lubrication; 24 pounds of cord for repairing the wagon hoods; one 27-pound sledge hammer; and assorted nails, bolts, washers, cleats, linchpins, ribs, hammers, saws, adzes, and crowbars.[9]

Some of the Spanish governors of New Mexico did not hesitate to profit from their official position by engaging in private business on the side, even though this was specifically prohibited by the law of the realm. In 1638, for example, Governor Luís de Rosas dispatched to merchants in the silver mining town of Parral, which was located about 125 miles southeast of Chihuahua, a sizeable personal consignment. This consisted of 17 boxes and 10 bales of goods, 2,000 yards of coarse woolen dress fabric, 46 drapes, 70 other hangings, 408 blankets, 24 cushions, 8 overskirts, 79 doublets and jackets, 124 painted buffalo hides, 207 antelope skins, 900 candles, and 57 bushels of pine nuts. Local authorities politely turned a blind eye to this illegal transaction, which on departure was duly notarized at Santa Fe and on arrival was officially recorded at Parral.[10]

The caravan contractors themselves were not slow to profit from the mission supply service they were running. In 1665 the friars complained that a contractor had squeezed the entire three-year supply for the missions into one section of the train and had then sold the free space thus generated to passengers and merchants who wanted to ship their own commercial freight. This ruse not only overloaded the wagons but resulted in long delays in loading and discharging unauthorized freight. Such inefficiencies played havoc with the already-uncertain shipping schedule. In one case, northbound wagons were delayed so long that they reached the Rio Grande just in time for the spring floods and had to wait there for three months until the waters receded.[11]

When Friar Francisco de Ayeta, the commissary (a senior official) of the New Mexican missions, returned to Mexico City with the caravan of 1676, he gave the viceroy a candid and depressing report of conditions in New Mexico. A drought lasting several years had produced conditions verging on starvation. The caravan trade had been unable to bring enough provisions for the Indians dependent on the missions. To borrow a descriptive term from British colonialism of a much later time, the natives were getting restless. Given the increasing hardships they faced at the missions, the Indians became more and more inclined to abandon missions and return to their old religion and former way of life. These disconcerting trends prompted the friars to resort to harsher measures to discipline their flocks: in 1677, for example, the mission caravan brought to New Mexico additional troops and horses to strengthen Spanish control. But this surge was not enough. Aided by roving bands of Apaches, in 1680 the Pueblo Indians rose in great revolt against the Spaniards under the leadership of a charismatic medicine man named Popé.[12]

During this rebellion, the Indians killed 400 Spaniards, including 21 missionaries, and compelled 2,200 Spaniards and other survivors to flee—most of them afoot—330 miles down El Camino Real to the safety of El Paso. An emergency supply train of 24 wagons from Mexico City had been ordered for their relief by Friar Ayeta. The refugees, however, were waiting at Fray Cristóbal Mountain, at the northern approach to New Mexico's Jornada del Muerto. Literally the Jornada del Muerto means "the Day's Journey of the Dead Man" but a contemporary and more colloquial translation would be "the Day's Desert March of the Dead Man." (This will be discussed later.) The supply wagons, on the other hand, could not get further north than El Paso because of high water at the usual crossing on the Rio Grande. Undismayed, the ever-resourceful friar simply ordered the wagons to continue upstream for 10 miles, looking for an easier and safer crossing.

On the morning of 18 September 1680, a heroic attempt was made to get across the Rio Grande. Six spans of mules were hitched to the first wagon;

Friar Ayeta himself, accompanied by several Indian swimmers, drove the mules and wagon into the swollen river. The water was so high that it rose three feet over the wagon bed. The mules managed to find their footing on shallower ground but they were not able to pull the wagon out of the river, so Friar Ayeta had to cut them loose. Fortunately, at this point Governor Antonio de Otermín and his escort arrived from the north — just in time to rescue the friar from the river. The wagon was at last hauled ashore safely to the east bank. The friar and the governor decided to send the remaining supplies across the river on the backs of swimming horses. Thus the emergency provisions finally reached the refugees by pack train, as it were, rather than by wagon train.[13]

To get to El Paso, however, the refugees first had to cross the Jornada del Muerto. This is what the conquistadors called the arid stretch of El Camino Real de Tierra Adentro, which is located in a desert basin between the Oscura and San Andres Mountains on the east and the Caballo Mountains and Fra Cristóbal Range on the west. Today it remains a virtually pristine high-desert ecosystem, where the limited plant and animal life so well adapted to this harsh and unforgiving environment continues to thrive. The Jornada del Muerto, however, was always a potentially fatal passage for unprepared or weak human beings. Nevertheless, strong caravans led by experts could cross it safely enough.

U.S. Army Captain Randolph B. Marcy's authoritative and well-written account, *The Prairie Traveler* (1859), would become the principal manual for Westering pioneers. In it he assures prospective travelers: "There is one [desert crossing] in New Mexico called *Journada* [sic] *del Muerto*, which is 78½ miles in length [other estimates put the length at closer to 100 miles], where, in a dry season, there is not a drop of water; yet, with proper care, this drive can be made with ox or mule teams without loss or injury to the animals."[14]

The Jornada was named after a German merchant, Bernardo Gruber, who was fleeing from the Inquisition; his sun-dried corpse was found in the desert in 1668. The Jornada is so flat that, in theory at least, it should be easy to cross but it is very dry, very hot and without any grazing, shade, or firewood. Intervening ranges of small mountains make it impossible for the traveler to get water from the Rio Grande, the only reliable water source in the region. Crossing the Jornada — whether on foot, on horseback, or in wagons pulled by oxen — required careful planning and took from several days to one week to accomplish. Parties often traveled at night to avoid the heat. Part of the trip involved crossing a large lava field produced by the Jornada del Muerto Volcano. The rough surface of this lava flow made travel even more difficult. (The region is so desolate, in fact, that in 1945 it was chosen as the best location in the United States for the first atomic bomb test. Code-named

"Trinity," this successful test was conducted in the northern part of what is now the White Sands Missile Range. The resulting blast was the equivalent of about 20,000 tons of TNT. It made such an impression on Robert Oppenheimer, scientific director of the atomic bomb project, that he remembered a quotation from the *Bhagavad-Gita*, a Hindu classic: "If the radiance of a thousand suns were to burst at once into the sky, that would be like the splendor of the mighty one. Now I am become Death, destroyer of worlds.")

After the Spaniards reconquered New Mexico in 1693, more than 800 refugees, loaded into 12 wagons, began the long trek from El Paso to New Mexico. Because it had not been used for 13 years, the trail was now heavily overgrown with brush. The settlers dealt with the problem by driving 900 head of cattle ahead of them. These animals trampled down the undergrowth and, of course, also provided beef on the hoof. The next year Fray Francisco Farfán led another caravan — consisting of 76 families recruited from the mining center of Parral — from El Paso to New Mexico.

For several years after the reconquest, mission caravans continued to supply the bulk of the religious and secular supplies needed in New Mexico. This is clear from a lawsuit of 1714.[15] In January of that year, a caravan from Mexico City camped on the banks of the Río de las Nazas, which is located between Durango and Parral. Although it was the dry season, a flash flood raged through the wagons and ruined much of the cargo. This included a consignment of tobacco, chocolate, sugar, and imported fabrics owned by Juan N. Vallejo, a merchant of Parral. He brought suit against the custodian of the New Mexican missions, whom he held to bear the ultimate responsibility. Also named in the case were the wagon master, Antonio Sánchez, who held a power of attorney from the friars, and Nicolás Bustrín, who owned the wagons and mules. Vallejo hoped to be awarded the wagons and mules as security for his claim for damaged goods. Mission records do not show how the suit was adjudicated but the episode does confirm that mission supplies were still being carried in wagons leased by friars, that merchants still shipped their own goods in these wagons, and that the friars accepted some responsibility for the safety of the merchandise in the caravans.

Because of the ever-present danger of Indian attacks, the caravans were invariably protected by regular troops and other armed men. Nevertheless, the Indians were sometimes successful. In 1760, for example, a wagon train staffed by 200 men was attacked about halfway between El Paso and Chihuahua by a small band of Indians. Although the defenders of the caravan far outnumbered the attackers, in the confusion of the fight the Indians managed to stampede and then capture a large number of horses. There was no easy solution to this problem. The best that could be done was to take advantage of the very limited military protection available at any given time. Thus in 1800, when the governor left Santa Fe, he was escorted by 32 soldiers. They also provided protection for local ranchers and merchants accompanying his caravan. These men brought with them 18,784 sheep, 213 head of cattle, and assorted bales of woolen goods and peltries. Later, when 15,000 sheep were driven along the trail in 1807, these valuable animals were protected by 300 civilians (mostly New Mexican ranchers) and an escort of some 35 to 40 soldiers.[16]

Hostile Indians, however, were not the only problem, perhaps not even the most serious problem, faced by merchants using the trail. There was such a shortage of hard cash in New Mexico that trade was reduced to the level of barter. A treatise written by Fray Juan Agustín Morfi in the 1770s shows how bartering — normally a rather simple way of doing business — was rendered extremely complicated by the multiple standards of values imposed by Chihuahua merchants to line their own pockets. The bottom line was that the poorer classes of New Mexicans — and even some of the merchants themselves — became confused and found themselves cheated.

If it was hard to establish the values used in bartering, it was even more difficult for businessmen to deal with the lack of hard cash. The official monetary unit was the *peso de plata*, a silver coin worth eight *reales*. To get an idea of its value, we can note that, during his 1724–1728 inspection tour of northern New Spain, Brigadier Pedro de Rivera received a salary of 12 pesos per day.[17] In practice, however, since the *peso de plata* was extremely rare in the New Mexico of the eighteenth century there were three additional ways of assessing monetary value. Remarkably, these consisted of *three imaginary coins used only in bookkeeping*, namely, the *peso a precios de proyecto*, worth six reales; the *peso a precios antiguos*, worth four reales; and the *peso de la tierra*, worth only two reales.[18]

The scholar Max Moorhead explained how New Mexicans could easily be caught up in "a vicious circle of swindles." Moorhead wrote:

> For example, a merchant of Chihuahua could buy thirty-two yards of coarse woolen goods in the south for six *pesos de plata* and sell it in New Mexico at a *peso de la tierra* per yard, a real value of eight *pesos de plata* in all. Since he was paid in local produce, he could accept remuneration in El Paso brandy, which was worth only one *peso de la tierra* per bottle when exchanged for manufactured goods, and thus acquire thirty-two bottles for the bolt of cloth. However, in reselling the brandy to other New Mexicans, the merchant could charge a *peso de plata* a bottle and thus eventually receive thirty-two *pesos de plata* for goods that had cost him only six. But again, since silver money did not circulate in the province, he must be paid in goods, and should the purchaser of the brandy wish to pay in corn from some future harvest, he was charged the prevailing *peso de precios antiguos rate*, four *reales* for each short bushel (*costal*) of grain, or fifty-one short bushels for the thirty-two bottles. After the harvest,

when this was collected, he could sell it to the troops in the southern presidios for ten *reales* per short bushel, almost eighty-four *pesos de plata* in all, or more than ten times the original cost of his goods and freightage.

This sort of procedure ... had been going on for a long time, and the merchants of New Mexico, being continually shortchanged, could never accumulate sufficient capital to own their own goods. They were obliged to buy on credit from Chihuahua, where they were paid low prices for their local produce and were charged exorbitant ones for their mercantile purchases, and thus were barely able to pay freight costs and still sustain themselves.[19]

Despite the difficulty of making an adequate profit, merchants continued to ply their trade. Traversing the long trail required patience and fortitude. Even under the best conditions, travel along this trail was painfully slow. It was rarely possible to make more than 15 miles a day. A letter mailed in Santa Fe took 26 days to reach Chihuahua and 40 days more to get to Mexico City. There were no taverns with overnight accommodations, so travelers had to bring their own cooks, provisions, and bedding. Their food, packed into *cantinas* (large leather pouches or boxes) carried by the mules, was spartan in the extreme. *Chili colorado con carne* (a fiery stew made of beef, chilies, and tomatoes), tortillas, and *frijoles* (refried beans) constituted the standard fare. In fact, this was all that an *arriero* (muleteer) could expect in 24 hours, except perhaps for a cup of chocolate and a piece of bread sometime in between.[20] Despite their scant nourishment, these muleteers were strong and highly skilled workers. Josiah Gregg reported:

> It is truly remarkable to observe with what dexterity and skill the *Arrieros*, or muleteers, harness and adjust the packs of merchandise upon their beasts. Half a dozen [muleteers] usually suffice for forty to fifty mules. Two men are always engaged at one time in the dispatch of each animal, and rarely occupy five minutes in the complete adjustment of his *aparejo* [pack-saddle] and *carga* [load]. In this operation they demonstrate a wonderful degree of skill in the application of their strength. A single man will often seize a package, which, on a "dead lift," he could hardly have raised from the ground, and making a fulcrum of his knees and a lever of his arms and body, throw it upon the mule's back with as much apparent ease as if the effort cost him but little exertion.[21]

Commercial activity along the trail to New Mexico improved only slowly. In 1803, for example, Governor Chacón reported that there were 12 to 15 local traders in New Mexico, but they were neither licensed nor skilled in commercial matters. Most of them had to operate on borrowed capital. Conditions did not get much better until a few years after the Santa Fe Trail opened in 1821 and began to send a flood of American goods to Chihuahua, Sonora, Durango, and other cities in Mexico.

These American goods would be much in demand in Mexico because they were more plentiful and therefore cheaper than Mexican goods. In 1826 the trader Charles Beaubien sent to Mexican markets 2,000 yards of various fabrics, five dozen mirrors, umbrellas, a hundred pairs of shoes, ribbons, buttons, leather combs, beads, and other items. In 1831 the trader William Wilson sent an even wider assortment of in-demand goods, including 30,000 yards of cloth, 150 dozen shoes, 22 dozen socks, silk, scarves, ribbons, combs, hairpieces, mirrors, hairpins, parasols, lace, belts, thread, knives, pocket knives, razors, snaps, saws, files, scissors, tin boxes, soap boxes, inkstands, ink, stoneware, crystal, shawls, threads for sewing and embroidery, thimbles, needles, paper, and cinnamon.[22]

The Santa Fe trade was certainly profitable. In 1846–1847, for example, Colonel Abert reported that "the profits of the Santa Fe traders are in this proportion: Goods, such as calicoes or prints that are bought for 10 cents, sell [in Santa Fe] for 37 and a half cents; and cazinets [cazinet was a fabric used, among other things, to make men's trousers], costing about 25 cents, sell for $2. A wagon contains from two to three thousand dollars worth of goods."[23]

This trade was conducted on a grand scale. As shown in Appendix 2, sometimes as much as $100,000 worth of new merchandise was offered for sale in Santa Fe. As American-Mexico trade blossomed, however, the Santa Fe market gradually became saturated with American goods. This fact encouraged American traders to send their goods south into Mexico itself. After about 1831, we must therefore think of El Camino del Tierra Adentro and the Santa Fe Trail not as two entirely different trails but, instead, as one continuous trail. A good indication of this fact is that when Yale University Press published the 1846–1847 diary of the 18-year-old traveler Susan Shelby Magoffin, Yale gave it this title: *Down the Santa Fe Trail and into Mexico*.

El Camino de Tierra Adentro itself would soldier on until 1882. In that year the Atchison, Topeka and Santa Fe Railroad extended its track from Santo Domingo (about 25 miles south of Santa Fe) to El Paso, where it crossed the river and connected with the just completed Mexican Central Railroad. This event brought the trail's usefulness to an end.

CHAPTER IV

The Old Spanish Trail

The Old Spanish Trail linked Santa Fe and Los Angeles. Because of intervening deserts, canyonlands, and hostile Indians, however, it did not run east to west directly between these two locations. Instead, it traced a giant parabola from Santa Fe northwest into central Utah — where its northernmost point was near Castle Dale, Utah, about 115 miles southeast of Salt Lake City — and then turned southwest to Los Angeles.

This parabola was not its only geographic complexity. When the trail left Santa Fe, it split into two routes. The south or main branch headed northwest past Colorado's San Juan Mountains to near Green River, Utah. The north branch ran north into Colorado's San Luis Valley and then crossed west over Cochetopa Pass to follow the Gunnison and Colorado rivers, finally joining the south branch of the trail near Green River.[1] If both routes are counted, the total length of the Old Spanish Trail comes to about 2,700 miles.[2] In the interest of simplicity, however, only the main branch is shown on the map.

Its origins are lost in prehistory but this trail probably grew out of a network of Indian trade paths linking the Ute settlements of the Great Basin, e.g., near the Great Salt Lake, with the pueblos of the upper Rio Grande. When astute Ute traders realized that rich strangers, the Spanish, were settling among the Pueblo Indians in the wake of Oñate's colonization program in 1598, this old trail may have come into new use.[3] The first Spanish reference to it does not appear until 1686, when Friar Alonso de Posada wrote:

> Taking from this villa [Santa Fe] a straight line to the northwest between north and south and crossing the *sierras* [mountains] called *Casafuerte* or *Nabajo*, one reaches the large river [probably the Río Chama] which runs directly west for a distance of sixty leagues which are possessed by the *Apacha* [Apache] nation. Crossing this river, one enters the nation called the *Yuta*, a warlike people. Beyond this nation some seventy leagues in the same northwest direction one enters afterwards between some hills at a distance of fifty leagues more or less, the land which the Indians of the North call *Teguayo* [that portion of Utah

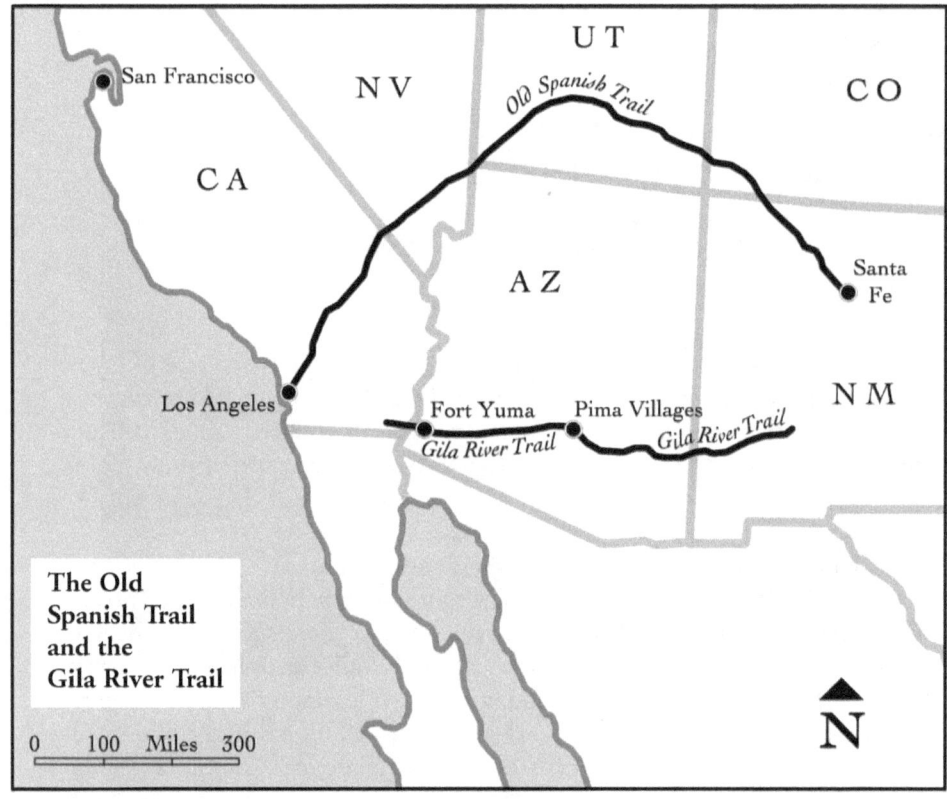

The Old Spanish Trail and the Gila River Trail

lying west of Salt Lake City], and the Mexican Indians by an old tradition call *Copala*.[4]

Posada's estimates of distances are remarkably accurate. He gives the distance to Teguayo as about 180 Spanish leagues, roughly 468 miles; a modern atlas shows the line-of-sight distance between Santa Fe and Salt Lake City to be about 475 miles.

Although Posada was aware of this "new" region in 1686, the Spanish government did nothing to explore or exploit it until the late 1700s, when they realized how much to their advantage it would be to use a trail there to link two of their most remote colonial outposts — Santa Fe and Los Angeles. The Spanish knew that their hold on California was tenuous indeed. Spanish missions there could not support themselves single-handedly: they were forced to wait for the infrequent arrivals of ships bringing goods up from the west coast of Mexico. This supply system, however, was quite unreliable. Because of adverse winds and currents, ships could make only slow progress sailing toward California. Moreover, the ships themselves were too small to carry the families of settlers and the livestock herds needed to establish permanent Spanish settlements in California. Gradually, an overland link between Santa Fe and Los Angeles was therefore carved out of the wilderness. It would become known to later scholars as the Old Spanish Trail.

The American historians LeRoy Hafen (1893–1985) and his wife, Ann Hafen (1893–1970), did a great deal of archival research and consulted many contemporary sources for their classic work, *The Old Spanish Trail* (1954). This book is a gold mine of information on historic trails, trade, and travels and is the source for many of the verbatim "I-was-there" accounts quoted here. Indeed, it appears that the Hafens were single-handedly responsible for rescuing this trail from the scholarly oblivion into which it had fallen. More recently, Joseph P. Sanchez and other scholars have also studied Hispanic efforts to establish trail routes from New Mexico to the Great Basin or immigration routes to California, but the Hafens' book is still immensely valuable.

The Hafens introduce the trail to the reader in these memorable words: "The Old Spanish Trail was the longest, crookedest, most arduous pack mule route in the history of America."[5] Despite its challenges, a trail from New Mexico to California seemed to Spanish officials to be the solution to two thorny problems. As the Hafens put it, "If Spain could open and maintain a line connecting these frontier outposts, such a link would not only tie together the far projecting lines of Spanish settlement and consolidate the northern frontier of New Spain, but would also bring new heathen peoples into the fold of the church. Thus could both national and ecclesiastical ends be served by one bold venture. Such was the background and inception of the Old Spanish Trail."[6]

The first recorded expedition to explore what would later become the eastern end of the Old Spanish Trail dates from 1765. Acting on orders from Governor Cachupín of New Mexico, the Spanish explorer Juan María de Rivera set out on a prospecting and trading expedition from Abiquiú, located about 40 miles northwest of Santa Fe. This little village would later achieve more lasting fame as the home of the great American artist Georgia O'Keeffe (1887–1986). Rivera found outcrops of mineral ore (later assumed, incorrectly, to be silver ore) in the mountains of the southwestern corner of Colorado. This ore gave the mountains their name: the La Plata (Silver) Mountains.[7]

An early and vigorous explorer of some of the western lands crossed by the Old Spanish Trail was Fray Francisco Garcés, a Franciscan priest assigned to the mission at San Xavier del Bac, which is located in the Santa Cruz Valley nine miles south of Tucson, Arizona. (The present mission church which stands on this spot was built between 1783 and 1797 by the Tohono O'odham tribe under the direction of Franciscan missionaries. It is romantically known as the "white dove of the desert"—a reference to the dramatic contrast between its white walls, the browns of the desert soil, and the cloudless blue skies.)

Beginning in 1774, Fray Garcés set out from the Yuma villages along the Gila River in southern Arizona. His objective: to find a trail to the California missions. First he made his way north to the Mojave Indian villages along the Colorado River. There he was given four guides, who led him along Indian trails to the Mojave River. Garcés then followed the Mojave for several days, finally reaching Mission San Gabriel Arcángel. Some of the indigenous routes he followed through the Mojave Desert would later become part of the western segment of the Old Spanish Trail.[8]

Often characterized as "restless," Fray Garcés was not only as tough as old rawhide but he was also a competent ethnographer. When making his way north along the Colorado, he at last reached the Mojave villages near Needles at the extreme southern tip of Nevada and was the first foreigner to report on the Mojave Indians:

> I can say with entire truth that these Indians have great advantages over the Yumas and the rest of the Nations of the Rio Colorado; they are less molestful, and none are thieves; they seem valiant, and nowhere have I been better served....
>
> The men go entirely naked, and in a country so cold this is well worthy of compassion. These [men] say that they are very strong; and so I found them to be, especially in enduring hunger and thirst.... [Fray Garcés was astounded to learn that the Mojave Indians routinely crossed the desert into California carrying nothing to eat and no bows for hunting. The Indians told him they could "endure hunger and thirst for four days" during this crossing.]
>
> There came to visit me about 20 hundred [i.e., 2,000] souls. Abound here certain blankets that they possess and weave of furs of rabbits and otters brought from the west and northwest, with the people of which parts they keep firm friendship.... They talk rapidly and with great haughtiness.... During the harangues that they make they give smart slaps with the palms on the thighs.[9]

Fray Garcés is credited today with being the first foreigner to cross the desert from the Mojave villages on the Colorado River to the mission at San Gabriel. One reason for his success was that by build and temperament he was perfectly suited to be a missionary to these Indians. His colleague, Fray Font, described him thus:

> Father Garcés is so well fitted to get along with the Indians and to go among them that he appears to be but an Indian himself. Like the Indians he is phlegmatic in everything. He sits with them in the circle, or at night around the fire, with his legs crossed, and there he will sit musing for two or three hours or more, oblivious to everything else, talking with them with much serenity and deliberation. And although the foods of the Indians are nasty and dirty as those

outlandish people themselves, the father eats them with great gusto and says that they are good for the stomach and very fine. In short, God has created him, as I see it, solely for the purpose of seeking out these unhappy, ignorant, and rustic people.[10]

As discussed in the chapter on Spanish explorations, Fray Silvestre Vélez de Escalante and Fray Francisco Atanasio Domínguez had set out from Santa Fe in 1776 bound for California. Heavy snows, however, had forced them to abort their westward journey in the Great Basin and return to New Mexico. Thus neither they nor Fray Garcés ever succeeded in opening a trail from Santa Fe all the way to Los Angeles. Nevertheless, the Spanish missions and ranches of California not only had survived but had visibly prospered, thanks entirely to their livestock. Herds multiplied rapidly on the open range due to the mild climate; the abundant, nutritious grasses; and the absence of predators. The end result was a large surplus that could profitably be traded. Indeed, as the Hafens concluded, "The existence of such a surplus would ultimately induce and promote a commercial traffic between New Mexico and California, that would be the outstanding feature of the Old Spanish Trail."[11]

This surplus generated a sizeable trade with New Mexico. Business began in 1829 when the New Mexican trader Antonio Armijo led a group of men from Abiquiú to Santa Barbara, California. An article published in 1830 in the *Registro Oficial del Gobierno de los Estados-Unidos Mexicanos* (*Official Government Register of the United States of Mexico*) reads in part (the word order has been has been lightly edited here in the interests of clarity):

> On the 6th of November of the past year [1829], there left from the village of Abiquiú 31 men, [all of whom were inhabitants of the territory of New Mexico, including the commandant Citizen Antonio Armijo] wishing to discover a route to Upper California and to sell therein some manufactures of their country, traveling towards the Northwest, and a month later reaching the Rio Grande, or Colorado, which they forded without difficulty, despite its being 2,000 *varas* wide [this is an exaggerated estimate because it is roughly equivalent to 1,800 yards].... [I]t took them three months less six days to arrive at the first village in California, which is Santa Barbara; they were delayed so because the route was unknown and they had to make numerous detours of the impassable mountains and canyons which impeded a straight course....[12]

During this difficult journey, they had to pick their way gingerly across country, traveling north of the Grand Canyon but south of the Old Spanish Trail. Near the Crossing of the Fathers, where Escalante and his men had forded the Colorado in 1776, the going was so hard that Armijo's men were forced to unpack their pack animals, carve steps into the canyon wall to provide footing for themselves and for their animals, and carry on their own backs the woven woolen goods (*serapes*, blankets, and quilts) which were in demand in

California.[13] The Californians were quite impressed by what Armijo had accomplished. The 1830 report quoted above goes on: "Upon arriving in California they were hospitably received by the inhabitants, who were very surprised to see them arrive from the direction which until then was unknown: they [the inhabitants] traded the products which the thirty [sic] travelers took with them for mules, horses, and stock…. It is hoped that in other trips a shorter road may be discovered and that from this discovery great usefulness will accrue to this territory and to all the Mexican nation."[14] In later years, traders heading east from California would drive bands of horses and mules — many of them stolen from California missions and ranches — back to Santa Fe, where some of these animals were put into service along the Santa Fe Trail.

The first party to explore the entire route of what would become the Old Spanish Trail consisted of American trappers led by William Wolfskill and George C. Yount in the winter of 1830–1831.[15] Both men had been traders in New Mexico during the 1820s and knew the West well. Wolfskill had already made three trips over the Santa Fe Trail, Yount, one trip. No one on their expedition was assigned the role of chronicler but some of the men did write about their experiences after the trip. In addition, modern scholars have been able to piece together a fairly accurate account of the journey, thanks to the fortunate survival of Wolfskill's financial records.

These records show that the Wolfskill-Yount company consisted of about 20 men. Wages paid to them varied greatly, in some cases reflecting longer prior service. One man, David Keller, was credited $91.93 for "service from Taos to California." Jose Archulate was paid for "3½ months service at $7 per month." Blass Greago earned a flat $8 per month. (In 1867 — more than thirty years later — $8 per month was also the going rate for 16-year-old José Librado Gurulé and other teenage boys traveling back and forth along the Santa Fe Trail.[16]) In addition to their wages the men and boys were provided with modest rations: flour, beef, and, when the beef was finished, horse meat. Yount and his "free trappers" (i.e., men trapping beaver on their own account rather than as company employees) had to pay for their beef and horse meat rations. Entries in the records show such per-man charges as "To his part of 4 beeves [sic] $2.25" and "To his part of 2 horses $4.50."

In an interview he gave in 1859, Ziba Branch, one of Wolfskill's hired hands, told Mrs. Day, a reporter for a journal called the *Hesperian*, about the difficulties the expedition had faced and the help that the California Indians had kindly provided. He said:

> [The Wolfskill party] made the journey from New Mexico towards Big Salt Lake, across the head waters of the Red [Colorado] River, and struck a stream called the "Pooneca," supposed to be [the] Severe River, which they followed until it emptied into Little Salt Lake near the California mountains.

It being the month of November [1830], the country was covered with snow, and they found it impossible to cross the Sierra Nevada Mountains, and consequently struck off for [the] Red River [the Colorado River]. They were nine days crossing, and had to break a path through the snow, which was two or three feet deep. They found but few beaver and no game, and soon run [sic] entirely out of provisions. When they started from New Mexico, they had four oxen; near Little Salt Lake they killed the last ox, and then had to subsist upon the flesh of their horses and mules, each man being put upon short allowance of the food, which, at best, was very poor.

They traveled along the Red [Colorado] River till they reached the country of the Mohaves [Mojaves], a treacherous tribe of Indians, who, however, treated them kindly, and gave them some bread which was made of pounded corn and baked in the ashes. They also had dried pumpkins, and some small white beans. The party tarried here for two days and traded with the Indians for such things as red cloth, knives, etc., and for food. They were a little apprehensive of an attack by the Indians, but finally got off in safety and traveled on to San Bernadino, where they arrived in February, 1831. From thence they proceeded to Los Angeles, where the party disbanded.[17]

Wolfskill and Yount, and presumably some of their men as well, settled permanently in California. While not all sections of the Old Spanish Trail and its several shortcuts can now be determined with certainty, the Wolfskill-Yount expedition was the first to go its full distance. Blazing this trail was indeed an impressive achievement but the route had some notable limitations. It was so rugged that it could be used only by horses and by mule caravans, not by wagons. It was never safe either for winter travel (too much snow) or for summer travel (too little water). On the plus side of the ledger, however, spring and autumn were fine seasons for travel.

This route was in its heyday in the 1830s and 1840s, when annual caravans carried woolen goods from New Mexico to trade for California horses and mules. These animals, which had often been stolen from California ranchlands, were driven east to Santa Fe, where there was a ready market for them. The long, parabolic course the trail followed was designed to give a comfortably wide berth to the lands of potentially hostile Indians further south. The Hafens summarized the Old Spanish Trail's usefulness in these words: "[While] acknowledging its limitations, and conceding its demands, the Trail constituted a travel route that for some two decades was to carry a unique commerce not insignificant in the development of Western America."[18] The surplus of horses and mules in California attracted not only thieves but also many legitimate traders. One well-documented case of the latter, in the 1830s, is that of Jacob P. Leese, who had been employed in New Mexico by the veteran trader Ceran St. Vrain at Taos and Abiquiú.[19] Before long, however, Leese succumbed to the siren call of California and decided to try his luck at cornering the market on the mule trade between California and New Mexico. He therefore negotiated contracts in California with the missions of San Miguel and San Luis Obispo, enabling him to buy mules at $14 each. By September 1834 he had about 450 horses and mules ready to be driven to Santa Fe. This bold venture, however, ended in failure.

Twenty-five years later, in 1859, Leese reviewed for Mrs. Day, the reporter for the *Hesperian*, exactly what had happened. He had left Los Angeles with nine riders in October 1834, planning to join up with a group of New Mexican traders at the Mojave River. When he got there, however, he found that the traders had left a few days earlier. Nevertheless, he continued his journey across the desert, believing that he was only a few days behind them. Here we will let Mrs. Day continue the story:

> [Leese] had now arrived at that part of the plains where for many miles there was no water to refresh the weary traveler; but by traveling all night and the next day until midnight he reached a place where water could be obtained.... Here, by the cool refreshing stream, they camped, and as all were very much fatigued, concluded to keep no guard that night, feeling the more secure for the thick fog which overhung the place. All slept soundly and the hours of the night passed quickly.
>
> Mr. Leese awoke with the early dawn, and his experienced eye immediately observed that there was something wrong about camp. The animals were confused and scattered — fresh Indian tracks were to be seen.... At ten o'clock the fog cleared off, and in looking about they found many of the poor animals with arrows sticking into their sides, and of the four hundred and fifty could collect but twenty-seven head. They succeeded, however, in finding the trail indicating the direction in which they had been taken, and immediately concluded to pursue their enemies, and, if possible, regain their animals.
>
> They were mounted and ready for pursuit, when one of the men came into camp and reported that the New Mexicans had been camped but a few hundred yards above; that they had been attacked by the Indians, and five of them had been massacred. This of course created more alarm in the small party, and they hurriedly proceeded to the scene of disaster. The place bore every appearance of a long and hard-fought battle. They were informed that the Indians [had] numbered about three hundred, while the [New] Mexican party contained but nineteen persons. They [had] fought all day and part of the night, losing five of their number; the remainder, it was afterward ascertained, reached home in safety. From this place Mr. Leese returned to California, thankful to escape with his life.[20] [He subsequently prospered in business in Los Angeles and San Francisco but had nothing more to do with the mule trade.]

As stated earlier, many of the horses and mules driven east to New Mexico and beyond had been stolen in California. In 1841 Rufus B. Sage, one of the most reliable chroniclers of the beaver trade, encountered near the Big Blue River in Kansas a party of men led by Philip Thompson, a former mountain man (beaver trapper) who had turned to stealing livestock when the beaver trade failed. (Beaver trapping became unprofitable when silk replaced beaver fur as the preferred material for men's hats; at the same time, intensive trapping had reduced the beaver population to very low levels.) Thompson and his men were driving horses to the Missouri River. Sage wrote:

> Their horses had been mostly obtained from Upper California, the year previous, by a band of mountaineers, under the lead of one Thompson. This band, numbering twenty-two in all, had made a descent upon the Mexican *ranchos* and captured between two and three thousand head of horses and mules.
> A corps of some sixty Mexican cavalry pursued and attacked them, but were defeated and pursued in turn, with the loss of several mules and their entire camp equipage; after which the adventurers were permitted [by the Mexican soldiers] to regain their mountain homes, without further molestation; but, in passing the cheerless desert, between the Sierra Nevada and Colorado, the heat, dust, and thirst were so intolerably oppressive, that full one half of their animals died. The remainder, however, were brought to rendezvous [that is, to a place where they could be sold], and variously disposed of, to suit the wants and wishes of their captors.[21]

A good description of the trade between Santa Fe and Los Angeles was written by Eugène Duflot de Mofras, a nineteenth-century French diplomat who was posted in Mexico City. He was sent by his government to explore the west coast of North America and its possibilities for French businessmen. While investigating California in this light during 1841 and 1842 he reported the following:

> Caravans travel once a year from New Mexico to Los Angeles. These consist of 200 men on horseback, accompanied by mules laden with fabrics and large woolen covers called *serapes, jerzas,* and *cobertones,* which are valued at 3 to 5 piasters each. [The piaster was a unit of currency originally equal to one silver dollar or one peso.] This merchandise is exchanged for horses and mules, on a basis, usually, of two blankets for one animal.
> Caravans leave Santa Fé, New Mexico, in October, before the snows set in, travel west ... and finally reach the outlying ranchos of California, from where the trail leads into El Pueblo de los Angeles. The trip consumes two and one-half months. Returning caravans leave California in April in order to cross the rivers before the snow melts, taking with them about 2,000 horses. The expedition that reached El Pueblo in November, 1841, included in addition to some 200 New Mexicans, 60 or more North Americans.[22]

During the Mexican-American war, the conquest of New Mexico by U.S. soldiers in the summer of 1846 apparently prevented the departure of the annual trade caravan for California. The arrival of American soldiers in California, did, however, encourage one final and large group of Mexican traders to set out on the Old Spanish Trail. This group reached California at the end of 1847. The *San Francisco Californian* reported on December 29, 1847, that it consisted of some 212 New Mexicans (60 of them boys), who were driving about 150 mules packed with blankets and other trade items. They left on their return journey to New Mexico in April 1848.[23]

Shortly thereafter, one of the most famous frontiersmen of American history — Christopher Houston "Kit" Carson (1809–1868) — rode out of Los Angeles along the Old Spanish Trail, together with U.S. Army lieutenant George Douglas Brewerton, carrying U.S. government dispatches for Washington, D.C. Carson is such a bigger-than-life character and his career is so well documented and so colorful that we would be remiss if we did not chronicle some of his exploits here.[24]

Raised in Franklin, Missouri, Carson was one of 15 children. When he was only seven, his father was killed by a falling tree while he was clearing land. This plunged the family into such poverty that Carson had to drop out of school. He never learned to read or write and would become the only illiterate general in the history of the U.S. Army. At age 14 Carson was apprenticed to a saddle maker in Franklin but he detested this trade, so two years later he ran away and joined a large caravan heading to Santa Fe, tending the horses, mules, and oxen to pay his way. He spent the winter of 1826–1827 living in Taos with a trapper and explorer named Matthew Kinkead, who taught Carson the skills needed to be a mountain man. Over the years, Carson also learned to speak Spanish, Navajo, Apache, Cheyenne, Arapaho, Paiute, Shoshone, and Ute.

In 1829 Carson signed on with Ewing Young and 40 other mountain men to trap in unexplored Apache country along the Gila River. During a clash with the Apaches, Carson shot and killed one of them — the first of a number of men he would kill. The initial installment in what would become the enduring legend of Kit Carson dates from 1835, when he attended a mountain man rendezvous along the Green River in southwestern Wyoming. (The annual rendezvous was the major economic and social event in a mountain man's life: there he sold his furs at low prices, bought new supplies for the coming trapping season at high prices, and wooed the Indian belles.)

At this particular rendezvous Carson was smitten by the charms of an Arapahoe woman named Waa-ni-beh (Singing Grass), who was also a favorite of Joseph Chouinard, a French-Canadian trapper. When Singing Grass chose Carson over his rival, Chouinard became very aggressive. The end result was a duel on horseback between the two men. The mountain man Samuel Parker was present at the fight and has left us this account:

> A hunter who technically goes by the name of the "great bully of the mountains" mounted his horse and with a loaded rifle challenged any Frenchman, American, Spaniard, or Dutchman to fight him in single combat. Kit Carson,

an American, told him that if he wished to die he would accept the challenge. Shunar ["Shunar" is an approximate pronunciation of Chouinard's French name] defied him. Carson mounted his horse, and with a loaded pistol, rushed into close contact, and both almost at the same instant fired. Shunar's ball passed over the head of Carson; [another account says that Carson's shot blew the thumb off one of Chouinard's hands] and while he [Carson] went for another pistol, Shunar begged that his life be spared.[25]

Later, accompanied by Singing Grass, Carson worked as a trapper for the Hudson Bay Company. These years were, he remembered, "the happiest days of my life." Singing Grass developed a fever after the birth of their child and died. At that time, as Carson later put it, "Beaver was getting scarce, it became necessary to try our hand at something else." He then became a hunter at Bent's Fort[26] and married his second wife, a Cheyenne, in 1841. She died after the birth of their daughter, Adeline. The next year Carson married Joséfa Jaramillo, the 14-year-old daughter of a prominent Taos family. They would raise 15 children of their own.

Carson decided to take Adeline back to Franklin for an education, leaving her with his relatives there. On a steamboat in Missouri, he met John C. Frémont, who would lead five expeditions into the West. Frémont was then looking for a guide to lead his first expedition (to South Pass, Wyoming) and soon hired Carson for the job. The expedition was such a success that Frémont's report to Congress set in motion a wave of caravans filled with optimistic emigrants heading West. Carson also served as the guide for Frémont's second expedition (1843), which proved that the long-sought "Great River of the West," believed to flow from the Rocky Mountains west to the Pacific Ocean, did not exist. A congressional report in 1845 on this expedition made Frémont and Carson nationally famous.

A second installment in the Kit Carson legend dates from this time. Somewhere along their route, Frémont and his men encountered a Mexican man and a boy who had just survived an Indian ambush. The Indians had killed two men, had staked two women to the ground and mutilated them, and had stolen 30 horses. Carson and Alex Godey (a fellow mountain man) decided to retaliate. They tracked the Indians for two days, attacked their camp, killed two of them, scattered the rest, and returned safely to Frémont's camp driving the stolen horses.

Carson was also the guide for Frémont's third expedition (1845). Its stated goal was to map the source of the Arkansas River on the eastern slope of the Rocky Mountains; instead Frémont led his men to California, trying to position himself to be a hero when the Mexican-American war broke out. Faced with superior numbers of Mexican troops, however, Frémont had to retreat to Oregon, where his group was attacked by Indians who killed three of Frémont's men. To avenge their deaths, in 1846 Frémont attacked a village of the Klamath tribe — believing, incorrectly as it turned out — that it was the Klamaths who had attacked his expedition. During this attack, Carson was nearly killed by a Klamath warrior: his own rifle misfired and the warrior was about to skewer him with an arrow. Frémont saved Carson's life by forcing his horse forward and trampling the warrior.

Returning to California that same year, Frémont encouraged American settlers there to rebel against Mexican rule. During this "Bear Flag Revolt," a group of Mexicans murdered two American rebels. Frémont intercepted three Mexican men and ordered Carson to execute them in revenge for the deaths of the Americans, which Carson did. When war with Mexico broke out, Frémont made Carson a lieutenant, thus beginning Carson's military career. After Colonel (later Brigadier General) Kearny rode into Santa Fe on August 18, 1846, with his "Army of the West" (the Mexican-American war will be discussed later), Frémont and Commodore Robert Stockton were eager to announce the conquest of California, too, and asked Carson to carry official tidings overland to President Polk in Washington.

After leaving Los Angeles, however, Carson encountered Kearny, at Socorro, New Mexico, and Kearny ordered him to guide Kearny's troops back to California so that they could stabilize the situation there. Thus, while another courier carried the mail to Washington, Carson led Kearny and his dragoons west along the Gila River. (Dragoons were soldiers trained to fight both on foot and on horseback. Their name comes from the French word "dragon" and refers to an early type of firearm whose muzzle was decorated with the head of a dragon.) They traveled at such a rapid pace that their mules died at the rate of about 12 animals per day.

During one battle in California, Kearny sent out Carson and Edward Beale (a colleague), accompanied by an Indian guide, at night to get urgently needed reinforcements. Because their boots would make too much noise, Carson and Beale had to take them off and tuck them into their belts. They then traveled — part of the way barefoot — through the rocks and cactus of the desert for 25 miles to San Diego, where they roused the garrison.

In 1847 Commodore Stockton appointed Frémont to be governor of California. Frémont directed Carson to carry official dispatches back to Washington, where Carson delivered them to secretary of state James Buchanan and met with secretary of war William Marcy and with President Polk. Having completed this assignment, Carson then received orders to do it all over again: to go back to California with new messages and to bring the replies back to Washington. Carson did all this but then decided to settle down with his wife, Joséfa, and take up ranching in Taos.

Carson was a public hero in his own time. The first of many novels written about him was Charles Averill's *Kit Carson: The Prince of the Gold Hunters* (1849). Mass consumption books of this kind were known as "dime novels" or "blood and thunders." In Averill's work, Carson promises the distraught parents of a girl who has been kidnapped by Indians that he will not rest until he finds her — which of course he manages to do. Tragically, however, real-life events in 1849 did not work out so well.

That year Jicarilla Apaches attacked a family camped along the Santa Fe Trail. The husband, a Santa Fe trader named James White, was killed outright; his wife was taken prisoner. A rescue party was organized in Taos, commanded by Major William Grier and accompanied by Carson as one of the guides. They tracked the Indians for 12 days to their camp on the Canadian River. Carson wanted to attack the camp immediately but Grier wanted to negotiate with the Indians and stopped for this purpose. This gave the Indians the chance to flee. They were clearly in no mood to talk. In his (dictated) autobiography, Carson relates what happened:

> Just as the halt was ordered, the commanding officer [Grier] was shot; the ball passed through his coat, his gauntlets that were in his pocket, and his shirt, stopping at the skin, and doing no other damage than making him a little sick at the stomach. The gauntlets had saved his life, sparing a gallant officer to the service of his country. As soon as he had recovered from the shock given him by the ball, he ordered the men to charge, but it was too late to save the captives. [Mrs. White's daughter and a servant were also seized by the Indians but their fate is unknown.]
>
> There was only one Indian left in the camp, who was promptly shot while he was running into the river in a vain attempt to escape. At a distance of about 200 yards, the body of Mrs. White was found, still perfectly warm. She had been shot through the heart with an arrow not more than five minutes before. She evidently knew that some one was coming to her rescue. Although she did not see us, it was apparent that she was endeavoring to make her escape when she received the fatal shot.
>
> I am certain that if the Indians had been charged immediately on our arrival, she would have been saved.[27]

The most remarkable thing about this tragic incident is that when Carson and Grier searched the camp abandoned by the Indians, they discovered a book that the White family had carried with them from Missouri. It was Averill's paperback novel starring Kit Carson. Carson said of it, "We found a book in the camp, the first of the kind I had ever seen, in which I was represented as a great hero, slaying Indians by the hundred. I have often thought that Mrs. White must have read it, must have prayed for my appearance in order that she might be saved. I did come, but I lacked the power to persuade those who were in command over me to follow my plan for her rescue. They would not listen to me and they failed."[28] This episode was the first time that the real Kit Carson came into contact with the mythic Kit Carson.

At the outbreak of the Civil War in 1861, Carson resigned his post as federal Indian agent for northern New Mexico and joined the Union volunteer army, which was under the command of Colonel Edward R.S. Canby. Carson was appointed colonel of volunteers. The Confederates won the day-long Battle of Valverde, set along the Rio Grande about 50 miles north of Santa Fe in 1862, but Carson, together with other volunteer officers, was commended for his "zeal and energy."

Later, acting under the orders of the new commanding officer, Brigadier General James H. Carleton, Carson conducted a scorched earth policy designed to drive the Navajos, who had been raiding New Mexican settlements, out of their traditional homeland. Carleton was not a respected or beloved leader. A local newspaper, the *Weekly New Mexican*, reported on 27 October 1866 that "The General has indeed gained 'the detestation and contempt of almost the entire population of the territory.'"[29] Moreover, a modern biographer describes him in these unflattering words: "He had an aggressive, jutting chin, and his eyes were wide, dark, and piercing. His flowing sideburns and thick, heavy mustache added to the arrogance of his countenance. Most of the army regulars who served under him found him arbitrary and sometimes cruel in his dealings with others. He was an unscrupulous, ambitious, selfish man, whose bearing radiated an abrasive, tyrannical personality."[30]

There were only a few skirmishes in this campaign but it resulted in widespread destruction of Navajo livestock and crops, ultimately forcing the Indians to surrender. The end result was that in the spring of 1864 more than 8,000 Navajo men, women, and children were compelled to walk or to ride in wagons over 300 miles to Fort Sumner, New Mexico. This fort was active from 1862 to 1869 as an agricultural experiment to test the U.S. Army's new theory, which was summarized jokingly as "we can feed the Indians cheaper than we can fight them."[31] Known as "The Long Walk," the Navajo exodus and return will be discussed in detail later.

In November 1864, in western Texas, Carson fought a combined force of Kiowa, Comanche, and Cheyenne warriors numbering over 1,500 men. This fight, known as the Battle of Adobe Wells, resulted in a victory for Carson and his men. Carleton recommended in 1865 that Carson be awarded the brevet rank of brigadier general. (A brevet rank was an honor which gave a military officer a higher nominal rank than the rank for which he was actually being paid.) Carson's citation for promotion read in part: "For gallantry in the battle of Valverde, and for distinguished conduct and gallantry in the wars against the Mescalero Apaches and against the Navajo Indians of New

Mexico."[32] When the Civil War ended in 1865 Carson resigned from the army and took up ranching, settling in Fraksvill, Colorado. He died of an aneurysm at Fort Lyon, Colorado, in 1868 and is buried alongside his wife in Taos.

Despite efforts in modern times by a few revisionist historians to discredit him, Carson's fame has survived intact. Indeed, as one Carson biographer, Harvey L. Carter, wrote in 1968, "In respect to his actual exploits and his actual character ... Carson was not overrated. If history has to single out one person from among the Mountain Men to receive the admiration of later generations, Carson is the best choice. He had far more of the good qualities and fewer of the bad qualities than anyone else in that varied lot of individuals."[33]

A later Carson biographer, Clifford E. Trafzer, added some revealing comments in 1982:

> Kit was a simple man of "sound character".... He was not formally educated but he knew the American West better than most other white men of his day. Kit was easily impressed by people like Carleton who were formally educated and had social "upbringing" and rank. He often yielded to casual adulation and could be persuaded and maneuvered through words of praise, flattery, and commendation. Kit envied such frontier figures as Carleton and usually showed them the utmost respect, admiration, and loyalty. Indeed, despite Carleton's paternalistic lectures, scoldings, and directives during Kit's campaign against the Navajos, the colonel [Kit] never wavered in his feelings about his commander. Carleton was Kit's superior, and Kit never questioned the wisdom or necessity of the general's orders and policies....[34]

At one point Carson tried to resign in order to return to his family, but Carleton would not accept Kit's resignation and persuaded him to remain in the army and fight the Navajos. Carleton was able to convince Carson that he was the only man in New Mexico capable of directing a successful campaign against them.

Let us now backtrack to April 1848 and pick up the story of Lieutenant George Douglas Brewerton, who rode with Carson from Los Angeles along the Old Spanish Trail when Carson was carrying U.S. government dispatches destined for Washington, D.C. Brewerton was an able young army officer and a good observer who has left us an invaluable account of life on the Old Spanish Trail. His memoirs, initially published in three installments by *Harper's New Monthly Magazine*, a respected periodical which is still being published today as *Harper's*, were reprinted by the University of Nebraska in 1993 under the title *Overland with Kit Carson: A Narrative of the Old Spanish Trail in '48*. Brewerton tells us of his travels with Carson:

> Our general course was by the great Spanish trail, and we made as rapid traveling as possible, with the view of overtaking a large Mexican caravan which was

slowly wending its way back to the capital of New Mexico. This caravan consisted of some two or three hundred Mexican traders who go once a year to the Californian coast with a supply of blankets and other articles of New Mexican manufacture; and having disposed of their goods, invest the proceeds in Californian mules and horses, which they drive back across the desert. These people often realize large profits, as the animals purchased for a mere trifle on the coast, bring high prices in Santa Fé....

We finally overtook and passed this party, after some eight days' travel in the Desert. Their appearance was grotesque in the extreme. Imagine upward of two hundred Mexicans dressed in every variety of costume, from the embroidered jacket of the wealthy Californian, with its silver bell-shaped buttons, to the scanty habiliments of the skin-clad Indian.... The line of march of this strange cavalcade occupied an extent of more than a mile; and I could not help thinking that a few resolute men might have captured their property, and driven the traders like a flock of sheep. Many of these people had no fire-arms, being only provided with the short bow and arrows usually carried by New Mexican herdsmen.[35]

Here it is worthwhile to dip into the journal kept by Orville C. Pratt, an ambitious young lawyer who was en route to California and Oregon in 1848 via the Old Spanish Trail. This is the only surviving diary with entries for each day spent on this trail. Two of the last entries, written as his party was struggling to reach Los Angeles, make good reading and will be quoted below.

In 1848 Pratt had been appointed by Secretary of War Marcy to investigate charges levied against an army officer at Fort Mann (today's Dodge City, Kansas), on the Santa Fe Trail. After an investigation cleared that officer, new orders, brought by the courier Kit Carson, instructed Pratt to continue on to New Mexico and from there to carry government dispatches to California and Oregon. At Santa Fe he was given an official escort of 16 men for his trip to California via the Old Spanish Trial. Volume one of Pratt's diaries records his trip to New Mexico, volume two his journey over the Old Spanish Trail itself. Pratt was well prepared for this trip. In addition to his armed escort he was carrying in his saddle bags $5,000 in cash, to be used on government business. Men and money, however, were no antidote for the Mojave Desert — as these entries bear witness (spelling, italics, and punctuation are as in the original):

WEDNESDAY OCT 18th 1848 Left camp this morning the sun about an hour high under the impression that the next water was 15 m. off. Soon after leaving camp we found ourselves off the trail and lost! The sun soon became severely hot, the sand deep, and from the weak condition of the animals they soon began to fail. No water or grass in prospect — the men suffering from thirst — mules giving out by the way, & our provisions short — all united to give me one of the severest trials of my life. We kept on until about 2 o'clock in the morning, & between that and daylight the men all got into camp. Could find no water. Daylight came & the men were sent in all directions but no water still! Travelled full 50 m. this day & camped in a dry arroyo.

THURSDAY, OCT. 17, 1848 In camp which we made last night about 2 o'clock [Pratt's party camped in the desert near today's Oro Grande, California, about 75 miles northeast of Los Angeles]. No water during the early part of the day, but finally found some [i.e., a small water hole in the otherwise dry bed of the Mojave River]. And greater joy I never felt at any time of my existence. And although without much of anything to eat the men seemed to forget all their troubles! Never until now have I *really* known what *suffering is*. My feet are blistered from walking full 30 miles yesterday over the burning sand & flint rocks. Boots are all worn out — Coat and pants tatered from riding 2 m. through the muskeet [mesquite, spiny shrubs or trees growing in extensive thickets] — shirt filthy and five weeks of constant wear in the dirt — & to complete the compliment of misery (as if a burning sun & hard riding all day, laying upon the ground between horse blankets at night, to say nothing of the food, not sufficient) in addition to all else, my body is literally alive with vermin! This would seem almost incredible at home, but it is too true that not only am I annoyed with body lice but every man in the company is precisely in the same way. In 5 days more I hope to be in the "City of the Angels," but the poetry of the name and the far famed delights of California will be as nothing if these cursed lice stick to me! But, nous vermin [in ungrammatical French this is meant to convey the idea that "we are now lice-ridden"].[36]

Cotton goods, mules, and horses were not the only commodities moving along the trail. Slavery was a well-established practice in many Indian and New Mexican communities. Reporting on conditions as they existed in 1851, the trader Daniel W. Jones described how the slave business was conducted by New Mexican traders along the Old Spanish Trail. These men would set out on their journey with only a few goods, which they would trade on the way to the Navajos or Utes for old horses. Jones sketched out the trade in these words:

These used-up horses were bought through and traded to the poorer Indians for children. The horses were often used for food. The trade continued into Lower California, where the children bought on the down trip would be traded to the Mexican-Californians for other horses, goods or cash. Many times a small outfit on the start would return with large herds of California stock.

All children bought on the return trip would be taken back to New Mexico and then sold, the boys fetching an average $100, the girls from $150 to $200. The girls were in demand to bring up for house servants, having the reputation of making better servants than any others. This slave trade gave rise to the cruel wars between the native tribes of this country, from Salt Lake down to the tribes in southern Utah. Walker [the famous mountain man Joseph R. Walker] and his band raided on the weak tribes, taking their children prisoners and selling them to the Mexicans. Many of the lower classes, inhabiting the southern deserts, would sell their own children for a horse and kill and eat the horse. The Mexicans were as fully established and systematic in this trade as ever were the slavers on the seas and to them it was a very lucrative business.[37]

In its final days the Old Spanish Trail became a route favored by horse thieves and slavers. Selected portions of the trail's eastern end were mapped by U.S. government expeditions beginning in the 1850s. The western portion of the trail was used chiefly by Mormons heading to California and would become known as the Mormon Road. After that, traffic on the Old Spanish Trail dribbled to an end.

CHAPTER V

The Santa Fe Trail

During its 59-year history, the length of the Santa Fe Trail varied according to its starting point from different towns in Missouri. Initially, during the early 1820s, it began at Franklin. Later, as the frontier pushed westward and as steamboats navigated farther up the Missouri River, the trail started at Independence in the late 1820s and at Westport (now Kansas City) in the early 1840s. Today, Independence is generally taken as the jumping-off point for most of the travelers along the Santa Fe Trail.

There were two main branches of this famous trail. The first was the Mountain Route, also called the Bent's Fort Route or the Raton Pass Route. (*Ratón* is Spanish for "rat" or "mouse.") Calculating from Independence, this route was approximately 835 miles long and took, on the average, about 72 days to traverse. The second branch was the Cimarron Route, also called the Cimarron Cutoff. Its length varied between 770 and 800 miles, the difference reflecting the fact that wagon masters were not forced to follow a single well-defined trail but would usually choose the most promising, e.g., the least rutted, of several generally parallel tracks over the prairie.[1] Today it is believed that the Cimarron Route was about 780 miles long and took some 62 days to traverse.[2]

When heading west, the two routes diverged near Fort Larned, built on the prairie of western Kansas to protect travelers, mail coaches, and freighters traveling along the Santa Fe Trail and to serve as an Indian Agency. (In 1818 Congress had authorized the president to appoint "temporary agents to reside among the Indians.") Each route had its own advantages and defects. The Mountain Route was longer but was less risky than the Cimarron Route because it followed the well-watered Arkansas River for much of the way. The Cimarron Route was the original wagon path between Missouri and Santa Fe. It was shorter than its rival but over one long stretch known as La Jornada (not to be confused with the Jornada del Muerto in New Mexico) there were no reliable supplies of water but only a few widely scattered springs. As

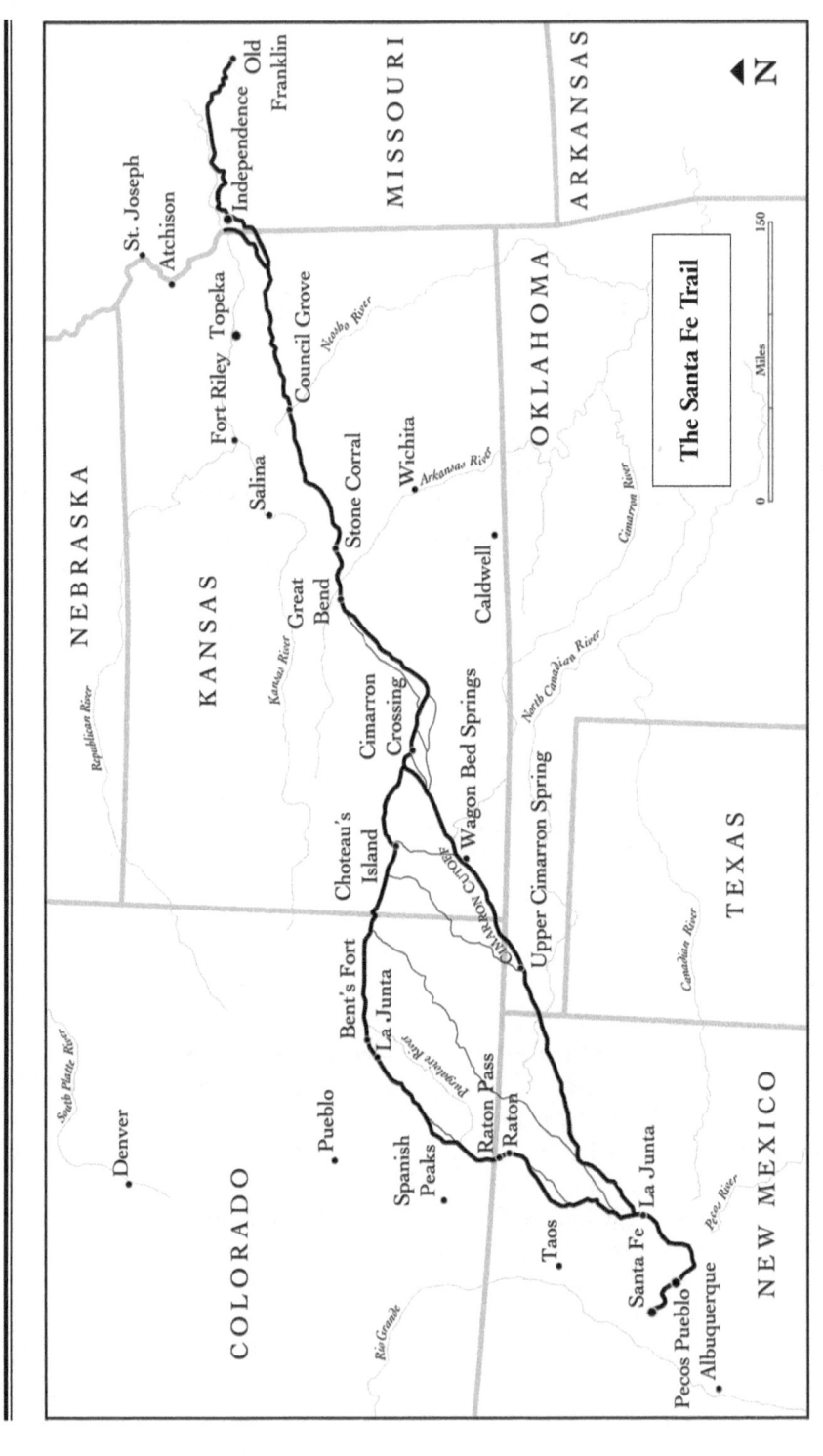

a result, it was riskier to use than the Mountain Route. The Cimarron Route usually took about eight or nine weeks to navigate.[3]

These two historic routes met near Fort Union, New Mexico, which will be discussed later, where three successive forts were built to protect travelers and to serve as a major military supply depot for the Southwest. After joining near Fort Union, the Mountain Route and the Cimarron Route then formed a single trail to Santa Fe.

In addition to these two main routes there was also a lesser-used third one. This was the 819-mile-long Fort Smith–Santa Fe trail. It began at Fort Smith, Arkansas, followed the Canadian River, and then crossed the Indian Territory of Oklahoma and the Texas Panhandle before finally reaching Santa Fe and Albuquerque. This trail was surveyed by Captain Randolph B. Marcy, who felt that he was never given formal credit for his effort. In *The Prairie Traveler* he complains:

> Another road leaves Fort Smith and runs up the south side of the Canadian River to Santa Fé and Albuquerque in New Mexico. [See appendix three.]
>
> This route is set down upon most of the maps of the present day as having being discovered and explored by various persons, but my own name seems to have been carefully excluded from the list. Whether this omission has been intentional or not, I leave for the authors to determine. I shall merely remark that I had the command and entire direction of an expedition which in 1849 discovered, explored, located, and marked out this identical wagon road from Fort Smith, Arkansas, to Santa Fé, New Mexico, and that this road, for the greater part of the distance, is the same that has been since recommended for a Pacific railway.[4]

The historical record, however, presents a more nuanced picture. It shows that in fact Josiah Gregg was the first to blaze this trail by leading over it, in 1839, a caravan of goods for trade in Santa Fe. It was a good ten years later, in 1849, that Marcy became the first one to survey this route officially — in his capacity as leader of a band of 500 men bound for California and as part of the search for a suitable railroad route to the West Coast.[5]

As mentioned earlier, after American-Mexico trade began to blossom in about 1831, we must think of El Camino Real del Tierra Adentro and the Santa Fe Trail not as two entirely separate trails but more or less as one single continuous trail. The Santa Fe Trail was the most heavily used. Its travelers included businessmen, soldiers, freighters, gold-seekers, emigrants, adventurers, mountain men, hunters, Indians, guides, packers, and translators competent in both English and Spanish.[6] This trail grew ever shorter as the railroad pushed ever further west. It finally came to an end when the Iron Horse reached Santa Fe in 1880 and, of course, later stretched all across the west.

The story of what would become the Santa Fe Trail begins with American fur trappers. Some of these men bought supplies or spent the winters in Santa Fe, Taos, Abiquiú, or in more remote villages before 1821, the year Mexico became independent of Spain. They knew that the Gila River and other streams of New Mexico had potential for beaver trapping, but the Spanish authorities specifically forbade foreigners, i.e., Americans and Europeans, to engage in any form of trade, including trapping, under pain of stiff penalties.[7]

This Spanish policy was based on the suspicion that foreign traders were really spies for France or Britain, Spain's keen rivals in the trans-Mississippi West. The "no trading" dictum was well known and was enforced rigorously. In about 1750, for example, the Spanish arrested an enterprising French trader, Pierre Mallet, who had made his way to Santa Fe. They deported Mallet to Mexico City for questioning. He was then sent on to Spain for further interrogation, at which point he disappears from the historical record. If he survived this long, slow process, he never returned to New Mexico.[8]

In 1821 newly independent Mexico reversed, virtually overnight, the long-standing Spanish policy of excluding foreign traders. As it happens, the Santa Fe Trail itself was born largely by chance. In 1821 William Becknell, a down-on-his-luck former soldier facing jail for debts, became a Missouri trader. He is now hailed as the father of the Santa Fe Trail because, with four other aspiring traders, he set out from Franklin, Missouri, to peddle goods to the Cheyenne Indians.[9] Becknell did not think a wagon could make this difficult trip, so he used instead a string of pack horses to carry the calico cloth, needles, knives, and other goods he planned to offer for sale. After crossing the plains of Kansas, he continued on into Colorado, only to find that his proposed customers — the Cheyenne — had already gone off on a horse-stealing foray much further south.

Becknell did not want to go back to Franklin with nothing at all to show for his efforts. He was therefore willing to risk his goods and perhaps his own liberty and that of his men by selling his wares in New Mexico. He crossed the Arkansas River and ventured into the Sangre de Cristo Mountains. Probably just north of Santa Fe, he met a group of soldiers who informed him that Mexico had just thrown off the Spanish yoke and was now independent. Cheered by this good news, Becknell drove his pack train into Santa Fe itself, where the governor assured him that American trade would now be most welcome. Becknell thereupon sold his goods for impressive amounts of Mexican silver.

Having turned such a nice profit, Becknell quickly decided that the next year he would transport even more goods to Santa Fe — this time not by pack train but in mule-drawn wagons. Although each wagon could hold six times the load a packhorse could manage, Becknell was not at all sure that his wagons could get through the Sangre de Cristo Mountains safely. Nevertheless, in 1822 he decided to risk putting the matter to the test: he went back to

Missouri, loaded his goods into wagons, and headed toward Santa Fe. During this trip into the west he managed to pioneer a new branch of the Santa Fe Trail, which would become known both as the Cimarron Route and the Cimarron Cutoff. This route avoided the mountains but in return had to cross 60 miles of inhospitable desert between the Arkansas and Cimarron rivers. Becknell was successful and in 1822 he became the first trader to ship goods to Santa Fe by wagons.[10]

The first caravans of pack mules — usually between 75 and 200 mules — traveled, on the average, about 15 miles per day along the trail. The later introduction of big canvas-covered freight wagons now known as Conestoga wagons, pulled by four to nine oxen or by four to eight mules, raised the average day's journey to some 17 or 18 miles. These big wagons were never standardized but many were about 16.5 feet long and 4.5 feet wide. They had hubs 16 inches wide, iron-rimmed tires 8 inches wide, and could transport loads of up to 16,000 pounds. For emigrants traveling to Utah, Oregon, or California, however, these huge wagons were too heavy and too hard to handle. Many Westering families preferred the lighter farm-type wagons (later dubbed "prairie schooners") which could be pulled by smaller teams.

By 1846, at least 375 freight wagons were employed in the Santa Fe Trail trade, along with 1,700 mules, 2,000 oxen, and 500 men. (It is said that local Indians called these freight wagons "goddams" because bullwhackers used this expression so frequently.[11]) At first the traders made only one trip per year but by 1860 caravans were leaving Missouri for Santa Fe every few days. The annual value of this trade, measured in terms of today's dollars, increased to more than $53 million. It is estimated that eventually there were then as many as 6,000 wagons, 9,000 men, 6,000 mules, and 28,000 oxen moving along the trail. Indeed, at the height of the trade, 50,000 ox yokes are said to have been in use every year.

The two-way flow of commerce over the Santa Fe Trail was quite remarkable. An overview by the modern author Susan Calafate Boyle emphasizes the need to understand this trail from a broad — indeed, from an *international* — perspective. She writes:

> The portion linking Missouri with New Mexico was only one segment of a complex transportation network of economic and cultural exchange that brought together two continents and several countries. The Santa Fe trade reached east well beyond Missouri to include New Orleans, New York, Baltimore, Pittsburgh, and other major cities; west, it extended as far as the California coast; and south, it stretched deep into the Mexican territory to incorporate most of its western and central provinces. The merchandise hauled across the prairies was often European in origin and arrived in the southwest as a result of the involvement of commission merchants in England, France, Italy, Spain, and Portugal, as well as the United States and Mexico.[12]

The frequency and severity of Indian attacks on the Santa Fe Trail has traditionally been overstated in books and films. The Indians knew very well that they would sustain unacceptably heavy losses if they attacked a wagon train driven by heavily armed men, so they preferred instead to lie in wait in hopes that one or two men — usually "greenhorns," i.e., newcomers to Western life — would foolishly leave the safety of the caravan and go hunting or exploring by themselves. Rather than attacking a caravan itself, the Indians hoped to be able to steal its horses and mules. To understand the real nature of the Indian threat, we should consider the balanced account provided by the greatest trader of the Santa Fe Trail — Josiah Gregg. He advised travelers that they should not be unduly frightened by the prospect of Indian attacks. Recalling one of his own skirmishes with the Indians, he assures his readers:

> We came off equally unscathed from the conflict [earlier, his men had fired two or three ineffectual shots at these Indians], barring a horse of but little value, which ran away, and was taken by the enemy. The Indians were about a hundred in number, and supposed to be Comanches, though they might have been a band of warriors belonging to the party we had just left behind.
>
> The novices [in Gregg's caravan] were not a little discouraged at these frequent inroads of the enemy, although it is very seldom that any lives are lost in encounters with them. In the course of twenty years since the commencement of the trade, I do not believe there have been a dozen deaths upon the Santa Fé route, even including those who have been killed off by disease, as well as by the Indians.[13]

That said, it is instructive to remember what happened to the peerless mountain man Jedediah Strong Smith, who was killed by Comanche warriors along the Cimarron Route in 1831. Dale L. Morgan (1914–1971), a pioneering historian of the fur trade and the trails of the American West, explains why Smith is deservedly so famous:

> In the exploration of the American West, Jedediah Strong Smith is overshadowed only by Meriwether Lewis and William Clark. During his eight years in the West Jedediah Smith made the effective discovery of South Pass [located in southeastern Wyoming, this 7,550-foot-high pass is one of the best places to cross the Rocky Mountains]; he was the first man to reach California overland from the American frontier [by crossing the Mojave Desert], the first to cross the Sierra Nevada, the first to travel the length and width of the Great Basin, the first to reach Oregon by a journey up the California coast. He saw more of the West than any man of his time, and was familiar with it from the Missouri River to the Pacific, from Mexico to Canada. He survived the three worst disasters of the American fur trade, the Arikara defeat of 1823, the Mojave massacre of 1827, and the Umpqua massacre of 1828, in which no less than forty men fell around him, only to die a lonely death on the Santa Fe Trail under the lances of the Comanches.[14]

In 1830 Smith had decided to embark on a trading venture to Santa Fe. In March 1831 the U.S. Department of State issued him a passport and a certificate of good character in preparation for his journey into Mexican territory. Smith's party, consisting of 74 men and 22 mule-drawn wagons, left St. Louis the next month and decided to follow the Cimarron Route. Because of an extreme drought, however, no trace of any wagon road across the bone-dry "water scrape," as it was called, could be seen. By late May the party was on the verge of dying of thirst, having by then been three days without water. With death hovering near them, a final effort was made to find water. Smith and a companion managed to discover a deep hollow in the prairie. In normal times it might have held some water but was now bone-dry. Still, there might be water hidden below the surface of the sand. Instructing his friend to stay there and dig for water, Smith set out alone, heading for a ravine about three miles away. He was never seen again.[15]

His friends managed to find water and survived. They learned about Smith's fate only when they finally reached Santa Fe. There they heard that some Comancheros had ridden into the city carrying Smith's rifle and his pistols. The Mexicans learned that a Comanche hunting party of 15 to 20 men had been lying in wait for buffalo at a water hole along the Cimarron. The Indians saw Smith approach and concealed themselves until he was too close to escape when they suddenly attacked him. He managed to kill one Indian with his rifle but was cut down before he could draw his pistols. (In this era, rifles in the trans-Mississippi West were almost always single-shot rifles. They took a long time to reload, so frontiersmen often carried two small pistols, also single-shot, as emergency backup weapons.)[16]

For a contemporary account of this incident it is instructive to read excerpts from two letters sent by Austin Smith, Jedediah's brother, from "Walnut Creek, on the Arkansas [River], 300 miles from the Settlements [of Missouri]." The first letter is to his father, Jedediah; the second is to his brother Ira. The spelling and punctuation in both letters are as in the originals. The first letter reads in part:

My Dear Farther
It is [pain]ful at [all] times to com[municate the death] of a friend,- but [when it f]alls to the lot of a son to communicate to a farther the death of a Brother, it is more so — Your son Jedediah was killed on the Semerone [Cimarron River] the 27th of May on his way to Santa fé by the Curmanch [Comanche] Indians, his party was in distress for water, and he had gone alone in search of the above river which he found, when he was attacked by fifteen or twenty of them — they succeeded in alarming his horse not daring to fire on him so long as they kept face to face, so as soon as his horse turned they fired, and wounded him in the shoulder then he fired his gun [his rifle], and killed their head chief it is supposed they then *rushed* upon him, and despatched him.[17]

The second letter gives the big picture of the event and then repeats it, giving more details to round out the story:

> [Jedediah Smith] saw the Indians before they attacked him, but [since he] supposed there could be no possible chance of an escape, he therefore went boldly up, with the hope of making peace with them, but found that his only chance was defense, he killed the head Chief.... The Spanish traders say that the Indians succeeded in alarming the horse he was riding so as to get his back to them [i.e., they frightened the horse so that it shied away from them, thus exposing the rider's back], which when effected, they then forced [fired] on him and wounded him in the shoulder; he then faced them and killed the Chief.[18]

Such an unprovoked and fatal attack by the Indians was what prompted an unnamed mountain man, who had spent the last 25 years of his life among the Indians of the Rocky Mountains, to offer this exaggerated but straight-from-the-shoulder advice to Captain Randolph B. Marcy in about 1859. Marcy tells us the mountain man said of the Indians:

> They are the most onsartainest varmints in all creation, and I reckon tha'r not mor'n half human; for you never seed a human, arter you'd fed and treated him to the best fixins in your lodge, jist turn round and steal all your horses, or ary other thing he could lay his hands on. No, not adzackly. He would kinder feel grateful, and ask you to spread a blanket in his lodge ef you ever passed that a-way. But the Indian he don't care shucks for you, and is ready to do you a heap of mischief as soon as he quits your feed....
>
> Don't they kill and sculp a white man when-ar they get the better on him? The mean varmints, they'll never behave themselves until you give um a clean out and out licking. They can't understand white folks' ways, and they won't learn um; and ef you treat um decently, they think you ar afeard. You may depend on't ... the only way to treat Injuns is to thrash them well at first, then the balance will sorter take to you and behave themselves.[19]

Despite these ferocious opinions, it seems clear that more travelers on the Santa Fe Trail were killed or wounded *by their own firearms*—through carelessness and accidents—than by the Indians. The case of a man named Broadus is much to the point here. When traveling along the trail in 1831 near Great Bend, Kansas, Broadus shoved a loaded rifle into the bed of his wagon, with the muzzle of the rifle pointing away from him, toward the rear of the wagon. Later, when he pulled the rifle out of the wagon, he did so from the rear, which meant that the muzzle was now facing him. In the process, the spring-loaded hammer of this powerful rifle caught on an obstruction and was shoved half-way towards the cocked position. As the rifle was pulled out of the wagon, the hammer cleared this obstruction, flew forward, and fired the rifle. There was a nearly fatal consequence: the bullet embedded itself deeply in Broadus' arm. Josiah Gregg, who may have been an eyewitness to the scene, tells us in graphic detail what happened next:

The bone being dreadfully shattered, the unfortunate man was advised to submit to an amputation at once; otherwise, it being the month of August and excessively warm, mortification would soon ensue. But Broadus obstinately refused to consent to this course, till death began to stare him in the face. By this time, however, the whole arm had become gangrened, some spots having appeared above the place where the operation should have been performed....

But being unwilling to resign himself to the fate which appeared frowning over him ... he obtained the consent of two or three of the party, who undertook to amputate his arm.... Their only "case of instruments" consisted of a handsaw, a butcher's knife and a large iron bolt. The teeth of the saw being considered too coarse, they went to work, and soon had a set of fine teeth filed on the back. The [blade of the] knife having been whetted keen, and the iron bolt laid upon the fire, they commenced the operation: and in less time that it takes to tell it, the arm was opened round to the bone, which was in an instant sawed off; and with the whizzing hot iron the whole stump was so effectively seared as to close the arteries completely. Bandages were now applied, and the company proceeded on their journey, as though nothing had occurred. The arm commenced healing rapidly.[20]

Such dramatic events were rare on the trail. What travelers usually had to cope with during their eight-week journey was much less exciting, namely, tedium, heat, dust, huge lightning storms, rain, mud, rattlesnakes, gnats, and mosquitoes.[21] The drudgery was occasionally broken by other unwelcome events, such as stampedes of the stock, swollen streams, prairie fires, hailstorms, or high winds.

Despite these difficulties, there were nevertheless many positive moments on the trail and more than enough time for pleasantries. When he was about to begin his trip along the trail in 1858, the traveler Hezekiah Brake remembered that "Far away from my wife and child, and six hundred miles of constant danger in an uninhabited region was not a pleasant prospect for contemplation. But I laughed with the rest, joked about roasting our bacon with buffalo chips, and the enjoyment we would derive from the company of skeletons that would strew our pathway."[22]

Travelers who, like Josiah Gregg, had been chronically ill before their journeys on the plains often found, as did Gregg himself, that the "purity of the plains" and the vigorous outdoor life quickly restored them to robust health. The plains offered not only health but scenic benefits as well. Easterners coming into the trans-Mississippi West for the first time were very impressed by the endless expanses of prairie grasses, punctuated by narrow ribbons of trees tracing the courses of the few waterways. One early traveler recalled how in spring "the vast plain heaves and rolls around like a green ocean."

Many others commented on the amazing mirages they encountered along the trail. (Mirages arise when light rays are bent and produce a displaced image of distant objects or the sky. Desert soils and sands can become very hot when exposed to the sun, easily becoming 20 degrees or more warmer than the air a few feet above. This is enough to cause mirages.) A trail traveler vividly evokes the effects of these mirages: "Horses and riders upon them presented a remarkable picture, apparently extending into the air ... 45 to 60 feet high.... At the same time I could see clear lakes of water ... with bulrushes and other vegetation."[23]

The daily routine of life on the trail was very predictable. At dawn, the teams were hitched up and a light breakfast was prepared. The wagon train got underway as quickly as possible, stopping only for a mid-morning "nooning" to unhitch the teams and let them graze and to gather "buffalo chips" (dried buffalo dung) for fuel. Lunch — the main meal of the day — was then prepared from a monotonous larder consisting primarily of flour, "sowbelly" (bacon preserved with salt), coffee, sugar, and salt. When available, beans, dried apples, or meat from buffalo or other game provided a welcome variety. After lunch, travel continued. By early evening the day's journey was done. Men then repaired their wagons, yokes, and harnesses; greased the axles of the wagons; doctored their livestock; and sometimes hunted buffalo or antelope. Later, by firelight, they ate a light meal; posted armed guards for the night; and, after a bit of socializing (accompanied, perhaps, by a little music) rolled up in their bedding under the stars of the open prairie.

From its very beginnings, traffic on the Santa Fe Trail grew rapidly. It did not take long for entrepreneurs to capitalize on this growing movement of people, livestock, and goods. Thus in 1833 the brothers William and Charles Bent, together with Ceran St. Vrain, set up Bent's Fort, located on the Mountain Route of the trail near La Junta, Colorado. Their initial goal was simply to trade with the Plains Indians for buffalo robes, and with the fur trappers for beaver pelts. Their adobe fort, however, soon became the center of an expanding commercial empire run by the Bent, St. Vrain Company.

This enterprise had stores in Santa Fe and Taos, where cloth, glass, hardware, and tobacco were traded for silver, furs, horses, and mules. Located 600 miles from Missouri, for most of its 16-year history, Bent's Fort was the only major permanent settlement along the Santa Fe Trail east of New Mexico. The fort was described in 1847 by a foreign traveler (the English hunter and explorer George F. Ruxton, who is an excellent source and who will be discussed later) as "a square building of adobe, flanked by circular bastions loopholed for musketry [that is, with small openings in the walls through which muskets or rifles could be aimed and fired], and entered by a large gateway leading into the corral or yard."[24] The fort provided food, water, supplies, and livestock, as well as rest and protection for explorers, traders, and the U.S. Army. The company's Mexican trade grew rapidly, too, as its wagon trains crossed and recrossed the plains, not only east-west but also north-south.

During the war with Mexico in 1846 the fort also became a staging point for Kearny's "Army of the West." When the trader William Bent (1809–1869) tried to sell the fort to the U.S. Army in 1849, he was so incensed by the very low sum offered to him that he filled the fort with gunpowder and explosive charges and, as he put it, literally "blew it to pieces." The remnants were designated as a National Historic Site and National Historic Landmark in 1960. The fort, restored in 1976 on the basis of archeological excavations and original sketches, paintings and diaries, is now known as Bent's Old Fort.

It should be noted here that many accounts of the Santa Fe Trail imply that commerce over it was the sole province of enterprising American (or, more occasionally, European) traders. By 1835, however, Hispanics formed the majority of those traveling from Santa Fe into Mexico and owned a sizeable portion of all the goods carried south. They also joined Americans in crossing the Great Plains and in business partnerships. After 1839 Hispanics played an even bigger role in the commerce between Mexico and the United States, expanding their Santa Fe Trail operations and traveling to the eastern United States, where they cultivated direct business relationships with American wholesalers and commission merchants.[25]

The international aspects of the Santa Fe Trail were evident in 1839 when Dr. F. Adolph Wislizenus (1810–1889), a German physician, decided to join a group of fur traders at Westport, Missouri, and travel with them into the Rockies. He described this trip in *A Journey to the Rocky Mountains in the Year 1839*, which was published in 1912. Many of the men in his group were Americans but there was also a scattering of French Canadians, Germans, and a Dane. Dr. Wislizenus would later make a separate trip to Santa Fe and Chihuahua in 1846 and 1847 (it will be discussed later) but at this point we can profit from his graphic description of his group's start down the Santa Fe Trail:

> The Fur Company transported its goods on two-wheeled carts, of which there were four, each drawn by two mules, and loaded with 800 to 900 pounds. The rest [of the men] put their packs on mules or horses, of which there were fifty to sixty in the caravan. Our first camp, Sapling Grove, was in a little hickory wood, with fresh spring water. Our animals we turned loose to graze in the vicinity. To prevent them from straying far, either the two fore feet, or the forefoot and hindfoot of one side are bound together with so-called "hobbles." ...
> After we had attended to our animals, and had eaten our supper, we sprawled around a fire, and whiled away the evening with chatting and smoking; then wrapped ourselves in our woolen blankets, — the only bed one takes with one — and slept for the first time under our little tents, of which we had seven. At dawn, the leader rouses the camp with an inharmonious: "Get up! Get up! Get

up!" Every one rises. The first care is for the animals. They are loosed from their pickets and allowed an hour for grazing. Meanwhile we prepare our breakfast, strike our tents, and prepare for the start. The animals are driven in again, packed and saddled.

We move off *in corpore* ["in a body," i.e., altogether]. We proceed at a moderate pace, in front the leader with his carts, behind him in line long drawn out [are] the mingled riders and pack animals. In the early days of the journey we are apt to lead the pack animals by rope; later on, we leave them free, and drive them before us. At first packing causes novices much trouble on the way. Here the towering pack leans to one side; there it topples under the animal's belly. At one time the beast stands stock still with its swaying load; at another it rushes off madly, kicking out till it is free of its burdens. But pauseless, like an army over its fallen, the train moves on. With bottled-up wrath the older men, raging and swearing [at] the younger ones, gather up their belongings, load the beasts afresh, and trot after the column.

Toward noon an hour or two of rest is made.... We unload the beasts to let them graze, and prepare a mid-day meal. Then we start off again and march on toward sunset. We set up the tents, prepare our meal, lie around the fire, and then, wrapped in our woolen blankets, commit ourselves to our fate till the next morning. In this way twenty to twenty-five miles are covered daily. The only food the animals get is grass. For ourselves, we take with us for the first week some provisions, such as ham, ship-biscuit, tea and coffee. Afterwards we depend on hunting. Such are the daily doings of the caravan.

In the first days our journey was straight west. The first day we marched over the broad Santa Fe road, beaten out by the caravans. Then leaving it to our left we took a narrow wagon road, established by former journeys to the Rocky Mountains, but often so indistinctly traced, that our leader at times lost it, and simply followed the general direction.[26]

Dr. Wislizenus was a careful observer and a good writer. During the early days of the Mexican-American war, in his *Memoir of a Tour to Northern New Mexico Connected with Colonel Doniphan's Expedition*, which was published in 1848, he paints vivid descriptions of lands and peoples. The large fold-out maps printed with this 1848 book depict numerous routes and are still useful today to students of the American West. For example, his "Map of a Tour from Independence to Santa Fé, Chihuahua and Matamoros" includes the now-long-forgotten track of the "Old Spanish military road from Santa Fé to San Antonio de Bexar."

Dr. Wislizenus's description of the Ciboleros (Mexican buffalo hunters) he met on the Santa Fe Trail is worth quoting here for local color (punctuation as in the original):

> While we were traveling to-day over the lonesome plain, men and animals quite tired and exhausted, on the rising of a hill before us there suddenly appeared a number of savage looking riders on horseback, which at first sight we took for Indians; but their covered heads convinced us soon of our mistake, because

Indians never wear hats of any kind: it was a band of Ciboleros, or Mexican buffalo hunters, dressed in leather or blankets, armed with bows and arrows and a lance — sometimes, too, with a gun — and leading along a large train of jaded pack animals.

These Ciboleros are generally poor Mexicans from the frontier settlements of New Mexico, and by their yearly expeditions into the buffalo regions they provide themselves with dried buffalo meat for their own support and sale. Their principal weapon is the lance, which, in riding they plunge so adroitly into the buffalo's flanks, that they seldom miss their aim. They are never hostile towards white men, and seem to be afraid of the Indians. In their manners, dress, and weapons, and faces, they resemble the Indians so much, that they may easily be mistaken for them. The company which we met with consisted of about 100 men and some women, and they felt rather disappointed when we told them how far they had to travel to find the buffalo.[27]

It is instructive here to look at Santa Fe itself in 1841. This account, which has been lightly edited, comes from an article in the 13 November 1841 edition of the *New York Tribune*, a weekly publication. It presents Santa Fe to us through the eyes of a traveler from Indiana whose name, alas, has not been recorded. The article reads in part:

[Santa Fe] is situated in a valley ten miles long, and from two to five wide, surrounded by immense mountains covered with pine and cedar trees, and affords the most beautiful scene the eye can conceive or the mind imagine. Santa Fe is the seat of Government of New Mexico, and is commanded by a Governor-General. It is also a military post, port of entry, and depository of all the ancient archives of the neighboring States. The houses are built of raw bricks [adobe], two feet long, six inches deep, and one foot wide, made with straw and mud, and dried in the sun, and such is the durability that many houses more than two hundred years old are standing and look well; they are only one story high, handsomely whitewashed inside, with dirt floors....

The ladies, certainly, are far more beautiful in this country than those of the same ranks in America, their jetty black hair, piercing black eyes, slender and delicate frame, with unusually small ankles and feet, together with their gay winning address, make you at once easy and happy in their company. Perhaps no people on earth love dress and attention more than the Spanish ladies, and it may be said of a truth, that their amorous flirtations with the men are matters to boast of among themselves. They did work but little, the Fandango and Siesta form the division of time. The Fandango is a lascivious dance, partaking of the waltz, cotillion, and many amorous movements, and it is certainly handsome and amusing. In this the Governor and most humble citizens move together, and in this consists all their republican boast. The men are honest — perhaps more so than those of the same class in the United States, proud and vain of their blood....[28]

Despite the reputation Santa Fe has enjoyed in our own times as a vibrant center of art and culture, daily life there in the mid-nineteenth century was probably remarkably dull. Aside from religious holidays, the major economic and social high-water marks during the year were the infrequent arrivals of the trading caravans. In his *Commerce of the Prairies* (1844), Josiah Gregg gives us a splendid account of one such event. The spelling is as in the original:

> The arrival produced a great deal of bustle and excitement among the natives. "*Los Americanos!*" ["The Americans!"] — "*Los carros*" ["The carts!"] — "*La entrada de la caravana!*] ["The arrival of the caravan!"] were to be heard in every direction; and crowds and women and boys flocked around to see what they could pilfer. The wagoners were by no means free from excitement on this occasion. Informed of the "ordeal" they had to pass, they had spent the previous morning in "rubbing up"; and now they were prepared, with clean faces, sleek combed hair, and their choicest Sunday suit, to meet the "fair eyes" of glistening black that were sure to stare at them as they passed. There was yet another preparation to be made in order to "show off" to advantage. Each wagoner must tie a bran new "cracker" on the lash of his whip [a "cracker," or popper, is a short thin braid at the tip of a whip which breaks the speed of sound and creates a vacuum; air rushing in to fill the vacuum makes a loud popping sound]; for, on driving through the streets and the *plaza pública* [town square], every one strives to outvie his comrades in the dexterity with which he flourishes this favorite badge of authority.[29]

In addition to the arrival of the caravans, there was another very popular diversion in Santa Fe: gambling. Writing of his experiences in 1846 and 1847, Colonel Abert tells us this about Santa Fe:

> The plaza was now our place of daily promenade, as one sees more of character being displayed in the market place than in any other public assembly. No one can visit this country without being struck by the inveterate habit of the people for gambling. The word "monte" [referring to a card game described below] is one of the first a stranger learns. In the market place, by the road side, nay, almost everywhere, you will see the "villanos" [uncouth farmers or herders] seated around, in little groups, deeply absorbed in their games. But, although they carry this vice to great excess, they are extremely temperate in their meats [i.e., in the amount of food they eat] and drink. The term "borrachon" (drunkard) is considered one of the most opprobrious epithets in their language.[30]

Of the many games of chance enjoyed by Mexicans, Indians, and foreigners alike in Santa Fe, "Spanish monte," which may date from seventeenth century Spain, had the most devotees. This game must not be confused with the better known "Three Card Monte," which is not a card game at all but merely a swindle and will not be discussed any further here.

In Spanish monte, as in all other similar casino games, the odds clearly favor the "house," i.e., the establishment where the gambling is taking place. The "house advantage" is a statistical measure of how much the casino expects to win, expressed as a percentage of the player's bet. The house advantage in many casinos today is typically between 0.5 percent and 12 percent. To use this latter figure as an example, this means that the player will lose, on average and over time, $12 dollars for every $100 dollars he or she wagers.[31] A modern expert humorously says of Spanish monte: "[This card game] largely consists of the Punters [gamblers] passing money back and forth between themselves, while the Bank [the house] remains relatively untouched; and then, every few hands, the Bank takes a bite out of the total pool of money being circulated by the Punters. Eventually, the Bank ends up with all of the money, and the Punters, providing they lacked the sense to get out while they were ahead, end up with nothing."[32]

Spanish monte is relevant to our story because it was the basis for the rise from poverty and obscurity of María Gertrudis Barceló, the most notorious lady of New Mexico and perhaps of the entire trans-Mississippi West. Nicknamed "La Tules" (said to mean "reed"), possibly because of her thin frame, Barceló was a celebrated monte card dealer who owned and operated a casino and bar in Santa Fe during the 1830s and 1840s. Details of her life remain sketchy but it appears that she got her start between 1825 and 1826 as a professional gambler in a remote gold mining camp located in the Ortiz mountains some 26 miles southwest of Santa Fe. Her lasting fame is due to the fortuitous arrival in Santa Fe of three American writers—Josiah Gregg, Susan Shelby Magoffin, and "Don Alfredo." Writing in 1844, Gregg paints what may be a biased picture of Barceló:

> The following will not only serve to show the light in which gambling is held by all classes of society, but to illustrate the purifying effects of wealth upon character. Some twelve or fifteen years ago there lived (or rather roamed) in Taos a certain female of very loose habits, known as *La Tules*.[33] Finding it difficult to obtain the means of living in that district, she finally extended her wanderings to the capital. She there became a constant attendant on one of those pandemoniums [casinos] where the favorite game of *monte* was dealt *pro bono publico* ["for the public good"—an ironic use of this classic phrase].
>
> Fortune, at first, did not seem inclined to smile upon her efforts, and for some years she spent her days in lowliness and misery. At last her luck turned, as gamblers would say, and on one occasion she left the bank [casino] with a spoil of several hundred dollars! This enabled her to open a bank of her own, and being favored by a continuous run of good fortune, she gradually rose higher and higher in the scale of affluence, until she found herself in possession of a very handsome fortune. [Her financial rise was due to a combination of personal charm and to the house advantage.]
>
> In 1843, she sent to the United States some ten thousand dollars to be invested in goods. She still continues her favorite "amusement," now being considered the most expert "monte dealer" in all Santa Fé. She is openly received in the first circles of society: I doubt, in truth, whether there is to be found in the city a lady of more fashionable reputation than this same Tules, now known as Señora Doña Gertrudes [*sic*] Barcelo.[34]

In 1846 Susan Shelby Magoffin, 18 years old and a bride of less than eight months, set out with her husband, Samuel, a veteran Santa Fe trader, on a trip from Independence through New Mexico south to Chihuahua. In her diary she describes Barceló as one of the guests present at a ball in Santa Fe (spelling as in the original): "There was 'Dona Tula,' the principal *monte-bank keeper* in Sant Fé, a stately dame of a certain age, the possessor of a portion of that shrewd sense and fascinating manner necessary to lure the wayward, inexperienced youth to the hall of final ruin."[35] The years had not been kind to Barceló, who in her youth probably had been very good-looking. By the time Susan saw her she was about 46 years old. In another section of the diary Susan uncharitably refers to her as "the old woman with false hair and teeth, (Dona Tula)."[36]

At one point, about 100 monte tables were operating in Santa Fe. Initially, the game was considered to be a *jeugo prohibido* (illegal game) but it was tolerated because the fines imposed on players immediately flowed into the pockets of local officials. Governor Manuel Armijo understood the advantages of legalized gambling. By 1839 gamblers' *fines* had become gamblers' *fees*; ten years later the sale of gaming licenses was contributing $1,700 to the Santa Fe "county treasury," i.e., to Mexican officials themselves. In contrast, "dram shops" (saloons) were generating only $1,256.66.[37] Mary J. Straw Cook, a modern historian, offers some advice to any ladies who might aspire to become monte dealers today:

> And a word of advice—no monte dealer on the street entered the business without immediate protection nearby. Manuel Antonio Sisneros, husband of Doña Tules, gambled and protected her in the early days of her career in the 1820s and 1830s. Following his abrupt disappearance after 1841, however, American James Madison Giddings and Mexican Santiago Flores became lookouts and guards for the monte-dealing Tules, often dealing the cards for her. After 1846 the scholarly Prussian August de Marle became her dealer, protector, and lover, following the arrival of the American army [during the Mexican-American war].[38]

De Marle was a good bodyguard. In late 1849 or early 1850 he showed his mettle during a fracas at an establishment in Santa Fe known as the United States Hotel. There a man by the name of Moore became violent because Barceló and de Marle had refused to lend him money. The reason probably was that Moore had lost money at Barceló's monte table; he had probably been drinking, too. In a fit of rage, Moore drew his pistol and fired a shot toward the monte table where Barceló and de Marle were at work. This shot broke up the game; at the same time, de Marle shoved Barceló under the monte table and shielded her with his own body. They never returned to gamble at the United States Hotel after this episode.[39]

La Tules also took the precaution of buying four adjacent properties in downtown Santa Fe. In a city where there were neither policemen nor banks, these buildings gave her colleagues a secure corridor to use when transporting heavy bags of gold dust and gold coins. The sources of this loot were the bulging pockets of the traders, soldiers, and trappers who had just come off the Santa Fe Trail and El Camino Real de Tierra Adentro.[40]

La Tules had a good head for business and recognized the importance of diversification. She had a hand in many other commercial ventures in addition to gambling. These included prostitution, mule trading, gold prospecting, and general trading.[41] But gambling seems to have provided the bulk of her income. She did so well financially from Spanish monte that by 1844 she was able to appear before Judge Tomás Ortiz and record a property deed for two houses — one of nine rooms, the other a smaller structure listed as having porches and an entryway. The main house was located not far from the central plaza of Santa Fe.[42]

Barceló's financial rise was matched by her social rise. An itinerant artist who styled himself "Don Alfredo" has this to say about Barceló in an article published in 1846 by a magazine called the *Messenger*:

> Gambling is practised by both sexes, and by none more than the Governor [Governor General Don Manuel Armijo] himself.
> There is now living in Santa Fe a certain lady known as LA TULES, who has made a handsome fortune by keeping a monte table. Although her early history cannot reflect much credit on her character, yet she is received into the highest circles of society, and, perhaps, there is not a female in that high-toned community who exercises more sway than she does. With this lady, who now assumes the more patrician title of Señora Doña Gertrudes Barcai [*sic*], his Excellency is very intimate; indeed, I believe, he is a partner in her business, and she still pursues the intellectual and profitable amusement [monte] with as keen a relish as in her younger days.
> To this Señora, the Governor communicates all the affairs of State, she then gives them to her adopted daughter, who is married to an American resident, and from the daughter they go to her husband, and thus they go from one to another until every movement becomes known to our people in the capital.[43]

When Barceló died in 1852 she was still very rich. She willed three houses to members of her extended family, together with cash and livestock, and also left money to the church and to city officials for charitable purposes.[44]

Santa Fe may have represented the bright lights of the Southwest but some adventurous souls were more attracted to exploits of the mountain men and tried to emulate them. In pursuit of the beaver, mountain men blazed trails to Taos, Bent's Fort, and later to Denver. The Taos Trail itself, also known as the Trappers Trail and Sangre de Cristo Trail, linked Taos with northerly regions such as Pueblo, Colorado, and Laramie, Wyoming. In its southern reaches the Taos Trail ran southwest from Bent's Fort to Rayado, New Mexico, where it turned due west towards Taos.[45]

One of the most readable commentators about life as an amateur mountain man is Lewis H. Garrard. The 17-year-old son of a wealthy and prominent family living near St. Louis, he left Westport, Missouri, in September 1846 via the Santa Fe Trail, bound for Taos, and returned to his home in July 1847. He published a journal of his trip in 1850 and, with youthful exuberance, gave it a sonorous title: *Wah-to-Yah and the Taos Trail, or Prairie Travel and Scalp Dances, with a Look at Rancheros from Muleback and the Rocky Mountain Campfire*.

The title of Garrard's book, "Wah-to-Yah" refers to a pair of volcanic mountains in south-central Colorado known as the Spanish Peaks, which are visible from as far away as 100 miles. They are located in the Sangre de Cristo Mountains as an eastern outlier of the otherwise nonvolcanic Culebra Range. Their Indian name means "Breasts of the Earth"; later travelers knew them as the Twin Peaks, Dos Hermanos, (Two Brothers), or as the Mexican Mountains. Regardless of what they were called, these twin peaks became valuable and unmistakable guideposts for travelers along the Mountain Route of the Santa Fe Trail.

Garrard's book is not a mature, scholarly, dispassionate work like Josiah Gregg's *Commerce of the Prairies* but, as we shall see, it has a pleasant, lighthearted touch which Gregg's book lacks. It is especially good on the unique jargon used by the mountain men who roamed through the Rocky Mountains and parts of the Southwest. See appendix four for an example of their speech. Largely thanks to his family connections, at Westport Garrard was accepted immediately as a member of a caravan commanded by a well known frontiersman, Ceran St. Vrain. Garrard describes him thus: "Mr. St. Vrain [was] an old mountaineer of the firm of Bent, St. Vrain & Co., Indian and Mexican traders. The firm is rich, and owner of several forts, of which Bent's or Fort William, on the Arkansas River, is the principal. Mr. St. Vrain was a gentleman in the true sense of the term, his French descent imparting an exquisite, indefinable degree of politeness, and, combined with the frankness of an ingenuous mountain man, made him an amiable fellow traveler."[46]

Of several good examples of Garrard's lighthearted touch, we will use here his account of what can accurately be called a "dog dinner." One of Garrard's companions on the trail was an experienced mountaineer named John Smith. As Garrard recounts the story, during a campfire conversation,

> Smith expiated at length on [Indian] customs, food, and easy life. Of the viands [meats], he lauded *dog's* flesh [a delicacy to the Indians] to the very skies; on my expressions of abhorrence at the bare thought, he said:

"I'll bet I make you eat dog meat in the village, and you'll say it's good, and the best you ever hid in your 'meatbag' (stomach)."

"No you will not," enjoined I; "the mere idea is enough to sicken one — slimy pup meat! Ugh! not enough of the carnivorous in me for that; besides buffalo meat, in my opinion, cannot be surpassed for delicacy of flavor in this or any other country."

[Smith replied:] "Well, hos! [literally "horse"; in this context it means "my friend"] I'll dock off buffler [I'll grant you the virtues of buffalo meat], and then if thar's any meat that 'runs' [if there is any other kind of meat] that can take the shine outen 'dog' [that can surpass dog meat], you can slide [you will win this discussion]."[47]

Later, at an Indian camp, Garrard was quite hungry and eagerly asked Smith and another mountaineer what the Indians were cooking on the fire. "Tarrapins!," Smith replied, and went on to explain how the Indians carefully prepared these terrapins for the table. He then gave Garrard a choice piece of the meat. Garrard writes:

I ate it with much gusto, calling "for more." It was extremely good, and I spoke of the delicacy of the meat, and answered all their questions as to its excellency in the affirmative, even to the extent of a panegyric on the whole turtle species.... Smith looked at me a while in silence, the corners of his mouth gradually making preparations for a laugh, and asked:

"Well, hos! how do you like dog meat?" and then such hearty guffaws were never heard.... I broke the shackles of deep-rooted antipathy to the canine breed, and, putting a choice morceau [piece] on top of that already swallowed, ever after remained a staunch defender and admirer of dog meat.[48]

Another young man who traveled lightly and widely and who wrote well is the English explorer and adventurer George Frederick Ruxton (1821–1848). He was expelled from a British military academy but finally became an officer in the British army and served in Ireland and Canada. Independently wealthy, he resigned from the army to become a hunter in Canada and then spent time in Africa and Mexico before moving to the United States, where he traveled as a mountain man. Ruxton wrote a series of articles on *Life in the Far West* for *Blackwood's* magazine, an Edinburgh journal. His *Adventures in Mexico and the Rocky Mountains* was published in London in 1847. Unhappily, after surviving many near-death experiences in the wilderness, Ruxton died of dysentery in 1848 in St. Louis at the age of only 27.[49]

Ruxton's *Wild Life in the Rocky Mountains*, covering his travels in 1846 and 1847, forms part of *Adventures in Mexico and the Rocky Mountains*. It provides unusually good reading because of its attention to detail and its "I-was-there" authenticity. Let us now profit from some aspects of his travel along El Camino Real de Tierra Adentro. Concerning the Jornada del Muerto, Ruxton tells us:

> I was now at the edge of this formidable desert, where along the road the bleaching bones of mules and horses testify to the dangers to be apprehended from the want of water and pasture, and many human bones likewise tell their tale of Indian slaughter and assault....
>
> Near the Perillo [a tiny water hole] is a point of rocks which abuts upon the road, and from which a large band of Apaches a few years since pounced upon a band of American trappers and entirely defeated them, killing several and carrying off all their animals. Behind these rocks they frequently lie in ambush shooting down the unwary traveler, whose first intimation of their presence is the puff of smoke [a gunshot] from the rocks, or the whiz of an arrow through the air. One of my mozos [muleteers], who was a New Mexican and knew the country well, warned me of the dangers of this spot, and before passing it I halted the mules and rode on to reconnoitre; but no Apache lurked behind it, and we passed unmolested....
>
> At sunrise we halted for a couple of hours on a patch of grass which afforded a bite to the tired animals, and about three in the afternoon had the satisfaction of reaching the river [the Rio Grande] at the watering place called Fray Cristoval, having performed the whole distance of the jornada, of ninety-five, or, as some say, one hundred miles, in little more than twenty hours.[50]

The capital of Santa Fe did not make a very favorable impression on him. He writes:

> The town is a wretched collection of mud-houses, without a single building of stone, although it boasts a *palacio* [palace] — as the adobe residence of the Governor is called — a long low building, taking up the greater part of one side of the plaza or public square, round which runs a portal or colonnade supported by pillars of rough pine. The appearance of the town defies description, and I can compare it to nothing but a dilapidated brick-kiln or prairie-dog town. The inhabitants are worthy of their city, and more miserable, vicious-looking population it would be impossible to imagine. Neither was the town improved, at the time of my visit, by the addition to the population of some three thousand Americans, the dirtiest, rowdiest crew I have ever seen collected together.... Under the portales were numerous monte-tables, surrounded by Mexicans and Americans. Every other house was a grocery, as they call a gin or whisky shop, continuously disgorging reeling drunken men, and everywhere filth and dirt reigned triumphant.[51]

Later, on his journey through northern New Mexico between Red River (about 75 miles northeast of Santa Fe) and Costilla (on the New Mexican side of the Colorado border), Ruxton paints a grim picture of late-season travel in the high country. He followed a trail which headed north from Red River. Today, according to a local expert in Red River, this trail no longer exists but it probably ran through Malette Canyon, where in the late 1800s a stagecoach track passed through what is still called Trail Canyon. This track ended at the now-abandoned mining town of Midnight, New Mexico.[52] These are some of the harsh conditions Ruxton faced: "The cold of these regions is more intense than I have ever experienced, not excepting even lower Canada; and when a northerly wind sweeps over the bleak and barren plains, charged as it is with its icy reinforcements from the snow-clad mountains, it assails the unfortunate traveller, exposed to all its violence, with blood-freezing blasts, piercing to his very heart and bones."[53]

To eat well on this trip, Ruxton had to be a good shot and a good hunter. He tells us (the spelling is his):

> Such was the state of congelation I was in, on this day, that even the shot-tempting antelope bounded past unscathed. My hands, with fingers of stone, refused even to hold the reins of my horse, who travelled as he pleased, sometimes slueing round his stern to wind, which was "dead ahead." Mattias, the half-breed who was my guide, enveloped from head to foot in blanket [sic], occasionally cast a longing glance out of its folds at the provoking venison as it galloped past, muttering at intervals, "Jesus, Jesus, *que carne*—what meat we're losing!"
>
> At length, as a band of some three thousand [a large herd of antelopes] almost ran over us, human nature, although at freezing point, could no longer stand it. I jumped off Panchito [his mule], and kneeling down, sent a ball from my rifle right into the "thick" of the herd. At the report two antelopes sprang into the air, their forms being distinct against the horizon above the backs of the rest; and when the herd had passed, they were lying kicking in the dust, one shot in the neck, through which the ball had passed into the body of another. We packed a mule with the choice pieces of the meat, which was a great addition to our slender stock of dried provisions.[54]

Ruxton was not, however, the only traveler who savored antelope meat:

> As I was butchering the antelope, half a dozen wolves hung round the spot, attracted by the smell of blood; they were so tame and hungry at the same time, that I thought they would actually have torn the meat from under my knife.... I threw a large piece of meat towards them, when the whole gang jumped upon it, fighting and growling, and tearing each other in the furious melee. I am sure I might have approached near enough to have seized one by the tail, so entirely regardless of my vicinity did they appear. They were doubtless rendered more ravenous than usual by the uncommon severity of the weather....[55]

Southwestern travelers like Ruxton normally could not get very far in a single day. They were forced to proceed relatively slowly because they had to lead pack mules, drive horses or other stock, or make their way carefully along narrow mountain trails where a fall could be fatal. There is at least one exception to this general rule, however. The Santa Fe trader Francis Xavier Aubry (1824–1854) made many lightning-like trips over the Santa Fe Trail and repeatedly broke speed records between Independence, Missouri, and Santa Fe. His exploits are worth noting here.

Aubry grew up on a farm in Quebec but left Canada to seek his fortune in the United States at the age of 18. In 1846 war with Mexico was imminent and businessmen in St. Louis began to talk about new opportunities to trade with Santa Fe and Chihuahua. At the age of 22 Aubry joined the Santa Fe trade and did well at it. Although he was a small man, standing only five feet two inches tall and weighing little more than 100 pounds, he proved to be a horseman of uncanny ability and endurance. In late 1847 and early 1848, for example, it took him only 14 days to ride from Santa Fe to Independence — a record for a trip that took wagon trains two months or more to finish. Not content with this achievement, that same year he repeated the trip in the spring of 1848 in eight days and ten hours.

Then, wanting to make three round-trips between Missouri and St. Louis in one year, in August 1848 Aubry returned to Santa Fe with 30 wagons packed with goods. He announced that after selling his wares he would try to break his own record on the way back to St. Louis. At a time when a laborer was making about one dollar a day, Aubry bet $1,000 that he could make the trip in only six days. The celebrated American folklorist J. Frank Dobie recounts the story:

> For sustained endurance, speed and distance, I rank a ride made by François Xavier Aubry as supreme in the whole riding tradition of the West....
>
> Before dawn on September 12 [1848], he left Santa Fe in a swinging gallop, and he ate only six meals on the ground, stopped only once to sleep — for two hours — before he reined up his final horse, heaving and atremble, at Independence on the Missouri. On the way he killed six horses [by riding them to death] and broke down six others.... He ate little while riding, and after the first day and night tied himself to the saddle so that he could doze without falling off....
>
> It was the rainy season of the year; for a whole day and night rain fell on him continuously, and high winds were blowing most of the time.... At ten o'clock on the night of September 17 he halts [in St. Louis] in front of the Noland House, called also the Merchant's Hotel.... Men rush out from the bar and "lift" him from his saddle. It is "caked with blood".... He has won his bet....
>
> The next summer in Santa Fe, Captain R.B. Marcy met Aubry at a supper being paid as a debt to the great rider. Aubry wrote down and signed a short account of his ride. "I made the trip," he said, "travelling time only counted, in 4 days and 12 hours, though the time spent between Santa Fe and Independence was 5 days and 16 hours. I made a portion of the trip at the rate of 250 miles to the 24 hours; made 200 miles on my yellow mare in 26 hours."[56]

Aubry remained in the Santa Fe trade until 1853. He then transported goods and drove herds of sheep, horses, and mules to California, where the gold rush had created a booming market. The next year he drove 14,000 sheep to California. His good luck ran out, however, when he returned to Santa Fe. There he stopped at a bar on the south side of the plaza and got into a fight with Colonel Richard H. Weightman, a former newspaper editor in

Albuquerque. Weightman stabbed Aubry and killed him. Arrested and tried for murder, Weightman was acquitted on the grounds of self-defense. Aubry was buried in Santa Fe.[57]

Travelers on the Santa Fe Trail in New Mexico valued the support and protection afforded by Fort Union, which was founded in 1851 near Watrous, about 90 miles northeast of Santa Fe. The ruts of the trail can still clearly be seen at Fort Union today. This historic site now preserves the second of the three forts built there, as well as the ruins of the third. The Santa Fe trader and author William Davis has left us a good snapshot of the fort as it appeared to him when traveling along the trail in 1857:

> As we crossed the ridge some three miles distant, the fort came into view, which at first sight appeared like a cluster of dark spots upon the white surface, close to the foot of a range of mountains. As we drew nearer we could distinctly see the quarters of officers and men; soon the flash of the sentinels' muskets caught the eye, and objects could distinctly be seen moving about. We reached the fort about eleven o'clock, and were landed at the sutler's store, that being the post-office. [A sutler was a civilian who sold foodstuffs and goods at an army post, where he usually had a shop.]
> Fort Union ... is situated in the pleasant valley of the Moro. It is an open post, without either stockades or breastworks of any kind, and, barring the officers and soldiers who are seen about it, it has much more the appearance of a quiet frontier village than of a military station. It is laid out with broad and straight streets crossing each other at right angles. The huts are built of pine logs, obtained from the neighboring mountains, and the quarters of both officers and men wore a neat and comfortable appearance.... I dined at the hospitable board of Colonel Cook [the commanding officer], and, after having eaten but one meal for the past forty-eight hours, the reader will readily believe that I did full justice to the repast.[58]

Fort Union was the first of the three successive forts built here. One of its earliest campaigns was directed against the Jicarilla Apaches, who in 1854 surprised and nearly wiped out a company of dragoons. Soldiers from Fort Union drove the Apaches back into the mountains west of the Rio Grande. In 1855 the soldiers also conducted operations against the Utes of southern Colorado and, in 1860 and 1861, against the Kiowas and Comanches raiding the plains east of the fort. This fort became an important stopping point on the Santa Fe Trail. There travelers could rest and resupply their wagon trains at the sutler's store before continuing their journey. The fort was also the principal quartermaster (supply) depot of the Southwest.

The second Fort Union, built in 1861, was a massive earthwork designed to defend the Santa Fe Trail against an anticipated Confederate invasion. It did not survive for long. The parapets were washed away by rains and tumbled into a surrounding ditch; the pine-log barracks rotted and became nesting places for insects; and the rooms were unhealthy, being damp and unventilated. This fort was abandoned in 1862 after Union forces from Fort Union and elsewhere halted a Confederate attack during the Battle of Glorieta Pass (roughly 20 miles southeast of Santa Fe).

The third and final Fort Union was begun in 1863, was modified in the 1870s, and was finally abandoned in 1891, thanks to the coming of the railroad. During its heyday it served as the principal supply base for the Military Department of New Mexico. Shipments of food, clothing, arms, ammunition, tools, and building materials arrived at the fort over the Santa Fe Trail and were then distributed to other forts in the Southwest. A British traveler wrote in 1867: "Fort Union is a bustling place; it is the largest military establishment to be found on the Plains, and is the supply center [for] the forty or fifty lesser posts scattered all over the country within a radius of 500 miles."[59]

Despite its practical uses, Fort Union left much to be desired as a place to live. Mrs. Orsemus B. Boyd, the wife of an army officer, remembered what it was like to live there in 1872: "Many ladies dislike Fort Union. It has always been noted for severe dust storms. Situated on a barren plain, the nearest mountains ... three miles distant, it has the most exposed position of any military fort in New Mexico.... The hope of having any trees, even a grassy parade-ground, had been abandoned long before our residence there.... Every eye is said to form its own beauty. Mine was disposed to see much in Fort Union, for I had a home there."[60]

The Santa Fe Trail would remain the most important route linking the settlements of the Mississippi Valley with New Mexico until 1880, when the Atchison, Topeka and Santa Fe Railroad (discussed later) was extended from Chicago to the Rio Grande. Ironically, this line bypassed Santa Fe itself but that same year the Denver and Rio Grande Railroad built a track coming from the north which passed through Santa Fe. It connected with the Santa Fe line at Lamy, which lies 15 miles south of Santa Fe.[61] Thus it was an ever-expanding railroad network that brought this historic trail to an end.

The closure of the Santa Fe Trail was a harbinger of the closure of Fort Union. When the U.S. Army finally abandoned the fort in 1891, it passed into private hands. The new owner was the powerful Union Land and Cattle Grazing Company. However, the company had no use for military buildings, which were allowed to fall into ruin. Conservationists, on the other hand, never abandoned their efforts to have the fort restored. Ultimately, they were successful: in 1954 President Eisenhower signed into law a bill establishing the Fort Union National Monument. By 1959 the National Park Service had turned the ruins into a site which is well worth visiting today.[62]

CHAPTER VI

Military and Cultural Perspectives on the Mexican-American War

The historic trails of the Southwest played a vital role in the Mexican-American War, a conflict between the United States and Mexico which arose in large part over the annexation of Texas by the United States in 1845.[1] The war took place in Texas, New Mexico, California, northern, central, and eastern Mexico, and Mexico City. It ended in a complete American victory. The most important result was the Mexican Cession, by which the Mexican territories of Alta California and Santa Fé de Nuevo México were ceded to the United States under the terms of the Treaty of Guadalupe Hidalgo (1848). As mentioned earlier, the present-day states of California, Nevada, Utah, and parts of Colorado, Arizona, New Mexico, and Wyoming were carved out of this Mexican Cession. Because of the great importance of this war to the American West, it is worth reviewing briefly here.

Politically, the war was always highly controversial. In the United States, the Whigs strongly opposed it, while the Southern Democrats warmly embraced the concept of Manifest Destiny and the expectation of conquering new lands for the expansion of slavery. (The Whig Party functioned between 1833 and 1856. Its name was chosen to evoke the American Whigs of 1776, who had fought for independence and had opposed autocratic rule. Manifest Destiny was the conviction that the United States was destined to expand from the Atlantic seaboard to the Pacific Ocean and even beyond.)

Mexico, for its part, considered Texas simply to be a rebellious province and denounced the United States as a brutal aggressor. Indeed, patriotic Mexicans still refer to the war, which is commonly known in the United States as the Mexican-American War or simply as the Mexican War, in highly nationalistic terms. They know it, for example, as *La Intervención Norteamericana*

113

(The North American Intervention), *La Guerra de Defensa* (The Defensive War), *La Invasión Estadounidense* (The United States Invasion), or *La Guerra del 47* (The War of '47). By whatever name we refer to it, the results were clear enough: the Mexican government lost more than 500,000 square miles (55 percent of its national territory) as a result of this conflict. In return it received from the United States the sum of only $15,000,000—less than half the amount the U.S. had originally offered to Mexico for these lands before the war began. (The Americans also agreed to assume $3,250,000 in debts that the Mexican government owed to U.S. citizens.)

Two of the campaigns of the war — those led by Kearny and by Colonel Alexander William Doniphan — centered on Santa Fe. This city was strategically important because it was the hub of caravan trade along the Santa Fe Trail. To protect that trade and to capture New Mexico itself, Kearny's 1st Dragoons and Missouri volunteers — a total force of about 1,500 men — made a grueling 537-mile trek along the Santa Fe Trail from Fort Leavenworth to Bent's Fort and thence to Santa Fe. These troops marched about 100 miles a week for five weeks. However, once they got to Santa Fe in August 1846, they found that the New Mexicans offered them no resistance whatsoever. The Mexican governor, Manuel Armijo, simply abandoned his own defensive positions and allowed the American force to secure its objective without a fight. Thus Santa Fe was captured without a single shot being fired.

There seem to have been three reasons for this sudden and unexpected American success. The first was that many New Mexicans believed that an American victory would be very good for trade; indeed, it can be said that the conquest of New Mexico had actually begun many years earlier, with the opening of the Santa Fe Trail in 1821—thanks to the profitable commerce that flowed along this artery of transportation.[2] The second reason was that New Mexicans were tired of being ignored by their corrupt, incompetent national government headquartered in Mexico City, which had little interest in and little ability to influence events on its distant northern frontier.[3] Finally, Governor Armijo himself clearly never intended to fight. James Magoffin, an American trader and brother-in-law of the young diarist Susan Shelby Magoffin, persuaded Armijo, allegedly by offering him a bribe of 500 ounces of gold, that retreat would be the better part of valor.[4] Armijo was later tried in Mexico City for cowardice and desertion in the face of the enemy but was acquitted of these charges. While in Mexico City, he also interceded on behalf of James Magoffin, who had been arrested in Chihuahua as an American spy.

Kearny set up a civil government in Santa Fe headed by the trader Charles Bent and then divided his command into three groups. The first, under Sterling Price, was ordered to hold New Mexico. The second, under Colonel

Doniphan, was sent south to capture Chihuahua. The third, led by Kearny himself, would press on to California.

Kearny led his forces along the Gila River Trail (described later) to California. As we have seen, at Socorro, New Mexico, he encountered Kit Carson, who told him that California was already in American hands, a report which turned out to be quite premature. In fact, the Californios (Mexicans living in California) would soon rise in revolt against the Americans. Kearny decided that since the trail ahead was so difficult and so arid, he would send all but two of his companies back to Santa Fe. After a long, hard march along the Gila River and across deserts, Kearny and 100 exhausted dragoons, led by Carson, finally reached Warner's Ranch (near San Diego). There they found themselves facing—and outnumbered by—a Mexican army stationed near the village of San Pasqual.

Without pausing to recuperate, Kearny ordered a surprise attack in hopes of a quick victory. However, a death-or-glory saber charge on foot, led by Captain Benjamin Moore, nearly led to disaster for the Americans: the sabers of the dragoons proved to be no match for the long lances of mounted Mexicans. Only the timely arrival of artillery and of reinforcements finally evened up the tide of battle—but not before 18 dragoons, including Captain Moore himself, lay dead in the dust. The net result was that the Battle of San Pasqual was indecisive.

Kearny then moved on to San Diego, where he joined up with a body of U.S. Marines commanded by Commodore Robert Stockton. In January 1847 their combined forces put down the revolt and solidified American possession of California. At the end of that month, another American expedition, the Mormon Battalion, "half naked and half fed," reached San Diego. This was what remained of the 545 Mormon volunteers who, under Philip St. George Cook, had marched from temporary camps in Iowa and Nebraska to Santa Fe and then across the blistering deserts of southern New Mexico and Arizona.[5]

As mentioned earlier, one of the U.S. Army officers who accompanied General Kearny on his expedition to conquer New Mexico was Colonel Abert, an officer of the Corps of Topographical Engineers. Abert is remembered by historians today thanks to his very informative and well written journal, which is full of local color. His journal was republished in Albuquerque in 1962 under the title of *Abert's New Mexico Report 1846-'47*. Two excerpts will show his nice literary touch. The first excerpt is set on the Rio Grande near its junction with the Rio Puerco, a small river which joins the Rio Grande near the town of La Joya de Ciboletta, New Mexico:

> We were much amused at the laconic replies of some persons [Mexicans] that we met upon the road—whence do you come? "De abaxo" ["from below," i.e.,

from the lower section of the river]. Where are you going? "Arriba" ["above," i.e., up the river]. What news have you? "Nada" [nothing.] Men who can give such non-committal answers certainly possess considerable finesse.

There is much more wit in these replies than in the stereotyped joke of "comprendo pero no quiero" [a rough translation is: "I 'get it'—that is, I understand what you are saying, but I don't subscribe to it"], that is every where echoed through New Mexico. Alas the degeneracy of the times. O tempora! O mores! It would make Cervantes weep, and, in despair, burn up his works.[6]

"O tempora! O mores" is a famous sentence by the Roman rhetorician Cicero. It means "Oh, what a time! Oh, what customs!" and is used ironically to criticize current attitudes or trends. Miguel de Cervantes (1547–1616) was a Spanish novelist, poet and playwright. His greatest work, *Don Quixote*, is regarded as one of the best novels ever written.

The second excerpt is Abert's description of a grizzly bear hunt along the Mountain Route of the Santa Fe Trail. This took place just before his party reached the narrow confines of Raton Pass, which, at an elevation of 7,834 feet, provides the most direct land route between the valley of the Arkansas River to the north and the valley of the Cimarron River to the south. It would later serve as a toll road and then as a railroad route. (With grades over the pass approaching 3 percent, even in modern times freight trains would need an extra "helper" locomotive when climbing through this pass.) Abert writes:

> We had no sooner left camp than we commenced the ascent of a long hill, whose top forms the dividing ridge of the waters running north from those running south. From the top of this ridge one has a magnificent view. As the road is very tortuous, at one time one beholds the Spanish peaks directly in front; but it is only for a moment, as the road immediately bends to the south.
>
> The bottom of the gorge was not comparatively level; we travelled along quite rapidly, when we again encountered difficult ground. Whilst riding alongside in advance of the wagon, I discovered a sudden rise that screened three large grizzly bears ("ursus ferox") in the middle of the road, marching directly towards me. They were not more than 100 yards distant; I lowered my head to prevent being seen, and rode back and told Pilka [one of his men] to get his rifle; he hurried forward, and stooping behind a rock waited for their approach; they came to within fifty yards of him, but his rifle snapped twice; the third time he put on a fresh cap and stood up to take aim.
>
> At the loud report of the cap, the bears all rose erect, snuffing the air. [Pilka was armed with a muzzleloading rifle that used a small explosive percussion cap to ignite the charge of gunpowder in the barrel. A cap sometimes failed to detonate, as in Pilka's first two attempts to fire. At other times, it might detonate with a bang but would fail to ignite the powder charge itself, as in his third attempt.]
>
> At last they caught sight of the cause of their alarm, when they scrambled up the perpendicular sides of the rocky gorge and ran off. We often congratulated ourselves that the rifle did not go off, for had the bears been wounded they

would have created dire havoc amongst our mules; and they were all crowded in such a narrow pass, that it would have been very difficult to have saved any of them. There are few animals more to be dreaded than the grizzly bear.[7]

An equally memorable character is 18-year-old Susan Shelby Magoffin. She kept a detailed diary at a crucial time—in 1846 and 1847. It is important today not in military terms but in social and cultural terms. Her travels, which coincided with the early days of the Mexican-American war, give us unique insights into daily life in New Mexico and in northern Mexico during these turbulent years. We shall therefore look at her diary in some detail.[8]

Susan was born in 1827 and grew up on a prosperous family plantation in Kentucky. There in 1845 she married Samuel Magoffin, an older, wealthy Santa Fe Trail trader. By the time of Susan's trip to New Mexico and northern Mexico in 1846, Samuel and his brother James had been involved in the Santa Fe trade for almost 20 years. On her travels she was accompanied, as befitted a mid-nineteenth-century gentlewoman of high economic and social status, not only by her husband but also by various servants and employees, plus her dog, Ring.

Susan was the first Anglo-American woman to travel west from Independence, Missouri, along the Santa Fe Trail and then south down El Camino Real de Tierra Adentro to Chihuahua in Mexico. Her party subsequently turned east off this latter trail and traveled toward Saltillo (located about 55 miles west of Monterrey, Mexico) and Matamoros (on the coast of the Gulf of Mexico, south of Brownsville, Texas). She entitled her diary "Travels in Mexico Commencing June, 1846. El Diaro de Dona Susanita Magoffin." Her diary was finally brought to light by Stella M. Drumm, the Librarian of the Missouri Historical Society, who published it in 1926 as *Down the Santa Fe Trail and into Mexico*. Ever since then, it has been a nugget in the literature of the Southwest.

Some historians have faulted Susan for her girlish enthusiasm but this adds an appealing freshness to her account. Two examples may make this point. The first is that she was so deeply in love with her husband that she always refers to him in her diary as *mi alma* (my soul). The second is that she looked at travel along the Santa Fe Trail with eyes of wonder. She tells us (spelling and punctuation as in the original):

Thursday 11th [June 1846]. Now the Prairie life begins! We soon left "the settlements" this morning. Our mules travel well and we joged on at a rapid pace until 10 o'clock, when we came up with the waggons. They were encamped just at the edge of the last woods. As we proceeded from this thick wood of oak and scrubby underbrush, my eyes were unable to satiate their longing for a sight of the wide spreding plains. The hot sun, or rather the wind which blew pretty roughly, compelled me to seek shelter with my friends, the carriage & a thick veil....

We now numbered, of ourselves only, quite a force. Fourteen big waggons with six yoke [of oxen] each, one baggage waggon with two yoke, one dearborn [the Dearborn wagon, widely used from 1819 to 1850, was a light wagon with a top and sometimes with side curtains] with two mules ... our own carriage with two more mules and two men on mules driving the loose stock, consisting of nine and a half yoke of oxen, our riding horses two, and three mules, with Mr. Hall the superintendent of the waggons, together with his mule, we number twenty men, three are our tent servants (Mexicans). Jane, my attendant, two horses, nine mules, some two hundred oxen, and last though not least our dog Ring. A grey hound he is of noble descent; he white with brown spots, a nice watch for our tent door.[9]

Susan had more than her fair share of suffering but bore it stoically. During the trip from Independence she was pregnant; at Bent's Fort, she suffered a miscarriage on 31 July 1846. Despite the intense pain she had been in and her sorrow at the loss of what would have been her first child, she was still very alert to what was going on around her (italics and punctuation as in the original):

My situation was very different from that of an Indian woman in the room below me. She gave birth to a fine healthy baby, about the same time, *and in half an hour after she went to the River and bathed herself and it,* and this she has continued each day since. Never could I have believed such a thing, if I had not been here, and *mi alma's* own eyes had not seen her coming from the River. And some gentleman here tells him, he has often seen them immediately after the birth of a child go to the water and *break the ice* to bathe themselves![10]

On 27 August 1846, Susan received some good news. She reports that "The news from Santa Fé is that A[r]mijo [the Mexican governor] has fled, and Gen. Kearny, who is in possession of his house, is fortifying the city — so we may just fix ourselves there for the winter."[11] Four days later she and her party were safely lodged in Santa Fe. She was elated (italics as in the original):

It is really hard to realize it, that I am here in my own house, in a place too where I once would have thought it folly of visiting. I have entered the city in a year that will always be remembered by my countrymen; and under the "Star-spangled banner" too, the first American lady, who has come under such auspices, and some of our company seem disposed to make me the first under any circumstances that ever crossed the Plains.... Brother James [Magoffin], received us at our door, and supped with us on *oysters* and *Champaign,* for 'twas too late to prepare a warm supper, and this by the bye was not a very bad one, though cold.[12]

Susan took great pains to learn Spanish and get along with the Mexicans. The day after her arrival in Santa Fe she wrote that "This morning a

Mexican lady, Dona Juliana, called to see me. She is a woman poor in the goods of this world, a great friend to the Americans and especially the Magoffins whom she calls a *mui bien famile* [*muy buena familia*—"very good family"]. Though my knowledge of Spanish is quite limited we carried on conversation for half an hour alone, and whether correct or not she insists that I am a good scholar."[13]

Although Susan did not comment very much on the course of the Mexican-American war, she did share her fellow Americans' contempt for General Armijo's lack of valor (italics as in original): "A day or two before Kearny arrived [in Santa Fe], A[r]mijo collected a force of some three thousand men to go out and meet him, and even assembled them ready for a battle in the canyon some twelve miles from town, but suddenly a trembling for his own personal safety seized his mind, and he dispersed his army, which if he had managed it properly could have entirely disabled the Gen's [Kearny's] troops by blockading the road &c. and *fled himself!*"[14]

Leaving Santa Fe on 6 October 1846, Susan and her fellow travelers followed El Camino Real de Tierra Adentro into Mexico. She was always quick to note local conditions:

> *Wednesday 14th* [October 1846] In our travel today we have met many Indians with their backs loaded with *muchas cosas a vender* [many things to sell]. They fill their *serapes* [Mexican shawls for men] with whatever it may be, and start off in the trot natural to the Indian, and it is a remarkable thing that nearly every Mexican (of the lower class) and the Indians are either knock-kneed or pigeon-toed. And they have such an odd way, when asked where and how far to such a place, of tooting out their lips in the direction of the place, with a piggish grunt and *cuenta* [answer].[15]

Other contemporary observers explain that this unique "tooting out their lips" to indicate direction was due to the fact that Mexican men often wore a serape, which covered their arms, and therefore could not gesture except with their lips and chin.

In any case, the ebb and flow of the Mexican-American war made travel very dangerous. Susan wrote on 15 January 1847 when her party stopped at a small town during their travels:

> The whole company of us were on the look out—*mi alma* was often on the house top.... We remained at this camp all this day, making preparations for a constant travel from tomorrow, in the mean time all fire arms are being examined, shot off and reloaded to be all in readiness for an attack. And we are well prepared for it; all the wagoners are well armed.... [W]ithin our little tent we have twelve sure rounds [probably two six-shot revolvers], a double-barreled shot gun, a pair of holster and one pair of belt pistols, with one of Colt's six barreled [six shot] revolvers—a formidable core for only two people to muster. I hope and pray none of them may have to be used, though we have good

ground to expect an attack either from these [Mexican soldiers], or a party of Indians reported to be below us a little — and to paint the scene as frightful as possible — we may have both to attack us.[16]

Susan's group was not attacked and continued to make its way toward Matamoros. The last entry in her diary was written on Wednesday, 8 September 1847, in Cuidad Mier, a small town in northern Mexico near the Rio Grande about 90 miles northeast of Monterrey. It reads in part (italics as in the original):

> Such a place this is! The seat of so many country-men's wrongs, the most miserable hole imaginable; impossible to get a house we are stowed away in a room with a family of men, women and children. The town is in confusion. Last night a band of robbers entered, shot down a sentinel, rode through the plaza, hitched up and drove off five wagons loaded with merchandise belonging to a Frenchman who says "he go and publish one reward." A runner comes in this evening from the party of forty dragoons sent in pursuit of them by Col. Belknap saying that they had come upon the thieves, some hundred in number *dividing out the spoils and only twelve or fifteen miles from town*, have had a fight, killed fifteen of the enemy, retaken the goods with all the Mexican equipage, guns, blankets, saddles, &c., and all without any loss to our side; they are returning to town....[17]

Later, Susan fell ill with yellow fever and at the same time gave birth to a son in Matamoros. This child did not survive. After Samuel Magoffin's trip to Santa Fe and Mexico, he retired from the Santa Fe trade and settled in St. Louis. There Susan gave birth to a daughter, Jane, in 1851. Susan died four years later, in 1855 at the age of 28, soon after the birth of a second daughter.[18] Her life was short but her legacy has been a long one. In her diary, she deeds to us and to later generations a lively and very personal account of cultural and military events during the Mexican-American war.

CHAPTER VII

The Butterfield Overland Mail Route

California was admitted as a state in 1850 and immediately began clamoring for better mail service from the eastern United States: service by square-rigger (sailing ship) was painfully slow. One result was that in 1857 John Butterfield won a U.S. government contract worth $600,000 a year to carry mail twice a week overland from St. Louis, through Arkansas, the Indian Territory, New Mexico, and Arizona, to San Francisco.[1] At the peak of his operations, which began in 1858, he deployed in this enterprise between 100 and 250 large, heavy (2,500 pounds), expensive ($1,300), and well-made stagecoaches built in Concord, New Hampshire; 1,000 horses; 500 mules; and approximately 800 employees. This ambitious enterprise was variously known as the Butterfield Overland Mail, the Butterfield Overland Stage, the Butterfield Stage, or the Oxbow Route.

The Oxbow Route was so-named because Southerners in Congress had demanded that Butterfield plot out a circuitous southerly route that satisfied their own regional interests. They did not want a central route which bypassed the South entirely and went directly west through the Rocky Mountains. They asserted that snowstorms there would make reliable mail delivery impossible. Advocates of a central route, on the other hand, claimed that it would be much shorter and that it could be kept open in winter without too much difficulty. Regardless of the merits of these respective arguments, however, the fact remained that, politically, the Southerners had the upper hand.

The postmaster general was Aaron Brown, a proslavery Tennessean who could be relied upon to support Southern interests. The outcome of the congressional debate was predictable: until the Civil War intervened, Butterfield's coaches were required to follow a southern route that, on a map, has the shape of a broad, shallow U. For this reason, it was nicknamed the Oxbow Route.

(An oxbow was a U-shaped wooden frame supporting the collar and the yoke around an ox's neck.)

The route Butterfield had to take was 600 miles longer than the central route and needed extra relay stations and frontier forts to support it. Irate New York newspapers quickly denounced it as "the horseshoe," "the side line," and "one of the greatest swindles ever perpetrated upon the country by the slaveholders."[2] Nevertheless, Butterfield managed to make a commercial success of this apparently unpromising route. It had two eastern terminals on the Mississippi River, one at St. Louis, the other at Memphis. The two routes originating from these terminals converged at Fort Smith, Arkansas. From Fort Smith, the line then ran through Indian Territory to Colbert's Ferry on the Oklahoma-Texas border. From there it headed west over the plains of Texas to El Paso.

En route it crossed the extensive plains known as the Llano Estacado. This name is often mistranslated as the "Staked Plain," a reference to the erroneous belief that Spaniards had to drive wooden stakes into the arid, featureless ground to mark their way across it. A more accurate translation from the Spanish, however, is the "Palisaded Plains." This refers to a huge mesa, or tableland, in eastern New Mexico and northwestern Texas so flat and so featureless that Coronado labeled it, correctly, as "a sea of grass." It is not entirely flat but its slope — only about 10 feet per mile — is so gradual that it is imperceptible to travelers.

From El Paso, the route ran through the parched landscapes of New Mexico Territory and entered California near Fort Yuma, on the Colorado River. It then dipped south into Mexico for a brief spell; reentered California at the New River, near Calexico, California, and made its way to Los

Angeles. Finally, it headed north through the San Joaquin Valley and Pacheco Pass to reach San Francisco, its western terminal.[3]

The first Butterfield stagecoach left Tipton, Missouri, in 1858. This little town was about 130 miles west of St. Louis and marked the farthest advance of the Pacific Railroad at the time. The exact route changed slightly from time to time but was always about 2,700 miles long. It was run twice a week and took an average of 25 days to complete each way. The luxurious Concord coaches averaged between 5 and 9 miles an hour.[4] When the route became too difficult for them, the passengers were transferred to more rugged but less comfortable mule-drawn Celerity stagecoaches, also known as mud wagons. These were light stagecoaches with roller flaps on the sides to provide good ventilation in hot weather.

Because of the considerable dangers involved, Butterfield recruited only experienced frontiersmen to drive his coaches. He gave employees and passengers very clear oral and written instructions:

Remember, boys, nothing on God's earth must stop the mail! ...

Drivers and conductors are to be armed but to shoot only when the lives of passengers are in danger.... No shipments of gold or silver to be carried to cut down on the attacks by highwaymen.

You will be traveling through Indian country and the safety of your person cannot be vouchsafed by anyone but God.

Every person in the Company's employ will remember that each minute is of importance. If each driver on the route loses 15 minutes, it would make a total loss of time, on the entire route, of 25 hours, or, more than one day. If each one loses 10 minutes, it would make a loss of 16½ hours, or the best part of a day. If each driver gains that time, it leaves a margin against accidents and extra delays. All will see the necessity of promptness: every minute of time is valuable, as the Company are under heavy forfeit if the mail is behind time.[5]

This was never an easy or a very safe route, always being plagued by lack of water and sometimes by hostile Indians. Each driver was responsible for 120 miles of it, i.e., 60 miles going out and 60 miles coming back. These men were tough and had a great deal of authority. General J.F. Rusling, who traveled extensively by stagecoach later on (he was writing in 1875 but his comments apply to earlier times as well), said of the drivers:

We talked a good deal, or essayed to, with the drivers ... but they were a taciturn species. Off the box [off the driver's seat] they were loquacious enough, but when mounted with four or six in hand [when using long reins to control four or six galloping horses] they either thought it unprofessional to talk, or else were absorbed too much in their own business.... They each had their fifty or sixty miles, up one day and back the next, and to the people along the route they were important personages.... They were fond of tobacco and whiskey and rolled out ponderous oaths, when things did not go to suit them....

As bearers of the United States mail they felt themselves kings of the road and were seldom loath to show it. "Clar the road! Git out of the way thar with your bull teams!" was a frequent salutation.[6]

Passengers were charged $200 for the whole route and were usually limited to 25 pounds of luggage, two blankets, and one canteen.[7] By changing drivers and horses frequently, the coaches could travel at top speed for 24 hours a day. During the very brief stops when horses were changed, the passengers were offered hasty and usually unappealing meals, usually consisting of bread, coffee, cured meat, and sometimes beans. The trip west could be long and hard. In *Roughing It* (1872), Mark Twain gives us an accurate and humorous description of his own travels from St. Joseph, Missouri, to Carson City, Nevada, in one of Butterfield's coaches:

> By eight o'clock [on 26 July 1861] everything was ready.... We jumped into the stage, the driver cracked his whip, and we bowled away and left "the States" behind us.... Our coach was a great swinging and swaying stage, of the most sumptuous description — an imposing cradle of wheels. It was drawn by six handsome horses, and by the side of the driver sat the "conductor," the legitimate captain of the craft; for it was his business to take charge and care of the mails, baggage, express matter, and passengers....
>
> We changed horses every ten miles or so, all day long, and fairly flew over the hard, level road. We jumped out and stretched our legs every time the coach stopped, and so the night found us still vivacious and unfatigued....
>
> When the sun went down and the evening chill came on, we made preparations for bed. We stirred up the hard leather letter-sacks, and the knotty canvas bags of printed matter.... All our things now being ready, we ... placed the water-canteens and pistols where we could find them in the dark.... Whenever the stage stopped to change horses, we would wake up, and try to recollect where we were — and succeed — and in a minute or two the stage would be off again, and we likewise....
>
> [At one stagecoach station, the station keeper] sliced off a piece of bacon for each man, but only the experienced old hands made out to eat it [they pretended to eat it], for it was condemned army bacon which the United States would not feed to its soldiers in the forts, and the stage company had bought it cheap for the sustenance of their passengers and employees.... Then he poured for us a beverage which he called "*Slumgullion*," and it is hard to think that he was not inspired when he named it. It really pretended to be tea, but there was too much dish-rag, and sand, and old bacon-rind in it to deceive the intelligent traveler. He had no sugar and no milk — not even a spoon to stir the ingredients with....
>
> We gave up the breakfast, paid our dollar apiece and went back to our mail-bag bed in the coach, and found comfort in our pipes. Right here we suffered the first diminution of our princely state. We left our six fine horses and took six mules in their place. [Twain and his colleagues had just been transferred from a Concord coach to a lighter Celerity wagon built for fast travel over

rough terrain.] But they were wild Mexican fellows, and a man had to stand at the head of each of them and hold them fast while the driver gloved himself and got ready. And when at last he grasped the reins and gave the word, the men sprang suddenly away from the mules' heads and the coach shot from the station as if it had issued from a cannon. How the frantic animals did scamper! It was a fierce and furious gallop — and the gait never altered for a moment until we reeled off ten or twelve miles and swept up to the next collection of little station-huts and stables.[8]

A less humorous but more detailed contemporary account of stagecoach travel via the Butterfield route comes from the journalist Waterman L. Ormsby, who was the only through passenger on the first westbound coach. He published a series of eight articles about his travel in the *New York Herald* between September and November 1858. The whole book is worth reading but in the interest of brevity only a few of his comments about the New Mexico portion of his trip are given below. His coach made its way into New Mexico. At Mesilla (now Las Cruces), Ormsby was quite impressed by the crops, dikes and canals he saw en route but, like many Easterners, he regarded the local inhabitants with unqualified distaste:

[T]he people, mostly Mexicans, were squalid and dirty — their houses were built of adobe and sticks.... The people seemed to luxuriate in filth, and basked in the sun with all the complacency of overfed animals. How different, I thought, would this valley be were it peopled by a few of our steady eastern farmers; I could not but conclude that Providence knew just the right place to put the lazy men to keep them lazy, and the industrious ones to keep them industrious. Here is a vast valley whose soil will yield but for the planting two crops per year, and yet it does not bring forth a tithe of its productiveness, because the people are lazy and indolent, and prefer to live in mud houses and bask in the sunshine, when, by a little labor, they might live in palaces with eastern magnificence.[9]

Continuing westward across southern New Mexico, his coach approached the station at the New Mexico–Arizona border near Stein's Peak (5,867 feet). Here Ormsby became understandably nervous:

We had learned on our way that the station at Stein's Peak was a favorite camping ground for the Apache Indians, and that but a few days before a band of two hundred and fifty, headed by Chief Mongas [Mangas Colorado, a renowned Apache chief], had gone to the station and demanded the gift of twenty sacks of corn, telling the men that they had "better hurry it up d—-d [damned] quick"....
The location of the station was in a little hollow under the mountain, so that we could not see it until we were within a few hundred yards of it. I can assure you that it was with no little relief that, as we ascended the last hill, we saw the corral still safe and the men moving about. But for a moment we were in doubt — we had come in full view of the place and had not yet seen a man, and

several moments of the most anxious suspense ensued ere we were quite relieved.[10]

When Ormsby finally arrived in San Francisco, 23 days and 23 hours after his departure from Tipton, he was asked, jokingly, if he now would like to return to the east via the Butterfield line. He replied, "Had I not just come out over the route, I would be perfectly willing to go back, but now I know what Hell is like. I've just had 24 days of it."[11]

As mentioned earlier, Butterfield's line was a great success. On 13 June 1859 an overland passenger wrote in the *New York Post*:

> The blast of the stage horn as it rolls through the valleys and over the prairies of the West, cheers and gladdens the heart of a pioneer. As it sounds through the valleys of Santa Clara and San Jose, it sends a thrill of delight through the Californian. He knows that it brings tidings from the hearts and homes he left behind him; it binds him stronger and firmer to his beloved country. So regular is its arrival that the inhabitants know almost the hour and minute when the welcome sound of the post horn will reach them. The Overland is the most popular institution of the Far West.[12]

Butterfield, however, had to abandon the southern route early in 1861 when Texas seceded from the Union. He then began using a more northerly route, known as the Central Overland California Route, which ran from St. Joseph, Missouri, to Placerville, California. Thompson Turner, a newspaper reporter in Arizona, worried that the new course of the Overland Mail would be a "death blow" to the towns along the old route: "The prospect of a withdrawal of the Overland Mail from this route has caused a complete stagnation in business and enterprise. "What will we do? Where shall we go?" is in every man's mouth.... Private letters from Washington state that it is even now in contemplation by the new Administration to withdraw the troops from this country. If this should be done, we are ruined and Arizona will lapse into nothingness."[13]

The southern section of the Butterfield Road continued to be used during the Civil War — not by civilian travelers but by Confederate and Union armies. Public mail did not reach Tucson again until September 1865, when some mail arrived from California via horseback. It was not until the coming of the railroads in the 1870s and 1880s, however, that regular mail contact with the eastern United States was finally restored.[14]

CHAPTER VIII

The Civil War in New Mexico

On 12 April 1861 Confederate forces opened fire on Fort Sumter in South Carolina; President Abraham Lincoln declared war on the Confederacy three days later. The New Mexico Territory was soon caught up in the epic struggle between North and South. Settlers in the Gadsden Purchase cast their lot with the Confederate States of America; most residents of New Mexico, however, retained a rather passive loyalty to the Union. In this chapter we will review briefly some of the regional highlights of the Civil War in terms of their importance for New Mexico.

Our story begins on 28 April 1861, when Major Henry Hopkins Sibley, a hero of the Mexican-American war, resigned his U.S. Army commission to serve the Confederacy. He managed to persuade Confederate President Jefferson Davis that he (Sibley) would easily be able to raise a Confederate army in Texas and lead it on a victorious march through New Mexico. A Confederate invasion of New Mexico was accordingly authorized in early July. Sibley's real goals, however, were far more extensive. He did not confide them to Davis but it is clear that, ultimately, he wanted to conquer for the Confederate cause not only New Mexico itself but also Colorado and Nevada (for their gold and silver) and California (for its ports, which lay beyond the reach of the Union blockade).

Perhaps blinded by his own ambition, Sibley assumed that the residents of New Mexico would rise to support his invading troops and that despite the arid conditions he would not need to arrange secure supply lines: his troops, he believed, could simply live off the land. In fact, however, most New Mexicans had no burning interest in national affairs, including the great issues of the Civil War, and devoted their energies chiefly to local matters. Counting on widespread public support (which would fail to materialize) Sibley confidently expected to capture Fort Union, the principal supply depot on the Santa Fe Trail. This fort was strategically important because it provided the weapons, food and other supplies to all the U.S. Army posts in the Southwest. Sibley, however, would fail to capture it.[1]

When the Civil War broke out, territorial officials in New Mexico had been worried that a Confederate force from Texas would invade New Mexico. Indeed, a coded, unsigned, and undated letter in Spanish, believed to have been sent by Nicholas Pino, a prominent pro–Union figure who played active roles in commercial, military, and political events in New Mexico, clearly expressed this fear. As later deciphered and translated by the Los Alamos National Laboratory, Pino's letter reads as follows in English:

> Sir, rumors are that the Confederates are organizing a force that will march through New Mexico. This will need confirmation. If such news exists and gets to this remote area of mine [Pino lived in Galisteo, a small town about 20 miles south of Santa Fe], you shall be informed. Your servant.[2]

Pino's fears were soon realized. Confederate military operations in the Southwest began in the summer of 1861, when a 254-man detachment (Lieutenant Colonel John R. Baylor's battalion of the 2nd Regiment Texas Mounted Rifles) crossed into New Mexico from El Paso and seized Fort Fillmore (located about 35 miles northwest of El Paso). Union troops there had to abandon the fort on 25 July 1861, thus effectively surrendering all of southern New Mexico to Confederate control.

Alarmed by this development, on 9 September 1861 Henry Connelly, the U.S. territorial governor, urged New Mexicans to take up arms in defense of the Union cause. He got a very warm response. Pro-Union men (most of them Hispanics) stepped forward quickly and were soon organized into five regiments of volunteers, plus assorted militia and cavalry units.

Not to be outdone, the Confederates in Texas had also launched a recruiting campaign. The result was that on 22 October 1861 Sibley and his 3,700-man "Confederate Army of New Mexico" set out from San Antonio. They marched across Texas and headed for Fort Craig (about 200 miles north of El Paso), one of the largest forts in the West.[3] There U.S. Army Lieutenant Colonel Edward R.S. Canby had gathered a Union force of some 4,000 men, including a regiment commanded by now-Colonel Kit Carson, to repel the Confederates. Ironically, Sibley and Canby were good friends. They had both been cadets together at West Point; indeed, Canby had been best man at Sibley's wedding and was also married to Mrs. Sibley's cousin.

When Sibley's forces closed in on Fort Craig, Canby refused to give battle and instead ordered his men simply to hold the fort itself. Sibley — rather than launching a frontal charge on the fort, which would have incurred heavy casualties — decided instead to reposition his troops across the Rio Grande, on the eastern side of the river near Valverde Ford, six miles north of the fort.

In so doing he hoped to cut the Union lines of communication between the fort and Union headquarters in Santa Fe.

Canby, however, sallied forth from the fort and prevented the Confederates from crossing the Rio Grande. Fierce fighting erupted. When the smoke cleared and the Battle of Valverde (21 February 1862) was finally over, the Confederates were left in possession of the field and thus could claim victory — but in the process they had sustained heavy losses. Private William R. Howell, a 20-year-old Confederate soldier, wrote: "It's truly a sad day to hear the groans of the wounded and witness the burial of the lamented dead wrapped in a blanket as a coffin!"[4]

Despite their losses, the Confederates were now resolved to penetrate ever deeper into the heart of New Mexico. They continued to march up the Rio Grande Valley and captured Santa Fe without a fight on 10 March 1862. (Connelly, the territorial governor, had already left Santa Fe and had moved to a temporary seat of government in Las Vegas, New Mexico. At the same time, a 120-wagon U.S. Army wagon train, protected by Federal troops from Santa Fe, had shifted the Union's military supplies from Santa Fe to Fort Union.)

With the fall of Santa Fe, the Confederates' conquest of New Mexico was now nearly complete. All that remained for them to do was to capture Fort Union itself. If successful in this effort, they could then advance on Colorado. Sibley therefore marched toward Fort Union. He had been the commander of the fort the year before, knew its weaknesses well, and was very confident of success because he had more men under his command than the 800 troops Canby had to defend the fort.

What he did not know, however, was that after his own tour of duty at the fort, its earthwork defenses had been rebuilt and were now stronger. What was much more important, however, was that he did not know that Federal volunteers from Colorado, many of them tough-as-rawhide miners, were heading for New Mexico to repel the Confederate invasion. Indeed, by 10 March 1862 some 950 of these men were at the gates of Fort Union itself, having marched about 400 miles to Fort Union in only 13 days (an average of about 30 miles per day).

Canby's 800 troops huddled at Fort Union with explicit orders from him to stay put and defend the fort. The commander of the Colorado Volunteers, Colonel John P. Slough, countermanded Canby's orders (he could do so because he outranked Canby) and made plans to attack the Confederates. On 22 March 1862 he led his forces down on the Santa Fe Trail toward Santa Fe. At the same time, Sibley and his troops were moving up the Santa Fe Trail toward Fort Union. The two armies met on 26 March 1862 near the mouth of Apache Canyon, a narrow wooded pass about 10 miles southeast of Santa Fe. The Colorado volunteers charged the Confederates and forced them to retreat. This small-scale skirmish was the first Union victory in New Mexico.

Two days later, on 28 March 1862, Union and Confederate troops clashed again, this time near Pigeon's Ranch, a hostelry of adobe buildings on the Santa Fe Trail, located on the east side of Glorieta Pass, a strategic pass situated on the Santa Fe Trail at the southern tip of the Sangre de Cristo Mountains. This pass offered the most direct route through the mountains between the upper valley of the Pecos River to the east and the upper valley of the Rio Grande to the west. In the nineteenth century it constituted the route of the westernmost leg of the Santa Fe Trail, i.e., between Santa Fe and the High Plains.

Reporting on this fight, which is now known as the Battle of Glorieta Pass and is recognized as the turning point of the Civil War in New Mexico, U.S. Army captain Jacob Downing wrote: "Then came the grandeur of battle, the test of bravery, the madness of despair. With wild, fierce yells that reached far above the roar of artillery ... this mass of excited humanity rushed fearlessly on."[5] There was no shortage of brave men in the field that day. Just before he was shot between the eyes, Confederate Major John "Shrop" Shropshire yelled out to his men, "Come on and help me take that position or stay back and watch men who will."[6]

The Battle of Glorieta Pass raged for six hours. It involved 850 Union and 1,200 Confederate troops who used artillery barrages, cavalry and infantry charges, bayonet attacks, and even hand-to-hand combat with pistols and knives. Both sides fought hard to control a high rocky outcrop known as Sharpshooter's Ridge. At first, Union soldiers held the ridge but then the Confederates captured it and immediately used it as a vantage point from which to shoot down at the Union artillerymen. This deadly rain of fire soon forced the Union soldiers to retreat. At the end of the day, the Confederates held the field and assumed that they had won. Their tactical victory, however, would end in a strategic disaster.

During the battle, a unit of 400 to 450 Union troops led by Colorado Volunteer Major John M. Chivington and guided by Lieutenant Colonel Manuel Chaves, a New Mexican who knew the area well, had moved to the high ground of Glorieta Mesa. Pointing down to Johnson's Ranch, 500 feet below them, Chaves said to Chivington, "You're right on top of them, Major."[7] Two hours later, Chivington's battalion scrambled down the mesa and destroyed the entire 70-wagon Confederate supply train, which the Confederates had left behind so they could move as quickly and as quietly as possible. Many of the men assigned to guard the wagons had left their posts to join the fighting at Pigeon's Ranch. This loss proved to be a fatal blow to the Confederate strategy: they now lacked the supplies needed to continue their invasion of New Mexico. They realized, moreover, that Union troops were now marching out from Fort Craig to attack them. Under these conditions, they had no alternative but to fall back to Santa Fe.

The Battle of Glorieta Pass has been called the "Gettysburg of the West" because, like its eastern counterpart, it managed to stop a major Confederate advance. Sibley desperately tried to recoup his sagging military fortunes by begging the governor of Texas for more troops but these were not forthcoming. Canby, for his part, was working out a subtle strategy to expel the Confederates entirely, first from Santa Fe, then from Albuquerque and, finally, from the rest of New Mexico.

He did this by ordering troops from Fort Union to head for Santa Fe, while he and his men marched north from Fort Craig toward Albuquerque. Canby calculated that these Union redeployments would force the Confederates to abandon Santa Fe and to focus instead on protecting the supplies they had stored at Albuquerque. His plan worked well. The Confederates abandoned Santa Fe on 7-8 April 1862; Union troops entered soon afterward and then marched south to join Canby's troops near Albuquerque. Rather than fighting at Albuquerque, however, the Confederates decided to cut their losses, end the campaign, and withdraw from New Mexico entirely. Facing a desert climate and lacking supplies, reinforcements, and popular support, they evacuated Albuquerque on 12 April 1862 and began the long, tiring march back to Texas.

By the second week of July 1862, all Confederate troops were out of New Mexico. Canby never tried to stop them as they were leaving. His policy was to avoid a major battle which, if he had won, would have resulted in his capturing large numbers of Confederate soldiers and thus being responsible for them as prisoners of war.

The end result of Sibley's bold foray into New Mexico was that it destroyed, once and for all, any Confederate hope of expanding all the way to the Pacific. New Mexico would continue to be held by the Union until the end of the of the Civil War in 1865. In a personal letter to the father of a fallen soldier, Sibley summed up the problems of warfare in New Mexico: "My dear sir, we beat the enemy where we encountered them. The famished country beat us."[8]

CHAPTER IX

The Long Walk of the Navajos

The Long Walk of the Navajos was a forced march of more than 8,000 Navajos, in 1863, from their homeland in northeastern Arizona and northwestern New Mexico to the Bosque Redondo, a newly created Indian reservation located near Fort Sumner on the Pecos River in eastern New Mexico. This was a distance of more than 300 miles. The Navajos did not follow a single, well-known and well-beaten trail to get there; the map used in this book is only a rough approximation. They were virtually imprisoned at the Bosque Redondo for five years — until 1868, when a repatriation treaty was hammered out between the United States government and the Navajos. This agreement finally permitted them to begin the long walk back to what is now the Navajo Indian Reservation, which the government had carved out of their ancestral lands. It now embraces about 17 million acres of northwestern New Mexico, northeastern Arizona, and southeastern Utah.

Ironically, the genesis of the Long Walk lies not in New Mexico itself but in southern California.[1] The sudden and massive influx of outsiders — miners, adventurers, saints and sinners — into California during and after the 1849 gold rush took a murderous toll on the local Indians (traditionally and collectively described as the Mission Indians), whose indigenous cultures had already been decimated by Spanish and Mexican domination. There were, however, a handful of influential and sympathetic American observers in California who believed that these Indians were hovering on the very brink of extinction. As then-Major James H. Carleton, never a great supporter of any Indians, put it poetically, they were becoming "Children of the Mist."

A bold new idea had occurred to Carleton and to some others: they concluded that to ensure the survival of the Mission Indians, these natives must be *physically separated* from the non–Indian residents of California and must be taught the rudiments of agriculture so that they could support themselves and be acculturated into "civilized" society. To put this new theory to the test, a pilot project, i.e., a farm, was set up at Fort Tejon (north of Los

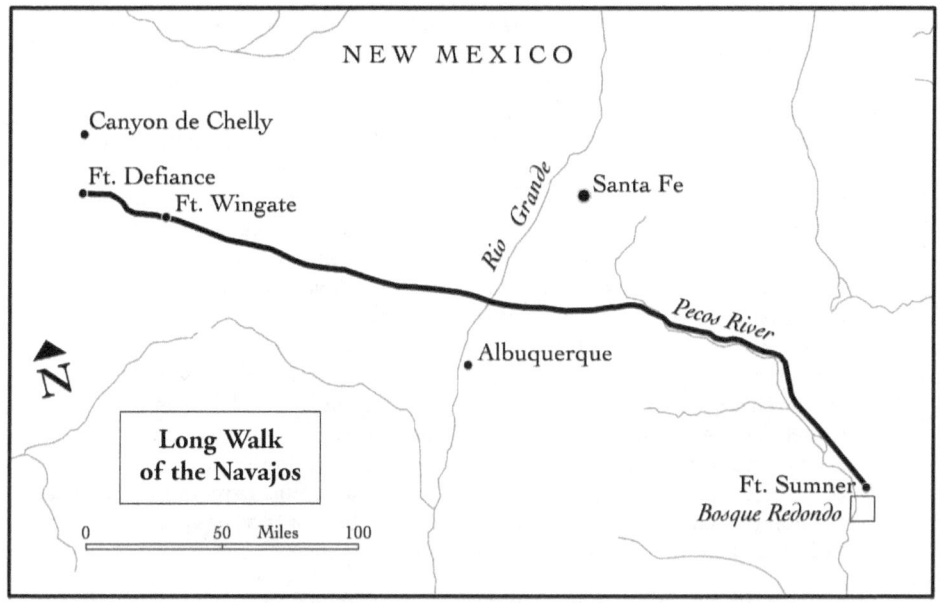

Angeles) in the early 1850s. This farm ultimately failed for two reasons: some Spanish-speaking land claimants proved that they held prior land grants, and the director of the pilot project fell victim to party politics. Nevertheless, the project did well enough during its brief life to suggest that it could indeed be successful elsewhere, given more favorable conditions.

When Carleton was promoted to brigadier general and was reassigned to New Mexico in the early autumn of 1862, he decided to take decisive action on "the Navajo problem." This problem was not a new one on the southwestern frontier: the Navajo Wars had begun in the early seventeenth century and continued into the mid-nineteenth century. These "wars" were actually a series of small-scale clashes, often punctuated by short-lived ceasefires and treaties, which involved (1) attacks by different Navajo bands on isolated ranches along the Rio Grande Valley, and (2) retaliatory military campaigns mounted both by the Spanish, Mexican, and United States governments and by their vengeful, well-armed citizens.

Carleton was certainly a biased commentator: he believed that all, or at least *most*, Navajos were untrustworthy brigands. He was thus presenting only one side of the story when in 1864 he gave a lecture to the Hispanic and Anglo inhabitants of New Mexico:

> From time immemorial these Indians had subsisted upon the flocks and herds of your fathers; had times without number, even in one single hour reduced whole families from comparative wealth to poverty. Your ancestors, under the

Spanish Government, made many campaigns against them, and many treaties of peace with them. But the Indians soon forgot the obligations to which they had pledged themselves, in each successive treaty. Then came other campaigns and other treaties, under the Mexican Republic. Again the Navajos forgot the punishment they had received, and over and over again broke their treaties. After the annexation of New Mexico to the United States, by the Treaty of Guadaloupe [sic] Hidalgo, the troops from the north commenced *their* campaigns. And now what was the result? ... [T]he treaties were broken, and on some occasions, even before the troops had been entirely withdrawn from the Navajo country. To cure this great evil from which your territory has been so long a prey, some new remedy must be adapted....[2]

When I came here this time, it not only became my professional business, but my duty to the residents and to the Government, to devise some plan which might, with God's blessing, forever bring these troubles to an end. [Here Carleton cited an estimate that in 1862 alone Navajos had stolen more than 30,000 sheep from Hispanic and Anglo ranches; such losses, he claimed, had cost the ranchers about $250,000.] These Navajo Indians have long since passed the point when talking would be of any avail. They must be whipped and fear us before they will cease killing and robbing the people.[3]

Carleton's solution was to move the Indians to a new reservation known as the Bosque Redondo (Spanish for "a round grove of trees"), which was located in east-central New Mexico on the Pecos River. Nearby, Carleton would build a military outpost known as Fort Sumner. He gave these stern orders to Kit Carson and told him to pass them on to the Navajos: "Say to them: 'Go to the Bosquae [sic] Redondo, or we will pursue and destroy you. We will not make peace with you on any other terms. You have deceived us too often and robbed and murdered our people for too long—to trust you again at large in your own country. This war shall be pursued against you if it takes years, now that we have begun, until you cease to exist or move. There can be no other talk on this subject.'"[4]

A board of U.S. Army officers, however, had examined the Bosque Redondo and advised Carleton that it was not at all suitable, for either a fort or an Indian reservation. They pointed out its clear deficiencies. It lacked grazing land for sizeable herds of livestock. Timber and other building materials were scarce and would have to be brought in from afar. The Pecos River was prone to flooding in the spring and its water was always alkaline and unpalatable. Carleton, however, beat down these naysayers, insisting instead that the Bosque Redondo was "the best pastoral region between the two oceans" and that within a decade the Navajos there would be living in "the most delightfully located pueblo of Indians in New Mexico, perhaps in the United States."[5]

It is unclear today precisely why Carleton attached such importance to the Bosque Redondo, especially after his fellow officers had given it a clear thumbs-down. He probably had three considerations in mind:

1. Like many other men of his generation, Carleton believed it was his Christian duty to tame the "savages" and turn them into peaceful farmers so that they could survive in American society. Despite its shortcomings, the Bosque Redondo must have seemed to him a good spot for this noble experiment.

2. He also subscribed to the aggressive doctrines of Manifest Destiny. (As noted earlier, Manifest Destiny was the conviction that the United States was destined to expand from the Atlantic seaboard to the Pacific Ocean and even beyond.) "Solving the Navajo problem" in New Mexico would be a clear step in this direction and would bring him lasting fame.

3. Carleton wanted to become a rich man. Without any geological or other proof to back his claim, he asserted that the Navajo homeland was rich in gold. Indeed, he argued that the Gila River itself was "one of the richest gold countries in the world" and that the Indians must be moved to another location so that "if the country contained veins and deposits of precious metals, they might be found."[6] He certainly wanted to be present when these alleged riches were found. Indeed, Carlton confided to a fellow army officer, Captain J.G. Walker: "My luck has always been not to be at the right place at the right time for fortunes."[7]

Carleton was not alone in believing that there must be gold on Navajo lands. Another ambitious official, William F.M. Arny, had served as chairman of the National Kansas Committee of the Republican Party and wanted to further the cause of the American Indians (and his own career). He represented a faction of the Republican Party that President Abraham Lincoln simply could not ignore, so in 1861 Lincoln appointed him to be the Federal agent to the Utes and to the Jicarilla Apaches. Once established in New Mexico, Arny would later serve as territorial secretary, acting governor, Ute agent, special Indian agent, and agent to the Pueblo Indians.[8] He wrote: "The country in which they [the Navajos] live is described as beautiful, and it is reported that the mountains contain as rich deposits of gold as can be found on this continent."[9]

Discovering these theoretical riches, however, would have to wait upon Carleton's military success. Early in 1863 Carleton had met in Santa Fe with 18 Navajo leaders and had given them a deadline of about six months in which to surrender. He had told them, "We [the U.S. Army] have no faith in your promises. You can have no peace until you give other guarantees than your word. If you do not return to Santa Fe [by a deadline of 20 July 1863] we will know that you have chosen the alternative of war. After that day every Navajo will be considered as hostile and treated accordingly. After that day the door now open will be closed."[10] This deadline came and went without any of these leaders returning to Santa Fe. Their failure to comply gave Carleton what was, to his mind, all the legal and moral justification he needed to launch a campaign against them. He therefore drew up a declaration of hostilities, which stated in part: "For a long time past, the Navajo Indians have murdered and robbed the people of New Mexico. It is therefore ordered that Colonel Christopher Carson, with a proper military force, proceed without delay to the Navajo country and there ... to prosecute a vigorous war upon the men of this tribe."[11]

Carson's expedition was the largest ever assembled to fight the Navajos.[12] It consisted of 736 soldiers, supported by an additional 326 soldiers under the command of Colonel Chávez at Fort Wingate, which was located about 80 miles west of Albuquerque. Making every effort to ensure success, Carleton hand-picked nine of his best officers and assigned them to Carson. This was a very prudent move because not all the U.S. Army's officers in the Southwest could inspire confidence among the troops. Major Arthur Morrison and Lieutenant David McAllister are good cases to the point.

Morrison had been in trouble even before he got to Navajo country. A junior officer (McAllister) had filed charges against him, alleging that Morrison had delayed leaving Los Pinos on the journey west to join Carson's campaign because he had been so drunk that he could not stand up. Moreover, added McAllister, Morrison had declared in a "loud and vulgar tone" that he would find prostitutes for his friends, announcing that "I am the damdest [sic] best pimp in New Mexico." Ultimately, given the choice of facing a courtmartial or resigning, Morrison would choose to resign. McAllister, for his part, came to a similar end. While serving as the officer of the day, i.e., as the officer formally responsible for the proper functioning of a military post, he was found drunk on duty — and in bed with an enlisted man. McAllister was forced to resign his commission.

Carson and his men set out on a reconnaissance trip on 5 August 1863. It lasted 27 days and covered nearly 500 miles of the arid mesa country where the Navajo lived — but without any tangible results. The Navajos simply refused to stand and fight: in most cases they wisely faded away into the wilderness. Captain Eben Everett, commanding officer of Company B, First New Mexico Volunteers, who kept the only private diary known to have come down to us from the campaign, recorded its hardships and one of the very few "victories":

> Left camp at 5 [thirty] A.M. [on 11 August 1863], proceeding very well for some 22 miles, when our troubles commenced. We were one hour climbing the first rocks. Killed Goats, Sheep, horses & mules [in this process]. One half mile on came to a still worse rocky ascent about as bad a place as I ever saw a trail made. Two and one half hours hard work accomplished the ascent with the loss

of one horse and One Mule and an awful amount of profane language in English Spanish & Dutch [one of the Army officers was originally from Holland]. On arriving at the top where were the ruins of an old Indian tower or house, here we met a party sent back from the advance to show us the way to the camp where we arrived about 7 P.M.[13]

[On the morning of 28 August 1863] a party of some thirty men were sent off to go round by way of an Indian village. They joined us at Camp about 3 o'clock bringing with them one scalp of an Indian they had shot. From its appearance the original wearer ... must have been an *hombre grande* [an important man].[14]

Since Carson could not bring the Navajos themselves to bay he turned instead to a scorched earth policy — systematically destroying the physical underpinnings of their way of life. Fields of wheat, corn, and melons were laid waste. Food caches were dug up and ruined. Water holes and salt deposits were guarded so the Navajos could not use them. Navajo livestock was captured or killed. Even clay pots and wicker baskets were destroyed, lest the Navajo continue to use them to cook, carry or store food. The scale of destruction was so great that Carson knew he was dealing a fatal blow to Navajo independence. The accounts he dictated from the field for onward transmission to Carleton reveal this clearly, as these examples show:

- The Wheat (about fifteen acres) we fed to the animals and the corn (about fifty acres) was destroyed....

- At about 10 A.M. the command [i.e., Carson's troops] arrived at a large bottom [a section of flat, low-lying land along a watercourse] containing not less than one hundred acres of as fine corn as I have ever seen. Here I determined to encamp that I might have it destroyed....

- They [the Navajos] have no stock [i.e., no stored supplies of food] and were depending entirely for subsistence on the corn destroyed by my command on the previous day. [The loss of their corn] will cause actual starvation, and oblige them to come in and accept emigration to the Bosque Redondo.[15]

In the autumn of 1863, Carson led two fruitless reconnaissance expeditions into the Navajo homeland. He then asked Carleton for leave so he could visit Joséfa, his pregnant wife, but was told that first he had to capture 100 Navajo men, women, and children. Carson realized that to do this he would have to invade the Canyon de Chelly, a Navajo sanctuary and stronghold (now a national monument) located near Chinle, Arizona.[16] This was a forbidding assignment because very few non-Navajos were then familiar with the torturous mazes of this canyon. The Spanish did know something about it. In 1805 Lieutenant Colonel Antonio Narbona had attacked Navajos living in the canyon and had killed 90 Navajo warriors and 25 Navajo women and children. He also captured three warriors, eight women, 22 boys and girls, and assorted livestock. What is more important for our purposes here, however, is that in his official report to Governor Fernando Chacón, Narbona stressed the enormous difficulties of the terrain itself. He said of the Canyon de Chelly that "[The Navajo had] entrenched themselves on an almost inaccessible point, and they had it fortified.... The Canyon de Chelly I scouted from its beginnings to its mouth. It is the fort on which the Navajo Indians had based their hopes of making themselves invincible, and as it is inhabited by many people, and fortified by nature with the cliffs that form it, that hope is not without reason."[17]

Narbona's knowledge of the canyon, however, never trickled down to the Americans: the first Anglo-American exploring party, led by Navajo guides, did not traverse the full length of the Canyon de Chelly until 1853. Carson himself did not know much about it when he and his troops reached the mouth of the canyon on 12 January 1864, but this did not deter him. After some sporadic fighting, the Navajos in the canyon realized that, militarily, their position was hopeless. They therefore surrendered and began to stream out of the canyon toward Fort Defiance,[18] about 7 miles north of Window Rock, Arizona. This post, established in 1851 by Colonel Edwin V. Sumner to create a U.S. military presence in the Navajo homeland, would later become a Navajo agency and the site of the first Navajo medical center.

Early in February 1864 Carson escorted an initial convoy of 253 Navajos from Fort Defiance to the Rio Grande River. There he headed north toward Santa Fe, where he received a hero's welcome. In the meantime, armed guards marched the Navajos hundreds of miles southeast to the Bosque Redondo. More than 8,000 Navajos made this long trek. About one third of them died en route or at the reservation itself.

It is impossible today to plot their route with 100 percent accuracy but an educated guess, based on the work of the historian Gerald Thompson, is that the Navajos were forced to walk southeast from Fort Defiance to Fort Wingate; southeast from Fort Wingate to the Rio Grande River; north along the Rio Grande to Albuquerque and, for some of the captives, further north to Santa Fe for public display there; north, east, and southeast from Albuquerque and Santa Fe to Fort Sumner; and, finally, south from Fort Sumner to the Bosque Redondo.[19]

The first supervisor of the Bosque Redondo was Kit Carson himself. He did not enjoy the job at all (being a bureaucrat was not one of his strong points) and, to make matters worse, he was faced with no end of intractable problems. In the summer of 1864, for example, the first corn crop was flourishing but the Navajos were not getting along at all well with the Mescalero Apaches, who shared the reservation with them. The Navajos were unhappy on other grounds, too. They did not want to live in the Pueblo-like apartments Carleton had provided for them. They refused to convert to Christianity. Once the distribution of free meal tickets for attending school was stopped, they refused to send their children to school. They complained that the drinking water was alkaline and that there was not enough firewood for cooking and heating. Navajo girls prostituted themselves to the soldiers and caught syphilis. Finally, the corn itself was laid waste by worms. As Carleton sorrowfully exclaimed, "We had a field of nearly three thousand acres which promised to mature finely, when, after it had tasseled and the ears formed, it was attacked by what they call here the cut worm or army worm, *and the whole crop was destroyed!*"[20]

These setbacks spurred Carleton to launch great efforts to correct these problems, but in the end all of his remedial measures came to naught. Many of the Mescalero Apaches fled from the reservation. Government officials in Washington and in Santa Fe finally concluded that the Bosque Redondo was an ill-considered and very costly failure. A new superintendent of the reservation was appointed in early 1865. He made no secret of his feelings: "If they [the Navajo] remain on this reservation, they must always be held there by force, not from choice. The sooner it is abandoned and the Indians removed, the better."[21]

Clearly, the Bosque Redondo was doomed. The Indians desperately wanted to leave. Cadette, chief of the remaining Mescalero Apaches, complained bitterly: "We have lost a good many of my people, and many are now sick. All but one of my horses have died from starvation. We could live better in our old country than in this. The water and grass are better there. Tell the Great White Father [i.e., the president of the United States] that we would like to go back to our old country."[22] One of the Navajo leaders, whose name is not known, was even more eloquent. He said, "We want to go back to [our own country]. We have done wrong, but we have learned better and if allowed to return to our Mountain homes will behave ourselves well. Cage the Badger and he will try to break from his prison and regain his native hole. Chain the Eagle to the ground, and he will strive to gain his freedom and though he fails he will lift his head and look up to the sky which is his home."[23]

This reservation became such a disaster that Carleton was relieved of his duties. Responsibility for the reservation was moved from the U.S. Army to the Indian Bureau, which was a branch of the Department of the Interior. On 28 May 1868, General William Tecumseh Sherman, a hero of the Civil War, visited the reservation in his capacity as commander of U.S. forces in the West. He discovered that the Navajos there were in desperate straits and agreed with them that they should be returned to their homeland as soon as possible. He later wrote of it: "I found the Bosque a mere spot of green grass in the midst of a wild desert, and that the Navajos had sunk into a condition of absolute poverty and despair."[24]

The end result was the Navajo Treaty of 1868, which gave the Navajos a huge reservation of nearly 3.5 million acres in their homeland. Fort Defiance was chosen as its headquarters. Soon, strung out in one 10-mile-long column along the trail, the Navajos began their long walk back home. Their leader, Manuelito — an intelligent, charismatic *rico* (wealthy man) — said later, "When we saw the top of the mountain [in their homeland] from Albuquerque we wondered if it was our [sacred] mountain, and we felt like talking to the ground, we loved it so, and some of the old men and women cried with joy when they reached their homes."[25]

CHAPTER X

The Goodnight-Loving Trail

Americans may like to think that they invented the cowboy but in point of fact the earliest well-documented cowboys very probably were the Scottish cattle drovers of the fourteenth century. Described by a contemporary observer as "great stalwart hirsute men, shaggy, uncultured and wild," they were driving Highland cattle to lowland markets as early as 1359.[1] The nineteenth century trail riders of the United States, however, drove much larger numbers of much wilder cattle over a much longer network of trails.

Today the trail riders' way of life may strike us as incurably adventurous and romantic but, in reality, driving cattle over an assortment of remote trails was basically a badly paid seasonal job for semiliterate young men. It was usually marked by long weeks of hard, boring, and often dangerous work in bad weather. Moreover, judged by historical standards, this way of life survived for only a very brief moment in time. It began in 1866 after the end of the Civil War and ended about 20 years later — in the 1880s, when the expansion of the railroads and the development of refrigeration made trail drives obsolete.

The saga of the nineteenth century American trail riders begins with the Spaniards.[2] It was they who brought the first longhorn cattle to America in 1493. Early Anglo-American settlers came to Texas chiefly to raise cotton but they also brought with them some cattle of northern European breeds. These foreign cattle mixed with the wild longhorns already in Texas: their progeny soon blossomed into huge semi-wild herds. These herds would provide the cattle for the first stocking of the central and northern plains.

During the Civil War, some Texans were interested in selling cattle to the Confederate forces, but Texas was simply too far away from the major paths of the Civil War armies for any kind of significant trade to develop. As a result, Texas cattle were left alone to multiply. This they did so successfully that by the end of the Civil War in 1865 there were between 3,000,000 and 6,000,000 head of untamed and unbranded cattle in Texas, worth as little as

$2.00 dollars each.³ This abundance of cheap beef seriously depressed the meat market in Texas itself. At the same time, however, beef prices were still very high in the territories north of Texas. Indeed, by 1866, cattle could be sold in northern markets for as much as $40 per head. Enterprising Texans therefore began to drive their cattle north along an extensive network of trails.

The best known of these were the Goodnight-Loving Trail, sometimes known simply as the Goodnight Trail; the Western Trail, also called the Great Western Cattle Trail, the Dodge City Trail, or the Fort Griffin Trail; the Chisholm Trail; and the Shawnee Trail.⁴ A huge tide of cattle would continue to flow north each year along these trails until distant markets were saturated and the northern plains were fully stocked with Texas cattle.

Cattle drives began in earnest in 1866 when about 260,000 head of cattle were trailed ("trailed" was the term cattlemen used to describe the process of driving cattle) out of Texas.[5] Total estimates vary but it is thought that between 1867 and 1881 approximately 5,000,000 cattle were driven north from Texas. What is even more remarkable is that the size and fecundity of the Texas cattle ranches was so great that, even after all these bovine exports were trailed to markets outside of Texas, about 6,000,000 cattle still remained in Texas itself.

One of the first cattlemen to make the long drive north was Charles Goodnight (1836–1929), a cofounder of the famous Goodnight-Loving Trail.[6] In this book we will focus only on this trail because it was one of the most heavily traveled trails in the entire Southwest and because it was the only one that ran through New Mexico itself. Its fame has endured into our own time. For example, the novel *Lonesome Dove* by Larry McMurtry (which won the Pulitzer Prize for fiction in 1986), its sequels, and a television miniseries were all loosely based on the lives of Charles Goodnight and his partner, Oliver Loving.

Goodnight himself was above all a man of action and an entrepreneur.[7] His eventful life can be summarized as follows:

> A cowboy who made it all the way up the ladder to cattle baron, Charlie Goodnight stole when he wanted to, lynched when he had to, and died having ruled millions of acres of Texas rangelands.... He presided over a herd that numbered upward of 100,000 head, from which he sold some 30,000 animals in an average season for a gross income of around half a million dollars. His hegemony over the area was as absolute as any medieval liege lord: when some armed neighbors appeared and said they intended to wipe out a harmless group of local sheepherders Charlie's curt order to desist was enough to send the abashed gunmen quietly back to their ranches.[8]

Goodnight came to the cattle driving business with the background of a fighter. He had served with the local militia in Texas during its long-running battles with the Comanches; had joined the Texas Rangers in 1857; had ranged his cattle across Palo Pinto, Parker, and Young counties in Texas during the late 1850s; and had fought for the Confederacy during the Civil War. At the end of the war he went back to Texas and took part in "making the gather." This referred to a nearly statewide roundup of all the cattle that had roamed free during four years of war. As a result of the gather, Goodnight now had a herd of cattle of his own but no market in which to sell them. He understood immediately that he would have to find a market somewhere outside of Texas and the war-stricken South.

Goodnight was apparently the first rancher to take the risk of driving his cattle west across a waterless stretch of west Texas to Fort Sumner, New Mexico, where some 8,000 hungry Navajos and Mescalero Apaches were being held on the reservation administered by the U.S. Army, and thence north to the boomtowns of Colorado, where mining was in full swing. To avoid hostile Indians, he had to piece together a safe route. In general terms, this began in Young County, Texas; followed the Butterfield Overland Mail stagecoach trail; crossed the Pecos River at Horsehead Crossing (described below); ran up the Pecos to Fort Sumner, New Mexico; and ultimately penetrated as far north as Cheyenne, Wyoming. The Texas cattle thus driven to the northern range (this was the drovers' term for the cattle lands lying north of New Mexico, i.e., Colorado, Wyoming, Montana, and the Dakotas) would be used to feed the Union Pacific Railroad's brawny tracklaying crews. Although this new trail was nearly twice as long as the more direct routes heading due north from Texas, it was much safer.

In the spring of 1866, when buying supplies and hiring hands in preparation for his initial journey, Goodnight happened to ride past the camp of Oliver Loving (1812–1867), an older and more experienced cattleman. Loving had heard about Goodnight's ambitious plan. When they met, Loving told him, "If you will let me go, I will go with you." Goodnight replied, "I will not only let you, but it is the most desirable thing of my life. I not only need the assistance of your force [your riders], but I need your advice."[9]

The two men decided to pool their herds and became partners. Their first combined herd totaled some 2,000 head and was driven by 18 well-armed men. Starting from their camp 25 miles southwest of Belknap (now a ghost town in north-central Texas) on 6 June 1866, they headed west for New Mexico, entering it through the Llano Estacado. Upon reaching the Pecos River at Horsehead Crossing (also called Dead Horse Crossing, so named because it was littered with the skeletons of horses, cattle and mules that had been poisoned by the alkaline river water or hopelessly bogged down in the quicksands), they turned north and followed the river to Fort Sumner, where they sold most of their herd for 8 cents a pound. This netted $12,000 in gold — a very handsome profit. At that point, Goodnight went back to Weatherford, Texas, with the gold and to get another herd; Loving, for his part, continued on north and sold the remaining cattle near Denver.

During his travels Goodnight had developed a hatred for the Pecos River because he lost hundreds of cattle in the surrounding desert and in the quicksands of the riverbed. The Pecos was, he proclaimed, "the graveyard of the cowman's hopes ... the most desolate country that I had ever explored."[10] This river earned, and kept, a very bad reputation among trail drivers. For example, twenty years later (in 1886), during what must have been one of the last drives up the Goodnight-Loving Trail, the Texas cattleman L.A. Franks wrote of his experiences as follows: "[W]e followed [the Goodnight-Loving Trail up the Pecos River] as far as Roswell, New Mexico [about 80 miles south of Fort Sumner]. We had a tough time of it, with no grass and no rain. We suffered heavy losses all the way up the Pecos, pulling and digging cattle out of bogs every day and losing some each day. We were a dilapidated looking bunch, cattle, horses and men."[11]

Despite the aggravations of the Pecos River, Goodnight and Loving would continue to use their trail for the next three years, until 1869. In September of that year, Loving was mortally wounded in New Mexico during an Indian attack. Accompanied only by "One-Armed" Bill Wilson, a trusted trail rider, Loving had ranged too far ahead of the herd, looking for potential buyers. Although he had promised Goodnight that he would travel through Comanche country only at night so he could not easily be seen, he became impatient and rode during daylight hours in order to make better time. When Loving was wounded, he sent Wilson back to the herd and then, with the help of some passing Mexican traders, managed to make his way to Fort Sumner, where he died of gangrene poisoning. Just before his death, he asked Goodnight to promise to take his body back to Weatherford, Texas, for burial. Goodnight immediately agreed.

Loving was first given a temporary burial in New Mexico while Goodnight and his men continued the cattle drive. Later, returning to New Mexico, Goodnight instructed his riders to flatten out all the used tin cans in camp (these cans held the oil needed by the cook) and solder them together to create a waterproof casket. Loving's body was first put into a wooden coffin, which in turn was placed inside the tin casket, which was sealed shut. A layer of powdered charcoal was packed between the two containers, which were then crated and transported back to Weatherford's Greenwood Cemetery for permanent burial. Writing in 1936, a historian of the Goodnight-Loving Trail felt that this procession was "the strangest and most touching cavalcade in the history of cow country."[12] Loving's grave is now the site of a Texas state historical marker.[13]

At different times there were four variants of the Goodnight-Loving Trail. According to a sketch map compiled by the Old Colorado City Historical Society, these variants were as follows[14]:

1. *The Loving Trail to Denver* (1866), which went through Las Vegas, New Mexico; crossed the New Mexico–Colorado border at Raton Pass; traversed Pueblo, Colorado, in the process passing just to the east of the Goodnight Ranch near Pueblo; and, finally, continued north to Denver.

2. *The Goodnight Trail to Cheyenne* (1868), which ran east of the Loving

Trail to Denver and generally paralleled it. This variant crossed the New Mexico–Colorado border at Trinchera Pass in order to avoid the toll road that that been established at Raton Pass by Richard Lacy "Uncle Dick" Wootton by 1867. (Uncle Dick will be discussed later.) The trail then continued on to Cheyenne.

3. *A New Branch of the Goodnight Trail* (after 1868), which generally paralleled the Goodnight Trail to Cheyenne but did not go all the way to Cheyenne. It terminated instead on the South Platte River at the ranch of John Wesley Iliff, who was known as the "cattle king of the Plains." Iliff had followed the railroads' tracklaying crews into Wyoming and had set up a string of small spreads (little ranches) along the way to hold the cattle he bought from drovers. The demand for beef became so great that some years he bought as many as 15,000 of the Longhorns which had wearily plodded their way north along the Goodnight-Loving Trail.

4. *A Final Variant of the Goodnight Trail* (1875), which ran from northeastern New Mexico to Granada, a small town in southeastern Colorado on the Arkansas River, not far from the Kansas border.

Goodnight was a great admirer of the longhorns he trailed north. He said of them:

> As trail cattle, their equal has never been known. Their hoofs are superior to those of any other cattle [because they did not crack easily when wet with morning dew]. In stampedes, [the Longhorns] hold together better, are easier to circle during a run, and rarely split off when you commence to turn the front. [During stampedes, rather than letting the cattle run in a straight line, the riders tried to force them to turn and to form a vast milling circle.] No animal of the cow kind will shift and take care of itself under all conditions as will the Longhorns. They can go farther without water and endure more suffering than others.[15]

The most famous longhorn was known as "Old Blue." He was always Goodnight's lead steer. At the end of each drive he was spared from the slaughterhouse and was driven back to Texas to lead another herd north. He did this for more than eight years, frequently wandering into the riders' camp in the evening in search of scraps of food. When Old Blue finally died at the age of 20, he was honored by having his horns mounted on a plaque in the headquarters of Goodnight's ranch.[16]

Trail riders had a hard life. They never got enough sleep or any tender loving care. In 1879, for example, when Baylis John Fletcher, a 19-year-old cowboy on the Chisholm Trail, complained to George Arnett, his trail boss, about the lack of sleep, Arnett shot back brusquely, "What the hell are you kicking about? You can sleep all winter when you get to Montana."[17] Arnett and all the other trail bosses were hard men: they needed to be if they wanted to keep their jobs. A trail boss was the ultimate authority on the trail — the captain of the ship — and at $100 to $125 a month, he was well paid. His job was to keep his cowboys in line and to negotiate with the Indians, who not infrequently demanded payment, e.g., one cow, as the price for letting the herd cross their tribal land. More important, the trail boss had to strike a fine balance between two conflicting objectives. On the one hand, he needed to move the herd along as quickly as possible so that the cattle were subjected to the hazards of the trail for the shortest possible time. (In 1886, the Texas cattleman L.A. Franks began with 2,200 cattle but had only 1,600 left when he finally reached the market at the end of the trail.)

On the other hand, however, the trail boss also needed to make sure that his cattle did not lose too much weight during their travels. If need be, they could be driven as far as 25 miles a day but in the process they would become so thin that they would be worth very little at trail's end. The trail boss usually had to compromise by driving the herd only about 15 miles per day, thus allowing the animals plenty of time to rest and to graze at midday and at night. This procedure would keep them at a healthy weight but, moving at such a slow pace, it could take two months or more for riders to drive a herd from home ranch to market.

Another "first" for Goodnight was his invention of the chuckwagon in 1866. "Chuck" was at that time a slang term for food. He devised a sturdy wooden wagon, drawn by mules or oxen, and covered with a rounded canvas top held up by metal hoops. The chuckwagon was an all-purpose vehicle which carried food, eating utensils, a water barrel, tools, bed rolls, and any rifles the riders may have brought with them. It was too dangerous on a drive to carry a rifle in a scabbard strapped to one side of the saddle: a lasso might easily snag on the stock, with potentially disastrous results for horse, rider and cattle alike. As a further safety measure, some trail bosses required riders to leave their pistols in the chuckwagon, too.

The chuckwagon served as a versatile kitchen on wheels, being fully equipped with drawers, shelves, and a "boot" (storage compartment) underneath. From the riders' point of view, the cook was the most important man after the trail boss himself. The cowboys had ravenous appetites after long hard days in the saddle; the best cowboys signed up only for the trail drives which had the best cooks. A good cook earned about $60 per month.

Chuckwagon cuisine was based on easy-to-preserve items, such as beans, salted meats, canned tomatoes (highly valued because they were very useful cooking ingredients, e.g., for chili, and because the men considered their juice to be quite refreshing), coffee, and sourdough biscuits. The men demanded that the cook provide ample helpings of everything. The fare included beef and buffalo steaks; "chuckwagon chicken" (bacon); "Pecos strawberries" (beans); "sourdough bullets" (biscuits); and strong, boiling-hot coffee. A later visitor to the West reported that he once had seen a cowboy drink coffee directly from the metal kettle which he had just taken off the campfire.

An unusual specialty of trail drive cooks was "son of a bitch stew." This consisted of the marrow gut of an unweaned calf (the marrow gut is a tube that connects the calf's stomachs), together with its brains, sweetbread (pancreas), heart, liver, and tongue — all stewed together in an iron pot for several hours. These internal organs had a very high vitamin content, which the cowboys relished — and needed — as an important dietary supplement to their vitamin-deficient diet of beef, beans and flour.[18]

Some of the best firsthand accounts of life on the cattle trails come from Andy Adams (1859–1935), who spent ten years in Texas, during eight of which he was punching (driving) cattle along the Western Trail. In his classic book, *Log of a Cowboy* (1903), he chronicled a fictional but wholly convincing and historically accurate five-month-long-drive of 3,000 cattle from Brownsville, Texas, to the northwest corner of Montana in 1882. Adams summarized the challenges of life on the trail in lyrical words which can stand as an epitaph to all Western cattle drives:

> It was necessary to keep several riders on duty when inclement weather was apparent, because in the event a storm set in the herd would tend to drift and during severe weather, would drift fast and far, unless held back. Then when thunder and lightening were persisting, there was always danger of a stampede starting, with its resulting losses, unless the riders were on hand to hold the run down to the minimum.
>
> I have experienced periods of two and three days and nights when our entire crew, of six to eight riders, was on duty the whole time without any rest. During the winter was the period of the year when inclement and threatening weather would persist for several successive days.... Occasionally, during the winter, a persisting sleet and rain storm, accompanied with cold, would set in. Such weather was the hardest weather to work in and also, required the most work, because the cattle would insist on drifting with the storm....
>
> Many things can scare a herd.... The herd may be bedded and arise instantly. Looking at a herd arising, it appears as if the earth is heaving up with an accompanying roar, a swish-like sound, and the clashing of horns. When the cattle are running, the pounding of their feet on the earth sounds as the roll of many muffled drums. The clashing of the horns gives off a sound similar to that of many muffled cymbals....
>
> Suppose it was dark and storming when a stampede was in progress, which it often was. Then imagine, if you can, riding at the head of several thousand wild, frightened cattle, and while riding, crowding your mount against the running cattle trying to force the animals off their course. Suppose your horse stumbled and threw you in front of the running cattle? Of course, the result of such an event is obvious. Talk about daring riders, that was one position the word daring does not express strong enough; *"sand in your gizzard,"* as the cowhand used to say, expresses such riders more accurately.[19]

CHAPTER XI

Steel Trails for the Iron Horse

The coming of the railroads would gradually but inexorably change beyond all recognition the historic trails, trade, and travels of the Southwest. There were only 23 miles of railroad track in the entire United States in 1830. During the coming decades a vast expansion of the railway network would take place — to such an extent that there were about 53,000 miles of track by 1870; 93,000 miles by 1880; and 164,000 miles by 1890.[1] In the East, beginning in the 1830s, railways began to replace canal boats and, to a more limited extent, animal-drawn wagons as the most efficient way to move people and goods over long distances. In the West, railroads took longer to gain a foothold but by the 1880s they would close down the historic Santa Fe Trail itself.

The earliest railroads west of the Mississippi River were the Red River Railroad in Louisiana, which linked Alexandria and Cheneyville in 1841, and the Pacific Railroad, the first part of which opened near St. Louis in 1852. Railroad history in New Mexico itself turns out to be surprisingly detailed and complex. In the 1880s, for example, more than 100 companies, most of them small, were involved in building and operating the railroads there.[2] For this reason, we will not attempt here to write a definitive account of the steel trails of New Mexico but will instead try to identify some of their most interesting points, arranging them, from time to time, in terms of their readability rather than their strict chronological order.

One key factor which spurred the great expansion of railroads in the West was the decision by Congress and the U.S. government to give away huge amounts of the public domain in the form of railroad land grants in order to encourage settlement and commerce. The *National Atlas of the United States* explains:

> The second half of the nineteenth century was the era of railroad land grants. Between 1850 and 1872 extensive cessions of public lands were made to states and to railroad companies to promote railroad construction. [During this

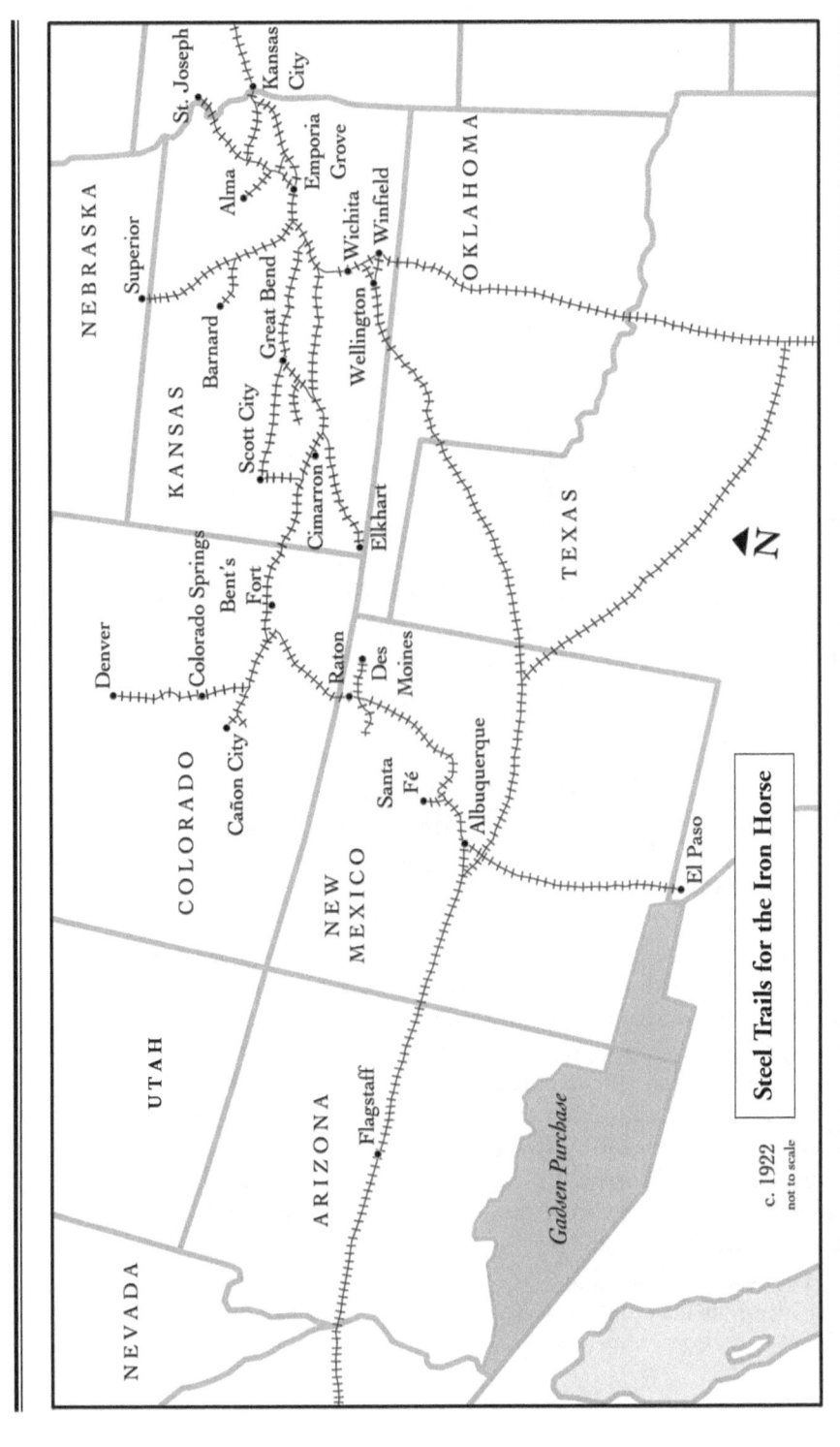

period, the railroads received more than 175,000,000 acres of public land.] Usually the companies received from the federal government, in twenty- or fifty-mile strips, alternate sections of public land for each mile of track that was built. [A section is a piece of land one square mile (640 acres) in area which forms one of the 36 subdivisions of an American township.] Responsibility for surveying and mapping the grants fell to the U.S. General Land Office, now the Bureau of Land Management. Numerous maps of the United States and individual states were made which clearly indicated the sections of the granted land and the railroad rights-of-way.[3]

To generate income, railroads set up real estate offices and sold land to the public from the land grants awarded by Congress. Discounted passenger fares were offered by a railroad to anyone who traveled west to inspect this land; if a traveler actually bought land, the price of his ticket was deducted from the cost of the land itself. Railroad real estate agents dangled a golden lure in front of prospective buyers. It would be a very wise long term investment, they claimed, for farmers and ranchers to buy up this land because the railroad offered not only passenger service but also a quick and safe way to get their goods to market.

In the 1840s and 1850s, many Americans were clamoring for a viable route for a transcontinental railroad line. Earlier in this book we met the Santa Fe trader Francis Xavier Aubry (1824–1854), who made many quick trips over the Santa Fe Trail and repeatedly broke speed records between Independence and Santa Fe. In 1853 Aubry started eastward from California on one of his several explorations of possible railroad lines from California to New Mexico. When he reached Albuquerque, he made this entry in his diary on 10 September 1853, explaining the purpose of the trip:

> I set out ... upon this journey simply to gratify my own curiosity as to the practicability of one of the much talked-of routes for the contemplated Atlantic and Pacific railroad. Having previously traveled the Southern, or Gila, route, I felt anxious to compare it with the Albuquerque, or middle route. Although I conceive the former to be in every way practicable, I now give it as my opinion that the latter is equally so, whilst it has the additional advantage of being more central and serviceable to the Union.[4]

The route followed by Aubry would be favored by traders, military men and surveying engineers—first as a wagon road and then as a preferred path for a railroad. It was well suited for transit and eventually became a major route for the Atlantic and Pacific railroad. In New Mexico, in 1888 the Atlantic and Pacific and its connections would extend from Las Vegas west to Lamy (near Santa Fe); southwest to Albuquerque and Isleta; and then northwest to Gallup. From there the line ran southwest and south across Arizona to Needles, California. At that point it joined the Southern Pacific Railroad (SP for short), heading for Mojave and other points west.

While Aubry was riding east from California, the American government had been negotiating with Mexico with two objectives in mind: to buy the land necessary for a transcontinental railway along a very southerly route, and to resolve the disputes that had simmered on after the Mexican-American War ended in 1848. The final result of these negotiations was the Gadsden Purchase, named for James Gadsden, the American ambassador to Mexico at the time. This treaty was negotiated in 1853 and ratified by the United States and Mexico in 1854.

Under its terms, the United States agreed to pay Mexico $10,000,000 for a 29,670-square mile portion of Mexico that later became part of Arizona and New Mexico. Traced on a modern map of Arizona and New Mexico, the Gadsden Purchase begins near Yuma, trends generally northeast toward Phoenix, and then makes its way southeast and east toward Las Cruces, New Mexico. This treaty did not resolve all the bilateral issues that troubled the two countries, e.g., financial claims and cross-border Indian raids, but it did create the southern border of the United States.[5] One unintended consequence was the danger of more frequent American clashes with the southern Apache, who were now living in what had suddenly become the territory of the United States.

There were many advocates for a railroad from the Midwest into New Mexico. As early as 1857, for example, a publicity circular on the merits of what was then termed the "St. Joseph and Topeka Railroad" had this to say:

> The greater part of the route [westward from Topeka] is over an ordinary level country, unsurpassed in fertility, and much resembling the interior part of Missouri.... The supply of timber is about equal and that of stone much better. There is ground for anticipating that such a road [the railroad] would yield a large percentage on the money invested in its construction, and that it can be built at less than average cost.
>
> But the greatest object to be secured at present by this enterprise is the trade to Santa Fe and New Mexico, which is annually very considerable, and will richly reward the earliest railroad communication that may be extended in that direction. The trade is increasing yearly, and is composed mainly of the manufacturers of the Middle and Eastern states; all of which, in the event of railroad communication west and south of St. Joseph, must pass over roads leading from the East to that place, affording them, in itself, a source of revenue by no means inconsiderable.[6]

The railroad company that would go down in the history of the Southwest simply as "the Santa Fe" was originally chartered in Kansas in 1859 as the Atchison & Topeka Railroad Company. It was founded by the promoter Cyrus K. Holliday. A history of Kansas described him in 1918 in these glowing words:

Mr. Holliday's greatest achievement was in projecting and building the first portion of the Atchison, Topeka & Santa Fe railroad. He was the first man to dream of a line of railway along the old Santa Fe trail to the Pacific coast. In 1864 he prepared a map showing the proposed road and tried to interest capitalists in the scheme. Everywhere he was met by rebuffs and sneers, but nothing daunted him, and he lived to see the realization of his dreams. He secured a charter from the Kansas legislature, and through the purchase and sale of Pottawatomie Indian lands raised money enough to built [sic] the first twenty miles of road — from Topeka to Carbondale — an event that was celebrated with appropriate ceremonies.[7]

After changing its name in 1863 to the Atchison, Topeka & Santa Fe Railway Company, this line greatly benefited from receiving, thanks to an Act of Congress in 1863 and a similar move by the Kansas legislature in 1864, a huge land grant totaling about 3,000,000 acres. A February 1893 article appearing in the *Cosmopolitan* (a weekly illustrated magazine), written by Charles S. Gleed, who was an expert on how the Santa Fe built and operated its rail lines, explained this grant as follows:

> The grant comprised alternate sections in a ten-mile strip on each side of the main line of the road through Kansas.... The lands were sold at an average of about five dollars per acre and netted the company something like five million dollars.... The railroad ... could not have existed except for the presence of this land as an attraction to settlers, and it could not have been built when it was if the possession of the land had not enabled the company to borrow money with which to build the road. The taxes on this railroad land grant built schoolhouses and court-houses from one end of Kansas to another.[8]

Under the terms of this land grant, the Santa Fe would receive 64,000 acres for every mile of track constructed — but only on the condition that within ten years time, i.e., by 1873, the line had been completed from Atchison to the Kansas/Colorado state line. The Santa Fe broke ground in Topeka in 1868 and began building westward. The first section of track opened in Kansas early the next year. It linked Topeka and Pauline, a distance of only 6 miles. Despite this unprepossessing start, by the end of 1873 the Santa Fe had indeed reached the Kansas/Colorado state line and thus qualified for the land grant.

Investors on the Pacific Coast were also eager to see the railroads expand. In 1865, for example, a group of businessmen in San Francisco, led by Timothy Phelps, had founded the Southern Pacific Railroad, initially in order to link San Francisco and San Diego. In the interests of brevity, we will not spend much time on the SP because it was less significant in terms of New Mexico itself than was the Santa Fe. Nevertheless, a very brief account of some of the SP's activities may be of interest here.

Beginning from Los Angeles, the SP laid tracks toward the east. In 1881 the second transcontinental railroad was completed when the SP's tracks from

Los Angeles met the Galveston, Harrisburg and San Antonio Railway's tracks in Texas, just west of the Pecos River. (The first, and more northerly, transcontinental railroad had been finished 12 years earlier, in 1869, when trains from the Central Pacific and the Union Pacific met at Promontory Point, Utah. There Leland Stanford, one of the prime backers of the Central Pacific and, later, the founder of Stanford University, had hammered in a golden spike to celebrate the union of these two lines.) The SP would eventually operate in some 15 Western, Southwestern, and Middle Western states.

Here we will break off, if only temporarily, our discussion of the railways themselves and will introduce some of the colorful men and women who played important roles in the multiphase projects involved in the construction and maintenance of these steel trails.

The earliest of these plucky individuals was Richard Lacy Wootton (1816–1893). Although not a railroad man himself, "Uncle Dick," as he was widely known, was instrumental in getting the first train into New Mexico. He had been, successively, a mountain man, a trapper, and a hunter at Bent's Fort. Subsequently, when we meet him, he had turned up in Trinidad, Colorado, armed with permission from both the territorial governments of Colorado and New Mexico to build a toll road over Raton Pass. In 1866, since there were no skilled workers at hand, he hired a tribe of Utes under Chief Conniache to build it. Uncle Dick improved some 27 miles of the toughest part of the trail over the pass. He later said of his achievement that "There were hillsides to cut down, rocks to blast and remove, and bridges to build by the score. But I built the road and made it a good one."[9]

By 1867, Uncle Dick had set up a tollgate in front of his house and was charging $1.50 for a wagon or a buggy and 25 cents for each horseman. Indians were allowed to use the road free of charge. His own home was near the toll road and was always open to stagecoach passengers, who could look forward to a hot lunch and extra helpings of good stories. It was clear because of the strategic location of this road that the Santa Fe would need to acquire Uncle Dick's right of way in order to run its railway over the pass into New Mexico. In 1879 the company therefore offered to buy his right of way, offering him the princely sum of $50,000. He turned down that offer. Instead, he altruistically sold his right of way to the railroad for the token sum of $1.00 for himself, plus a life grant of $50 per month in credit at a grocery store in Trinidad. (This grant passed to his wife when Wootton died in 1893 and then passed to a daughter.)[10]

Another memorable character in the history of the Southwest was the entrepreneur Fred Harvey. In 1876 he had opened a restaurant at the railroad depot in Topeka. Previously, railroad officials and train travelers alike had been forced to accept the filthy dining rooms, poor service, and bad food characteristic of the depots where steam locomotives had to stop for water and services. They were now amazed by the spotlessly clean surroundings, first class service, and the large portions of excellent cooking offered by Harvey and his able staff. Indeed, the Santa Fe had such confidence in Harvey that it gave him a blank check to set up a series of "eating houses" at depots along almost the entire route. By the late 1880s, there was a Fred Harvey dining facility at almost all the depots along the tracks of the Santa Fe railroad. Some of these restaurants evolved into hotels, some of which still survive today. In effect, Harvey had established the first restaurant chain in the United States.

The Harvey dinner menu listed in appendix five cost the traveler only 75 cents; wines and other beverages were available at extra cost. By 1888 Harvey was also offering "meals on wheels" — in other words, food service in dining cars on the trains themselves. Most memorably, he hit upon the brilliant idea of hiring as waitresses in his restaurants a large number of single, attractive, intelligent, well trained, and well behaved young women, aged between 18 and 30. These girls were all dressed in identically severe but very becoming black-and-white starched uniforms and were paid $17.50 per month, plus room, board, and tips — a generous income by the standards of the day. Many of these girls ended up marrying railroad employees or local ranchers or farmers and thus had to leave the ranks of the Harvey Girls, as they came to be called.

Passengers found these young ladies a very refreshing change from the rowdy male waiters of pre–Harvey days. Those young men, if they turned up for work at all, were likely to arrive drunk and were quick to pick fights with their customers. Frontier legend assures us that the Harvey Girls helped "to civilize the American Southwest."[11] Before they managed to do so, however, there was a most uncivilized era — that is to say, the years of the "railroad wars."

In 1878 the Santa Fe had authorized construction of a rail line running south from Trinidad, Colorado, over Raton Pass and on into New Mexico. The company's first and most important objective was to make sure that it had unquestionable legal control of Raton Pass itself. (The right of way it had obtained from Uncle Dick was not sufficient for this purpose. The railroad still needed to file papers with the Department of the Interior but had not yet done so. As a result, the pass was still legally "open," waiting the first fully qualified claimant.)[12] At the same time, however, another railroad company — the smaller Denver and Rio Grande Railroad (D&RG) — was also trying to get the sole right to use the pass. Indeed, the D&RG was about to claim physical possession of Raton Pass and to set its construction crews to work there.

The D&RG had reasoned — incorrectly, as it turned out — that there was no pressing need for it to file a plat and a profile for its line (that is, no need to take the steps necessary to give it legal control of the pass) because no rival company seemed to be near enough to dispute the right of way through this bottleneck. The Santa Fe, however, prevailed: its own construction crews unexpectedly began to work on the pass by lantern light in the predawn darkness of a wintry February morning in 1878. As the railroad historian L.L. Waters put it, "There was not much the D&RG men could do. Only one railroad could go through and the Santa Fe was [already] in possession."[13]

After legal action and threats of violence between rival gangs of railroad workers, the Santa Fe took the drastic step of hiring local gunfighters to enforce its own claim to the pass. The final result was that, outgunned and outmaneuvered, the D&RG had no choice but to back down and yield Raton Pass to the Santa Fe. Thus the "first railroad war" ended without a shot ever being fired.

The next year, however, a silver strike in Leadville, Colorado, ignited the "second railroad war." The issue here was control of the Royal Gorge — a narrow, deep canyon on the Arkansas River near Cañon City, Colorado. This conflict once again pitted the Santa Fe against the Denver and Rio Grande. At first, the Santa Fe had the upper hand because it had hired the legendary gunfighter Bat Masterson (1853–1921) to recruit about 70 other hardened gunfighters. In June 1879, however, the Fourth Judicial Circuit court ruled in favor of the Denver and Rio Grande, which, with the assistance of local sheriffs, then launched an attack on the Santa Fe's gunmen. Sharp fighting took place at the Santa Fe's garrisons in Denver, Colorado Springs, and Pueblo. Masterson's headquarters in Pueblo was the last to surrender but in the end it did. This second "war" ended with the Denver and Rio Grande in full control of the Royal Gorge.[14]

After triumphing at Raton Pass, the Santa Fe's construction teams began laying track in northeastern New Mexico in December 1878. Where it could, the line followed the well-traveled course of the Mountain Route of the Santa Fe Trail but the surveyors also had to thread their way through the mesas of northeastern New Mexico, hunting for a viable railroad route down to Santa Fe.

For many miles they followed the canyon cut by the upper part of the Pecos River. Then they crossed Glorieta Pass; entered the watershed of the Rio Grande; ran along Galisteo Creek, where the track still follows very steep grades today; and turned north at Galisteo Junction (which was later renamed Lamy to honor a local bishop) toward Santa Fe. The first train reached the capital in February 1880. It was welcomed by flowery speeches and a parade. With its arrival, the historic Santa Fe Trail would gradually be relegated to the dustbin of history.

The Santa Fe continued to lay track in New Mexico but the city of Santa Fe itself would ultimately be served only by a branch line because of the difficulties of the terrain. The Santa Fe's tracks reached Albuquerque in April 1880. They continued on to Rincon and there turned southwest toward Deming, where they met the SP's tracks coming from California in 1881. In New Mexico, the Santa Fe's own track-laying initially ended at that time and place. Acting through other corporate entities, however, the Santa Fe would continue to build and maintain steel trails for many years to come.[15]

Because of the Apache menace, railroad construction crews in the Southwest sometimes needed U.S. Army protection. In 1880, for example, Lieutenant Colonel Dudley took command of Fort Cummings, which was located about 20 miles northeast of Deming and which had been closed in 1873. It was opened again in 1880 after a band of Warm Spring Apaches led by Chief Victorio bolted from the San Carlos Reservation and began terrorizing southern New Mexico and western Texas. Dudley sent out detachments to guard the crews building west from the Rio Grande. One of these soldiers, Earl S. Hall, recalled in his later years that when he and his fellow soldiers went out on a 15-day expedition hunting for Apaches, the campaign proved to be so hot and so difficult that the soldiers lost an average of 15 pounds each.[16]

Apaches were not the only problem Dudley faced. In late 1880 a rancher named George Stevens was held up when traveling on horseback from the Rio Grande to Silver City, New Mexico. The bandits took his rifle, ammunition, and money — but, surprisingly, let him keep his loaded revolver "in case he ran into Indians." These or other outlaws also stole livestock from local ranches. When Dudley and the Silver City newspaper editor looked for the most likely culprits, they decided that these crimes were not the work of Indians after all but more probably of "either a gang of road agents or itinerant tramps waiting to help lay track for the railroad."[17]

By using the SP's tracks from Deming to Benson, Arizona, and then by building (via the New Mexico and Arizona Railroad) a track to Nogales on the Mexican border, the Santa Fe eventually was able to offer through service from Kansas City all the way to the Pacific Coast.[18] Such tracklaying in the Southwest faced many problems. One contemporary writer, whose name has been lost to us, joked that "The original builders of the Atchison followed the line of the Arizona trail [the "middle route" running west from Albuquerque] so religiously that if the trail skirted a ten-foot stream for a quarter of a mile to strike a shallow spot for fording, the railroad builders did likewise, instead of bridging the stream where they struck it, and where the trail ran up a tree or hid in a hollow rock to avoid the wolves or savages, the railroad did the same!"[19]

The Santa Fe's workforce mainly consisted of Spanish-speaking New Mexicans and Pueblo Indians on the one hand and English-speaking Irish immigrants on the other. The New Mexicans and Pueblo Indians, colloquially known as *traqueros*, were unskilled low-paid workers assigned to the dreary, repetitive tasks of track maintenance, e.g., removing weeds, tamping down ballast, and replacing rotten ties. In 1895 they were making between $1.00 and $1.25 per day.

The Irishmen, on the other hand, were earning twice as much. Because of their skills, Irish workers pocketed $2.25 per day in 1895.[20] They held the jobs which demanded care, training, and expertise — jobs where a single mistake could be fatal to the worker himself, to his colleagues, or to the passengers when the track was finished. The best example of such a task was drilling blasting holes into solid rock: explosive charges would then be placed in the holes and detonated to blast out railroad tunnels. Another job that required experience was laying down the rails themselves, not only in straight lines but also in sweeping curves. What was probably the longest straight stretch of track (47 miles) and the longest continuous curve (5 miles) were both built by the SP near Tucson in 1880. The most beautiful curve was the graceful, lovely Reverse Curve High Bridge on the line to Cloudcroft, New Mexico, built in the same era by the Alamogordo & Sacramento Mountain Railway.

Hands-on experience was needed to build the short "switching" segments which trains had to use to pull off the main line onto turnouts, or where they joined another set of tracks. The Irish could teach by example. In one case that has passed into railroad lore, a young American decided to look for a job on the railroad. Although he knew nothing at all about laying track, he confidently assured the foreman that he was an expert. On this basis he got a low-level supervisory job.

When he joined his crew, they were laying a straight section of track, so all went well. Our young man, however, could see that, up ahead, he would have to build a switching segment — something far beyond his very limited abilities. He therefore asked a burly, energetic Irish worker — let us call him Mick — to build this segment of the line because he (the young man) suddenly had to leave the scene to meet with the railroad's timekeeper. Mick was eager to please his new boss and readily agreed. The young man left but quickly hid behind a pile of railroad ties so that he could watch Mick at work. By doing this, he learned how to build switching segments and was soon able to return to his team, confident of his new-found knowledge.

A famous American folk song, initially composed in 1888 and performed in our own times by Pete Seeger and other singers, jokes about these Irish railroad men. One version of the song runs as follows:

Every morning about seven o'clock
There were twenty tarriers drilling at the rock.
The boss comes along and he says, "Keep still
And bear down heavy on the cast iron drill."
> [There are different opinions about the origin of the word "tarrier." Some believe that it comes from the verb *tarry*, to delay or to be tardy when doing something. Others say it refers to a burrowing, barking dog, a terrier.]

Chorus:
And drill, ye tarriers, drill.
Drill, ye tarriers, drill.
For it's work all day for the sugar in your tay [tea]
Down beyond the railway.
And drill, ye tarriers, drill
And blast, and fire.

The boss was a fine man down to the ground
And he married a lady six feet 'round.
She baked good bread and she baked it well
But she baked it harder than the hobs of Hell.
> [A hob is a projection at the back or side of a fireplace on which something may be kept warm.]

The foreman's name was John McCann.
By God, he was a blamed mean man.
Last week a premature blast went off
And a mile in the air went big Jim Goff.
And when next payday came around
Jim Goff a dollar short was found.
When he asked, "What for?" came this reply:
"You was docked for the time you was up in the sky."[21]

One of the most evocative descriptions of the workers who built and maintained the railroads of the Southwest (and undoubtedly those of other regions as well) is "gandy dancer." The origin of this term is uncertain but it is known that railroad work crews used specialized tools known as "gandies" to lever the tracks into position. Oral histories from railroad towns suggest that "gandy dancer" referred to a man who positioned the rails so they could be nailed down to the wooden ties, which were known as sleepers.[22] Each long, heavy rail weighed about 700 pounds and was carried by a crew of five men. First they straddled it, leaving spaces between themselves. Then, on command, they bent down, reached between their feet, picked up the rail, and moved it a short distance. In so doing, the men were said to look, from afar, like a line of waddling geese. They thus became known as "ganders" and their work as "gander dancing"—a phrase eventually shortened in use to "gandy dancing."

Gandy dancers had to be strong men and, equally important, they had to know how to work in unison. To help them do so, they invented simple songs with a strong sense of rhythm. Here is one of them. (The ejaculation "huh" marks the strenuous physical effort involved at a key moment of a given task):

>Pick an' shovel ... huh
>am so heavy ... huh
>Heavy as lead ... huh
>Heavy as lead ... huh
>Pickin', shov'lin' ... huh
>Pickin', shov'lin' ... huh
>Till I'm dead....[23]

Construction work on the Santa Fe line in New Mexico was described in graphic terms by the railroad expert and journalist Charles S. Gleed in a *Cosmopolitan* magazine article cited earlier:

>Financiers for the most part saw little to justify the faith of the soldiers, miners and other frontiers-men [*sic*] who urged that the old Santa Fe trail ought to be converted into a trail of steel, and some day would be....
>There has been much costly and unusual engineering work in the system. The great elevations in New Mexico and Colorado were reached by remarkably difficult work. The longest tunnel, that on Raton mountain, at the Colorado–New Mexico state-line is nearly two miles long. There are five notable bridges.... These bridges cost nearly one million dollars each.
>One of the chief difficulties encountered by the company building through New Mexico was the physical peculiarity of the country. Mr. Robinson [Alfred A. Robinson, the Santa Fe's chief engineer] left nothing undone to discover what must be guarded against in the work of construction. For example, the oldest inhabitants were consulted at great length as to what ought to be expected as to rain and water courses. But after the line was completed the water made light of all that had been said about it historically. It ran where it had never been before and it failed to appear when most expected.
>Mile after mile of track was lifted [by floods] from its place in the canyons and hung in graceful festoons on the trees and hillsides. Suddenly, on occasion, a shallow valley in which water never seemed to have been heard of before would contain a roaring torrent, which would run madly at the intruding railroad and reduce it to its primitive level. In the Rio Grande valley, the river, with all the capriciousness of the wind, ran first from one side of the valley and then to the other, each time leaving the track to sink or swim as its superintendent might manage.
>It was no uncommon spectacle, even as late at 1884, to see Superintendent George L. Sands, with his men, wading and swimming from bank to bank in a heroic endeavor to "make both ends meet." Iron bridges, longer spans, higher elevations, elaborate dikes and ditches seem to have fixed things so that water may [now] be defied. Parts of the system were built with incredible rapidity.

Track-laying at the rate of one mile a day was often achieved. The track across the Great Divide winds and climbs and crosses and redresses itself in a wonderful manner.[24]

In New Mexico, the Santa Fe offered service to Las Vegas, Santa Fe, and Albuquerque. Its steel trails then headed southwest for Deming, the connection point for California. At the same time, another track (belonging to the Atlantic & Pacific Railroad) was being built westward from Albuquerque in the summer of 1880. Henry Allen Tice (1855–1939) was a young surveyor working with the crew that laid out this railroad, which was to run from Isleta, New Mexico, to California. Tice gives us an amusing insight into Southwestern frontier society in this 1880 sketch of a Santa Fe dance hall, where a square dance was in progress:

> At the end of the bar nearest the door stood a big, two-fisted, fierce-mustached villain, wearing a big sombrero, a blue flannel shirt, no coat, his corduroy pants stuck into his boots, a bandana about his neck, and a forty-five in his belt holster.
> His "lady" [a dance hall prostitute] ran her elbow into his ribs and pointed her thumb over her shoulder at a countrified-looking boy who had taken his "lady" to a wall-flower seat where they were the sole floor spectators of the wet line [the bar]. The "ladies" had all called for cocktails for themselves and their partners — more money for the bar than in whiskey straights, and more commission for the "ladies."
> The aforesaid villain looked toward the lonesome couple on the side line, then proceeded rapidly across the room and, standing in front of the tenderfoot, addressed himself as follows: "Lookyee hyer, yuh ____, ain't yuh no gentleman? Where was you brung up, yuh ____? Why didn't yuh take yere lady up to the bar like the rest o' the gents did? Fer two cents and with yere lady's permission, I'd ventilate [shoot] yuh. What yuh goin' to do?"
> Safety first impelled the boy to follow the tough gent's mild suggestion. Two more cocktails disappeared....[25]

Another contemporary account of "villains" along the railroad comes from Charles S. Gleed. Here he was commenting chiefly about the railroad line in Kansas but his comments apply to New Mexico as well:

> "The end of the track," and many stations which had once been at the end of the track were for a long time very disorderly towns. Murder and the milder but more interesting crimes were of constant occurrence. Cowboys of the bad kind, Indians, railroad construction stragglers, and hard characters generally were at first largely in the majority in most of the Santa Fe villages [the towns along the Santa Fe's tracks] and made them more painfully active than they ever will be again. Judge Lynch [this refers to "lynch law," e.g., an extrajudicial hanging conducted by a mob] was a popular dispenser of justice, and without his help the regular courts could hardly have kept up their works.[26]

Even after the second transcontinental railroad was completed in 1881, horses, mules and oxen continued to be widely used for transportation. Indeed, it was not until after a number of railroads had begun serving the trans-Mississippi West that a newspaper could tell its readers, in 1893 and without fear of contradiction: "The prairie schooner has passed away and is [now] replaced by the railway coach with all its modern comforts."[27]

Transcontinental train travel certainly helped to change the United States from an agrarian society into a modern industrial power. Moreover, the railroads had a profound social effect, too: they made it much easier, faster, cheaper, and safer for women and children to immigrate to and settle in the West. The growing presence of women and children filed the rough edges off many of the wild frontier towns — thanks to the development of schools and churches, better law enforcement, and other institutions supporting family life.

Chapter XII

The Southern Trails

A number of lesser-known and now-obscure trails of the Southwest can be loosely lumped together as the southern trails. Different historical sources locate them in slightly different places and disagree on their names. As used here, "southern trails" will refer to the trails that ran to locations generally lying south or west of Santa Fe. Only a small sample of the southern trails will be discussed here — by no means all of them. Those mentioned here are the Southern Trail itself; the Zuni Trail; the Gila River Trail; the Apache Pass Trail; and the Upper and Lower Emigrant Trails, both of which ran through west Texas to El Paso.

Most of these southern trails were used by Indians long before the coming of the Spaniards. Between about 1276 and 1287, for example, the Mogollon people built the dwellings that are now part of the Gila Cliff Dwellings National Monument, located north of Silver City, New Mexico, near the headwaters of the Gila River. Making their own trails, these Indians exploited the abundant game and fertile soils of the Gila River valley, raising crops of corn, beans, and squash. By 1300, however, for reasons that are still not clear, they abandoned this settlement and moved elsewhere. Two hundred years later, they were replaced by the Apaches, who migrated to the upper Gila River in about 1500. The great Apache war leader Geronimo, who is described below, was born in the early 1820s near the headwaters of the Gila River in what is now the Gila Wilderness of southwestern New Mexico.

Other southern trails were blazed, extended, or altered by American trappers, prospectors, soldiers, emigrants, ranchers, and even by archeologists. Today all these trails remain of considerable interest to historians of the Southwest. Although these southern tracks are not nearly as well known as the more northerly routes and are much harder to locate today, they nevertheless carried an impressive tide of the Argonauts (contemporary slang for "gold seekers") so eager to seek their fortunes in the gold fields of California. Indeed, it is estimated that perhaps 20,000 of the 35,000 to 40,000 would-be prospectors bound for California after the discovery of gold there in 1848 traveled along the southern trails rather than along the more northerly routes.[1]

The Southern Trail Itself

Southbound travelers on El Camino Real de Tierra Adentro could join the Southern Trail near the small town of Garfield, New Mexico. This trail had the greatest number of emigrants passing through the region and is well documented: travelers have left us some 62 diaries and reminiscences about their experiences.[2] The Southern Trail followed a U-shaped course from Garfield to the Pima Indian villages of Arizona, dipping briefly into Mexico in the process to touch at Santa Cruz, before turning northwest into Arizona.

James Frederick Thibault, a traveler en route to the California gold fields in 1849 or 1850, wrote about the steep, dry, rocky, and brush-covered section of this trail as it led him out of Guadalupe Pass, a 5,424-foot-high pass located in Guadalupe Mountains National Park (situated near the border between New Mexico and Texas). Thibault greets his reader with the following salutation (phrasing as in the original): "Welcome to the brink of a descent that would make the head swim to look down. This our wagons had to descend probably 800 or 1000 feet in half a mile, and to pass over the ground that one would pronounce it for wagons impassible.... When I came to the brink of this frowning gulf, it was a sight that caused me to pause and gaze with admiring awe on a scene of black and terrible desolation.... [W]ell might the boys say, 'we have overtaken the elephant at last.'"[3] "Seeing the elephant" or some variant on this theme was a familiar expression for gold rush travelers. It arose before the gold rush when traveling circuses first began to display elephants to the public. So few Americans had ever seen a real elephant that to encounter one represented, figuratively speaking, the achievement of a person's most heartfelt desires. On 29 September 1849, for example, according to Benjamin Butler Harris, a traveler along the Gila Trail, "Alas, little we dreamed of the huge, colossal *Elephant* we were about to see!"[4]

At one especially difficult section of the Southern Trail as it was leading out of Guadalupe Pass, the Argonauts were obliged to use ropes to lower their wagons down a 1,000-foot decline. Thibault talks of this particular spot: "[O]ne miss drive [one mistake], and a wagon [would be] whirled to destruction.... [N]o one felt inclined to trust himself to the back of his animal for fear of performing a somerset [summersault] over its head. To take a seat on the verge of this descent, and view this mountainous and broken landscape, would fill the beholder with dread."[5]

From Santa Cruz the Southern Trail then ran northwest via Tucson to the Pima villages, where it joined the Gila River Trail. In summer, the trek from Tucson to the Pima villages could be deadly without enough water. Dr. David Jordan set out from Fort Smith, Arkansas, on 27 March 1849, bound for the gold fields. In his diary he recorded how local residents had kindly placed three buckets of water by the side of the trail, and as the thirsty travelers reached them "they rushed to them & drank like maniacs." Jordan reports that one man, upon reaching the Gila River, even jumped right into the river and "laid down and opened his mouth & let the water run in."[6]

The Zuni Trail

This route, also known as the Middle Route Trail, or in railroad parlance later on as the Arizona Trail, headed west from Albuquerque to Zuni on the New Mexico–Arizona border. It then turned southwest toward the junction of the Gila River and the Salt River west of Phoenix. The latter part of this trail was especially difficult. Lieutenant Edward Griffin Beckwith was assigned to escort James Collier, the newly appointed customs collector for the port of San Francisco, toward his new post. On 17 September 1849 Beckwith confided to his journal that they "were often without a trail — no one knows our whereabouts but the mountain man with us thinks we are on or near the Salt River."[7] The mountain man was the famous beaver trapper John L. Hatcher, whose jargon is captured in Appendix 4.

The Gila River Trail

The Gila River Trail (see map on page 72) was unique. It consisted of an ill-defined network of roughly parallel trails and tracks, not a single well-beaten path connecting one destination to another.[8] Used over many years by Indians, Spaniards, Mexicans, and Americans alike, these trails generally followed the 649-mile-long Gila River. As noted earlier, this river rises on the western slope of the Black Range Mountains in western New Mexico and ends at Yuma, Arizona, where it joins the Colorado River.

The Gila River, including its chief tributary, the Salt River, was once one of the largest perennial streams in the West. In modern times water diversion for both agricultural and urban uses has reduced its flow considerably. During the nineteenth century, however, the Gila River was navigable by small craft all the way from near the Arizona–New Mexico border to its mouth. The width of the river varied from between 150 to 1,200 feet and it was between 2 and 40 feet deep. In 1849 the California-bound traveler John Hudgins built a barge out of abandoned wagon beds, loaded it with 5,500 pounds of freight, and piloted his unique box-shaped craft down the Gila to its junction with the Colorado. That same year, too, another Argonaut, Joseph R. Simmons, built a raft to go fishing on the Gila River but ended up using it to carry supplies for his mining company instead. Except for running into some sandbars, Simmons made the trip down the river to the Yuma Crossing without incident.[9]

The eastern part of the Gila River Trail consisted of a rugged mule trail which ran from near Truth or Consequences, New Mexico, to the villages of the Hila Akimel O'Odham (Gila River People), an Indian tribe living along the Gila near Phoenix. During the Mexican-American war, General Kearny ordered Captain Philip St. George Cooke to lead heavy wagons full of supplies along this mule trail. By the time Cooke and his Mormon Battalion had reached the Big Burro Mountains, however, it was clear that travel over this branch of the Gila Trail was too rough to be practical for wagons. For example, Burro Peak (8,035 feet high) lies on the western edge of the Continental Divide.

Cooke was thus forced to swing south and enter Arizona. Upon reaching the San Pedro River (just south of the present international border), the battalion made its way north along the river to a point near the site of Benson and then swung westward toward Tucson. After a short break there to rest and obtain supplies, the troops turned northwest to the Pima villages. From there, Cooke was able to retrace Kearny's well-beaten route to California.[10]

In the process he and his men had a near-fatal encounter with a herd of wild cattle. These were cattle that had been left to multiply unhindered and had run wild after local ranchers abandoned their properties in about 1830 because of Apache depredations. Wild cattle were unpredictable, hard to kill, and very dangerous. For example, Daniel Tyler, a Mormon volunteer, described how a lone bull that repeatedly charged two of the Mormon volunteers had been hit six times by well-aimed musket balls, any one of which would have been fatal, before it finally keeled over and died.[11] Not long thereafter, a group of bulls were so audacious as to charge Cooke's column of soldiers. Cooke wrote of it (phrasing and spelling his):

> One [bull] ran on a man [Private Amos Cox of Company D], caught him in the thigh, and threw him clear over his body lengthwise; then it charged on a team, ran his head under the first mule, tore out the entrails of the one beyond, and threw them both over. Another ran against a sergeant, who escaped with severe bruises, as the horns went each side of him. A third ran at a horse tied to a wagon, and, as it escaped, its great momentum forced the hind part of the wagon from the road. I saw one rush at some pack mules and gore one so that its entrails came out broken.

I saw an immense coalblack bull charge on Corporal [Lafayette N.] Frost of Company A. He stood his ground while the animal rushed on for one hundred yards. I was close by and believed the man in great danger of his life and spoke to him. He aimed his musket very deliberately and only fired when the beast was within ten paces; and it fell headlong, almost at his feet. [Tyler, the Mormon volunteer mentioned above, said that the bull was charging Cooke and that Frost stood his ground to protect his commanding officer. Frost was a very brave man.] One man, when charged on, threw himself flat on the ground, and the bull jumped over him and passed on. I have seen the heart of a bull with two balls through it, that ran on a man with those wounds, and two others through the lungs.[12]

After these and other adventures, Cooke and his men successfully completed their trek to San Diego.[13] The 1,900-mile route he helped pioneer to southern California would later become known as "Cooke's wagon road."

The western portions of the Gila River Trail extended from the villages of the Pima Indians, which were located in south-central Arizona, to the Yuma crossing of the Colorado River. The Gila River Trail is of interest to us because it was the scene of some remarkable incidents which merit discussion here.

One of the most entertaining contemporary accounts of this trail can be found in James O. Pattie's journal, published in 1831 as the *Personal Narrative of James O. Pattie*. This work describes Pattie's travels and adventures as an energetic young fur trader in New Mexico between 1824 and 1830. It is evident, however, that many of Pattie's accounts were written chiefly to exaggerate his own importance and heroism. One of the best signs of this is that he took great pains not to identify by name most of the men he wrote about in his book. He almost certainly realized that if they were located they would only laugh at many of his claims.

Nevertheless, some of his accounts do ring true. For example, when his party was trapping beaver along the Gila River, this is what happened (punctuation and phrasing are his own):

> We passed a cave at the foot of the Healay [Gila] at the foot of the cliffs. At its mouth I remarked, that the bushes were beaten down, as though some animal had been browsing upon them. I was aware, that a bear had entered the cave. We collected some pine knots, split them with our tomahawks, and kindled torches, with which I proposed to my companion, that we should enter the cave together, and shoot the bear. He gave me a decided refusal.... Finding it impossible to prevail on him to accompany me, I lashed my torch to a stick, and placed it parallel to the gun barrel, so as that I could see the sights on it, and entered the cave. I advanced cautiously onward about twenty yards, seeing nothing. On a sudden the bear reared himself erect within seven feet of me, and began to growl, and gnash his teeth. I leveled my gun and shot him between the eyes and began to retreat.

Whatever light it may throw upon my courage, I admit, that I was in such a hurry, as to stumble, and extinguish my light. The growling and struggling of the bear did not at all contribute to allay my apprehensions. On the contrary, I was in such haste to get out of the dark place, thinking the bear just at my heels, that I fell several times on the rocks, by which I cut my limbs, and lost my gun. When I reached the light, my companion declared, and I can believe it, that I was as pale as a corpse.

It was sometime, before I could summon sufficient courage to re-enter the cavern for my gun. But, having re-rekindled my light, and borrowed my companion's gun, I entered the cavern again, advanced and listened. All was silent, and I advanced still further, and found my gun, near where I had shot the bear. Here again I paused and listened. I then advanced a few strides, where to my great joy I found the animal dead.... My father [who was also part of the expedition] severely reprimanded me for venturing to attack such a dangerous animal in its den, when the failure to kill it outright by the first shot, would be sure to be followed by my death.[14]

In addition to their sizeable population of bears, the wild highlands of the Gila River would become the last stronghold of the Apache Indians. Even after the Apaches had been subdued and put into reservations, bands of warriors would break out and roam the Gila country of New Mexico, part of which is still a remote and potentially dangerous wilderness. Nineteenth century newspapers bristled with accounts of prospectors and settlers killed by the "red fiends of Hell."[15] The survivors were not slow to retaliate.

In 1837, for example, an American scalp hunter and outlaw from Kentucky named John James Johnson heard that the governor of Sonora, Mexico, would pay 100 pesos for the scalp of an Indian man, 50 pesos for that of a woman and 25 pesos for that of a child. Near today's Gila River settlement of Cliff, located in southwestern New Mexico close to the Arizona border, Johnson invited Apache leaders and their families to meet with him for trade talks and to receive valuable gifts, among which were flour, blankets, saddles, and whiskey. As the Indians happily examined their presents, Johnson touched off a hidden howitzer loaded with slugs, nails, bits of chain, and other shrapnel. About 20 Apaches, including women and children, died in the blast. Their Apache chief, Juan Jose Compra, was also killed in the massacre. He was replaced by the formidable chief Mangas Colorado. Despite Johnson's treacherous "victory," however, he was never able to collect his reward from the Mexican government.[16]

During the Mexican-American War, in 1846 Lieutenant William Hemsley Emory led a topographical unit to explore and chart the territory between Fort Leavenworth to California. In the process, relying on the advice of one of his muleteers — who had trapped beaver along the Gila — Emory produced the first reliable topographical map of the Gila River Trail. This map was to prove very useful in the boundary negotiations of the Treaty of Guadalupe Hidalgo which ended the war.

Emory was an excellent writer as well as an excellent cartographer. He described, vividly and accurately, the trail near the present day town of Solomon in eastern Arizona. There the Gila River's deep gullies had forced Emory's band away from the river and into the surrounding mountains. It took him and his men eight and a half hours to travel 16 miles and get back to the river again. Labeling this stretch of the trail as the "Devil's Turnpike," Emory described it:

> The whole way was a succession of steep ascents and descents, paved with sharp, angular fragments of basalt and trap [trap rock, a plutonic igneous rock which resembles piles of blocks which are sometimes reminiscent of stairs]. The metallic clink of spurs, and the rattling of mule shoes, the high black peaks, the deep dark ravines, and the unearthly looking cactus, which stuck out from the rocks like the ears of Mephistopheles [the devil], all favored the idea that we were treading on the verge of the regions below [hell]. Occasionally a mule gave up the ghost, and was left as a propitiatory tribute to the place. This day's journey cost us some twelve or fifteen mules.[17]

Emory also recounted how after the Battle of San Pasqual he had tried to comfort the wounded 55-year-old U.S. Army scout Don Antonio Robidoux when Robidoux was suffering from loss of blood and was chilling in the sub-freezing temperature. Emory was able to bring some hot coffee to him; Robidoux was most grateful and rewarded him with a cake, which Emory describes in these words: "[It was] made of brown flour, almost black with dirt, and which had, for greater security, been hidden in the clothes of [Riboudoux's] Mexican servant, a man who scorned ablutions. I ate more than half without inspection, when, on breaking a piece, the bodies of several of the most loathsome insects were exposed to view. My hunger, however, overcame my fastidiousness."[18]

With remarkable prescience, Emory realized that an easier part of this trail would be the best southern route for a transcontinental railroad.[19] Later, he would publish, between 1856 and 1859, a three-volume *Report on the United States and Mexican Boundary Survey*. This magisterial work was highlighted by a definitive map and by well-illustrated sections on the topography, geology, zoology, and botany of the area.[20]

In 1853 Richard Dallam, a cattle drover, passed by a site on the Gila River about 15 miles west of Gila Bend, Arizona (so named because near there the Gila River makes a 90 degree curve), known as Murder's Camp; Dallam explained the reason for this name.[21] In 1849 a kind-hearted man from Arkansas named Elijah Davis was en route to the California gold fields. He took pity on another traveler, George Hickey, who was down on his luck. Davis had offered to give Hickey food and shelter on the trip to California but soon the two had an argument. Harsh words were exchanged. Hickey pulled a knife and stabbed Davis, who died almost instantly.

The other gold seekers seized Hickey, empanelled an informal jury, found him guilty, and recommended a military-style execution. Twelve rifles were loaded — six with both gunpowder and a lead ball (bullet), the other six with gunpowder alone. Twelve men drew lots to see who would be on the firing squad and then picked up rifles at random so it would not be clear who had the loaded weapons. A grave was dug for Hickey near where Davis had been buried. Hickey was forced to stand or sit in the open grave. At the command "Ready, aim, fire!" he was hit in the chest by several balls and slumped into the grave. The grave was then filled in and the men dispersed.

The lengths to which men would go to get gold is well illustrated by the following account. In the 1860s two prospectors were killed by the Apaches near Turkey Creek, which is located in the Gila Wilderness not far from Silver City, New Mexico. Learning of this event, four off-duty soldiers from Fort Bayard decided to visit Turkey Creek to see if they could find any gold there. One of these soldiers was named Sidman. He was the only soldier to return to the fort. The other three soldiers had, he claimed, been killed in an Indian ambush. However, when an army burial party was sent to Turkey Creek to inter the bodies, no human remains could be found. Moreover, Sidman himself seemed to be quite vague and disoriented. He soon left New Mexico for Missouri.

Years later a hungry camper on Turkey Creek was digging a hole in the ground for his bean pot when he unearthed a skeleton.[22] He then found two other skeletons buried nearby. When local residents learned about this, they remembered that from time to time Sidman would return to Turkey Creek from Missouri. They also remembered that at the end of each visit to Turkey Creek he always had plenty of high-grade gold ore to sell. The residents could not help wondering whether Sidman's three colleagues had indeed been killed by the Apaches — or by Sidman himself, who later was making off with the gold ore. This mystery was never solved.[23]

The Apache Pass Trail

This route ran for some 200 miles west from Soldier's Farewell Hill (west of Deming, New Mexico) to Tucson, Arizona, threading its arid way through a narrow 5,110-foot defile (Apache Pass) between the Dos Cabezas Mountains and Chiricahua Mountains. This pass is located about 20 miles east of Willcox, Arizona. A nearby freshwater spring, known appropriately as Apache

Spring, was considered to be such a vital water resource that after the Battle of Apache Pass in 1862, the U.S. Army built Fort Bowie there in the later 1860s. This fort is now the Fort Bowie National Historic Site.

The Apache Pass Trail was basically a shortcut along the Southern Trail. The '49er David Durie Demarest, traveling on the Upper Emigrant Trail (discussed later), tells us that this shortcut was known to two guides accompanying Mexican general José María Elías. On the general's instructions, they showed it to the famous Texas Ranger John Coffee Hays, who with his men was leading Demarest's group toward California. A short digression about this famous Texas Ranger may be of interest here.

Today Hays is known to students of American firearms for his leadership role in "Hays' Big Fight." To understand the importance of this frontier incident, we must remember that the earliest Colt revolver to make its mark on the frontier was the single action, .36 caliber, five-shot Patterson model. (In a single action revolver, the hammer must be cocked manually before each shot.) Captain Samuel H. Walker of the Texas Rangers vividly described the Patterson revolver in action (spelling and punctuation as in the original): "In the summer of 1844 Col. J.C. Hays with 15 men [all armed with Colt Pattersons] fought about 80 Camanche Indians, boldly attacking them upon their own ground, killing & wounding about half their number. Up to this time these daring Indians had always supposed themselves to be superior to us, man to man, on horse.... The result of this engagement was such as to intimidate them and enable us to treat [negotiate] with them."[24]

When we meet him on the Apache Trail in 1849, Hays had just resigned from the Texas Rangers and was on his way to take up his new job as Indian subagent on the Gila River. However, he felt himself destined for much better things, so instead of languishing on the Gila River he boldly pressed on to California. There he became sheriff of San Francisco and later founded the nearby city of Oakland.[25]

Apache Pass itself was sometimes used by the Indians for ambushes; indeed, Mexicans knew it as El Puerto del Dado (literally "The Gate of the Die," or more colloquially "The Pass of Fate") because after entering it a traveler was never sure of getting out alive. Usually, however, it was a peaceful place. In 1849, for example, Robert Eccleston, a gold seeker bound for California, called the pass "a romantic one" and described it as follows (spelling as in the original): "We followed the bed of a dry arroya [arroyo] where there was scarcely room for the wagon wheels, let alone room for the driver. This road was overshadowed by handsome trees, among which I witnessed the pecan, the oak, the willow, &c."[26]

Located near Apache Pass, Fort Bowie National Historic Site was established in 1972 to commemorate the conflict between the Chiricahua Apaches and the U.S. Army and to preserve the ruins of Fort Bowie. The most memorable military engagement there is known as the Bascom Affair.[27] It began on 27 January 1861, when Apaches raided the ranch of John Ward, ran off 20 head of his cattle, and kidnapped Mickey Free, the 12-year-old son of Ward's Mexican mistress. Ward, described by his contemporaries as a drunk and "in all respects, a worthless character," believed — erroneously, as it turned out — that Chief Cochise, one of the most famous Apache leaders, and his Chiricahua warriors were responsible for this attack. Ward therefore demanded that the Army punish Cochise and recover the cattle stolen from his ranch. Observers felt that Ward was much more worried about his livestock than about young Mickey.

The Army sent an inexperienced young officer, Lieutenant George N. Bascom, and 54 soldiers to try to capture Cochise. Bascom had graduated from West Point only two years before and had served in Indian Territory for less than four months. He invited Cochise, who was accompanied by six other warriors from his band and by his wife and children, into his camp. Cochise thought this was only a social visit but Bascom suddenly made it clear that he would hold all the Indians hostage until Ward's cattle and the boy were returned.

Cochise himself managed to escape immediately — by using his knife to slice his way out of the Army tent in which he was being held. While escaping, he was lightly wounded by a gunshot in the leg but still managed to get away. Bascom continued to hold as hostages the six warriors and Cochise's wife and children. In retaliation, Cochise then captured and held hostage a stagecoach driver named Wallace, plus three other Americans seized during an Indian attack on a wagon train. Bascom refused to negotiate the exchange of any hostages, so Cochise had the four hostages tortured and killed. Enraged, Bascom released Cochise's wife and children but, at the urging of his outraged soldiers, he hung the six captured warriors from the limbs of the four oak trees under which the Americans had been murdered.

Cochise, now further infuriated, retaliated by going on the war path with Chief Mangas Coloradas, the father of Cochise's wife. These two leaders launched a long series of attacks, during which the Apaches began to gain the upper hand. Their success prompted the Army to send an expedition under Brigadier General James H. Carleton to subdue them.

On 15 and 16 July 1862 the two sides came to grips at Apache Pass: a battle erupted between 500 warriors under Cochise and Mangas Coloradas on the one hand and a force of California volunteers under Carleton on the other. The Indians stood their ground manfully until the Army called in artillery fire on them. This was the first time the Apaches had ever experienced such a form of warfare. The son of a chief who had fought there said later, "After they turned cannon loose on us at Apache Pass, my people were certain that they were doomed."[28] Nevertheless, the Apaches fought on for several more hours before retreating. This clash resulted in the establishment of Fort Bowie to defend Apache Pass and Apache Spring. A temporary fort was built in 1862 and was replaced by a more substantial structure in 1868.

In January 1863 General Joseph Rodman West, under orders from Carleton, captured Mangas Coloradas by tricking him into a peace conference under a flag of truce. The Americans took Mangas Coloradas prisoner and then executed him. Cochise, further inflamed, led further Apache attacks on American and Mexican settlements throughout the 1860s. After many skirmishes, the army, under General George Crook, using Apache scouts and informants, finally captured Cochise in 1871 and forced him to surrender.

That year the Army ordered the Chiricahua to settle in the Tularosa Reservation in New Mexico but in 1872 Cochise escaped again and renewed his attacks. After a treaty was hammered out by General Oliver O. Howards (with the help of Tom Jeffords, an American who had become a blood brother to Cochise), Cochise retired to a reservation in Arizona, where he died of natural causes in 1874. His death, however, did not end skirmishes in the region. For example, in January 1877 Captain C.B. McLellan of the 6th Cavalry sent this report from Camp Bowie to Colonel J.F. Bennett in Silver City, New Mexico:

> Lieut. [John L.] Rucker returned to this post a few days since after a most successful scout. He struck the Indians about forty miles south of Ralston, killed ten, wounded quite a number, captured one boy, forty-five head of stock, a large amount of camp equipage, ten rifles, two six shooters, in fact everything the party had. His victory was complete; those who made their escape are destitute, as they left everything in their flight. The stock captured is Mexican, and evidently from Sonora; ... all the plunder captured was Mexican, including a large number of blankets of Mexican manufacture, which they had evidently taken from some Mexican train or store. [A subsequent report in the *Arizona Citizen*, a local newspaper, added that "three thousand dollars in Mexican silver coin was among the booty."][29]

The high point of Fort Bowie's existence came in 1886, when army campaigns culminated in the surrender there of Geronimo. This accomplished war-chief and later tribal chief lived, traveled, and fought in what is known as the Southern Four Corners area, which includes southeastern Arizona, southwestern New Mexico, northwestern Chihuahua, and northeastern Sonora. In his own time, Geronimo was a very well known and much feared Apache leader, famous for his daring exploits and his numerous escapes from capture between 1858 and 1886.

Legend has it that one such escape took place in the Robledo Mountains of southwestern New Mexico. When pursued by U.S. soldiers, Geronimo and his followers retreated into a cave, which is still known as Geronimo's Cave. The soldiers remained outside and patiently waited for him to surrender, but he never came out. Later they learned that he had escaped by a secret passageway.

The Mexicans nicknamed him "Geronimo" because during one battle he repeatedly attacked Mexican soldiers when armed only with his knife, ignoring the deadly rain of bullets hissing around him. His remarkable courage prompted the embattled Mexicans to pray for help from Saint Jerome by calling out in Spanish: "San Jeronimo!" This legend had such a long life that, during World War II, American paratroopers would sometimes shout "Geronimo!" as they parachuted from their planes.

Geronimo finally gave up in 1886 at Skeleton Canyon, Arizona, a natural passageway from Mexico to Arizona, which is located in the Peloncillo Mountains which straddle the Arizona-New Mexico border. He accepted the terms of surrender formally put forward to him by Brigadier General Nelson A. Miles. A marker has now been erected south of Rodeo, New Mexico, and northeast of Apache, Arizona, which commemorates this event. A Website covering the history of southern New Mexico has this to say:

> A short distance south of the marker is a road which leads east and then south/southeast to the actual surrender site [located on what is now private land]. This is four wheel drive vehicle country, and heavy rains can render the road virtually impassible in spots. Once at the site, the canyon road leads east and ends about two miles inside New Mexico. From there, travel is by foot following either the canyon floor (the creek bed) or a higher narrow trail. For one who wishes to understand the elusiveness of the Apaches and the difficulties in the Army's attempts to capture them, a day spent hiking Skeleton Canyon will be an invaluable lesson.[30]

Geronimo's surrender marked the end of the Apache Wars in the Southwest. When he finally gave up, his own band of followers consisted of only 16 warriors, 12 women, and 6 children. Geronimo and over 300 of his fellow Chiricahuas were later sent to Fort Marion, Florida. Many of them were then transferred to the Mt. Vernon barracks in Alabama; about one quarter of them would die there from tuberculosis and other diseases. Ultimately, the Chiricahuas were relocated to Fort Sill, Oklahoma. In 1913, about 200 of the surviving Chiricahuas elected to resettle in New Mexico on the Mescalero Reservation.

Geronimo himself was the ultimate survivor. He successfully conducted a hit-and-run guerrilla warfare campaign that for many years frustrated the best efforts of the Mexican and American forces sent against him. His knowledge of trails and travels in southern New Mexico, southern Arizona, and northern Mexico must have been encyclopedic. In his old age, Geronimo had become such a national celebrity that he even rode in President Theodore Roosevelt's inaugural parade in 1905.

That same year he agreed to tell his story to S.M. Barrett, superintendent of education in Lawton, Oklahoma. Translated into English, this autobiography was presented in the traditional style of an Apache warrior reciting part of his history. Excerpts from it can be found in appendix six. Geronimo finally died of pneumonia at Fort Sill, Oklahoma, in 1909, after falling from his horse and lying in a cold ditch all night. Today the Geronimo Trail National Scenic Byway in southwestern New Mexico preserves his memory.

Fort Bowie itself was finally abandoned in 1894. Declared a National Historic Landmark in 1960, its assorted ruins are now carefully preserved (it was also the site of a Butterfield stagecoach station) and are redolent of Southwestern history. The Fort Bowie site is located on the unpaved Apache Pass Road, which can be accessed from Interstate 10 near Bowie, Arizona.

The Upper and Lower Emigrant Trails to El Paso

These two trails traversed West Texas. The Upper Emigrant Trail, trending slightly towards the northwest, ran some 600 miles from Fredericksburg, a German settlement of about 300 people, to Benjamin Franklin Coons' ranch, which by 1858 would become the city of El Paso. The Lower Emigrant Trail, also trending northwest, was the link between San Antonio and El Paso del Norte; the latter would later be renamed Juarez.

We have already encountered one '49er on the Upper Emigrant Road — David Durie Demarest — whose account of travel over this route is clear and useful. Another articulate '49er was L.N. Weed, who recorded that Mexican women very much valued light-colored skin — to such an extent that the Mexican proprietress of a store in a small West Texas town even suggested that Weed marry her daughter. Weed wrote: "but as I had not intended to commit matrimony I declined."[31]

Travel on the Lower Emigrant Trail (also called the Military Road) was exceptionally difficult at first. The '49er Thomas B. Eastland traveled with John Coffee Hay, whom we have already met, while Hay and army engineers were surveying and working on this route. Eastland complained to his diary on 11 September 1849 (italics in original): "*Ninety-seven days*, of irksome delays and travel ... distance according to my own estimates, 693 miles, over a trackless, and hitherto unexplored wilderness, following in the wake of an Army, whose slow movements were made slower still by the engineers and Road Makers.... A shameful route...."[32] Ten years later, however, this trail was in much better shape and travel was much easier. In 1859, Captain Randolph B. Marcy gave an excellent description of it in his invaluable guidebook, *The Prairie Traveler*.

CHAPTER XIII

Historic Trails, Trade, and Travels Today

This chapter presents opportunities for interested readers to experience for themselves some of the historic trails, trade, and travels as their remnants are preserved today. A final section of this chapter offers some thoughts on their enduring significance.

Pecos, New Mexico

The major site here is the Pecos National Historical Park, which consists of an excellent Visitor Center and several interesting noncontiguous units. The main unit holds the ruins of Pecos Pueblo itself and the remains of the mission there, which was built in the early 1600s and was known as Mission Nuestra Señora de los Ángeles de Porciúncula de los Pecos. Other units of this park protect later historical artifacts, e.g., the site of the American Civil War battle in 1862 near Pigeon's Ranch (a stage coach station on the Santa Fe Trail) and Glorieta Pass; a stretch of clearly visible wagon ruts along the Santa Fe Trail; the Forked Lightning Ranch (formerly known as Kozlowski's Stage Station), once owned by Tex Austin, the "Daddy of Rodeo," and later by the actress Greer Garson. Kozlowski's Stage Station, warmly praised by travelers on the Santa Fe Trail for its excellent food, is now a National Historic Landmark.

On the environmental front, the Pecos Wilderness embraces 223,667 acres of unspoiled land. This inspiring wilderness, which lies at the southern end of the Sangre de Cristo Mountains, extends through two ranger districts in the Santa Fe National Forest and the Carson National Forest. Its terrain varies from the open meadows of the Pecos River Valley to the steep slopes of the Sangre de Cristo Mountains. Wildlife includes deer, mountain lions, elk, bighorn sheep, black bears, and smaller game. Outdoor activities, e.g., hiking, horseback riding, camping, fishing, and hunting, are the best and indeed probably the only ways for travelers to experience the Pecos Wilderness in any depth: motorized vehicles are not allowed within its boundaries.

Prehistoric Indian Trails and Trade

Chaco Culture National Historical Park is located in a relatively inaccessible canyon cut by the Chaco Wash in northwestern New Mexico. The nearest city is Farmington, New Mexico. Containing the most impressive collection of ancient ruins north of Mexico, this park was designated a UNESCO World Heritage Site in 1987 and is well worth visiting. One should not venture there, however, without a suitable, well-maintained, and well-equipped vehicle. Up-to-the-minute local information is also essential. Since many of the roads in the park are only rough, rutted dirt roads that are not carefully maintained, they can quickly become impassable in bad weather. Breaking down or getting bogged down on one of them would not be a pleasant experience.

Spanish Exploration, Settlement, and Inspection

Perhaps the most creative and evocative site under this rubric is the Coronado National Memorial, which is located in the southeastern corner of Arizona very close to the Mexican border. It commemorates and interprets Coronado's expedition and the resulting massive cultural impact of sixteenth-century Spanish colonial exploration in the Americas. The memorial does not safeguard any tangible artifacts surviving from the expedition itself but instead serves a much broader purpose. As the National Park Service explains, it encourages visitors "to reflect upon the impact the Coronado Entrada had in shaping the history, culture, and environment of the southwestern United States and its lasting ties to Mexico and Spain. The Memorial has two sister parks in Mexico. The location was chosen for the panoramic views of the U.S.-Mexico border and the San Pedro River Valley, the route believed to have been taken by Coronado. It was hoped that this proximity to the border would strengthen bi-national amity and the bonds, both geographical and cultural, which continue to link the two countries."[1]

The National Park Service warns visitors that drug smuggling and/or illegal entry is common in this region due to the proximity of the international border. It recommends that visitors be aware of their surroundings at all times and that they not travel alone in remote areas. It makes these additional suggestions:

- Visitors should remember that cell phone service is usually out of range within the boundaries of the memorial.
- They should not pick up hitchhikers.
- They should keep valuables, including spare change, out of sight; should lock their vehicle; should not travel on unofficial "trails"; and should avoid hiking in areas of major border activity.
- They should not make contact with any people who are in distress, even if they ask for food, water, or other assistance. Instead, visitors should report the location of such distressed people to the memorial's staff or to the Border Patrol. By the same token, visitors should not contact anyone who is behaving in a suspicious manner but should alert these authorities instead.[2]

El Camino Real de Tierra Adentro

This trail is the earliest Euro-American trade route in the United States. Tying Spain's colonial capital (Mexico City) to its northernmost frontier posts in distant New Mexico, it was blazed atop an ancient network of Indian footpaths.

Added by Congress to the National Trails System in October 2000, the U.S. portion of El Camino Real de Tierra Adentro National Historic Trail extends 404 miles from El Paso, Texas, to Ohkay Owingeh Pueblo, New Mexico, which is located about 25 miles north of Santa Fe. This section of the trail is now jointly managed by the Bureau of Land Management and the National Park Service.

An excellent El Camino Real International Heritage Center has been established about 30 miles south of Socorro, New Mexico. It is off the beaten path of Highway 25 but is still easily accessible by car. A few hours spent there will give the visitor a good sense of the desolation and, at the same time, the arid beauty of this remote area.

The Old Spanish Trail

In 2002 this 2,700-mile trail was officially recognized by the Bureau of Land Management and the National Park Service as the Old Spanish National Historic Trail. It winds its way through six states: Arizona, California, Colorado, Nevada, New Mexico, and Utah. Due to its recent authorization, this historic trail does not yet have many formally designated visitor facilities or services. There are, however, museums, historic sites, and historic markers sprinkled along it from Santa Fe to Los Angeles.

The Santa Fe Trail

The arrival of the Iron Horse in New Mexico in 1880 marked the end of commercial traffic along the Santa Fe Trail but the saga of this remarkable trail is far from over. In 1987 Congress established the Santa Fe National Historic Trail, which is administered by the National Park Service in cooperation with other agencies, interested groups, and private landowners. Moreover, a highway route that roughly follows the trail's path through Colorado and northern New Mexico has been designated the Santa Fe Trail National Scenic Byway. Americans and citizens of other countries will thus be able to follow the trail for many generations to come.

Counting both its routes, the Santa Fe National Historic Trail stretches for a total of 1,200 miles between western Missouri and Santa Fe. In the process, it visits five states: Missouri, Kansas, Oklahoma, Colorado, and New Mexico. The National Park Service has this useful advice for visitors: "When traveling along the Santa Fe National Historic Trail, please ask permission before going on private land. Please respect your hosts' hospitality when you visit their sites. Leave everything as you find it. Obey signs, use designated parking areas, and limit your stay to the time necessary to appreciate the site. Don't use metal-detectors, dig at sites, collect artifacts, or remove anything. Some sites contain burials; please respect these sacred places."[3]

Campaigns of the Mexican-American War

This war was fought with varying degrees of intensity in Texas; New Mexico; California; northern, central, and eastern Mexico; and Mexico City. Only six of the roughly 47 battles of the war took place in New Mexico itself. These "battles" (the word is used very loosely here) were[4]:

- Battle of Santa Fe (also known as the Battle of Cañoncito): near Santa Fe, 8–14 August 1846. No shots were fired because Governor Manuel Armijo and his forces retreated before General Stephen Watts Kearny's troops could attack them. Kearny's men occupied Santa Fe on 18 August 1846.

- Battle of El Brazito (also known as the Battle of Temascalitos): 9 miles from Las Cruces, 25 December 1846. Colonel Doniphan's forces held their fire until the Mexican army was only 50 yards away. At such close range the Americans' volleys were devastating: under this rain of lead, the Mexicans broke and ran.

- Battle of Cañada: Taos, 24 January 1847. U.S. commander Sterling Price began to put down the Taos Revolt, an uprising of local Indians and Mexican ranchers.
- Battle of Mora: about 45 miles southeast of Taos, 24 January–1 February 1847. After a failed attack by U.S. forces on 24 January, another American expedition, this time armed with cannons, razed the village of Mora on 1 February 1847.
- Battle of Embudo Pass: about 30 miles southwest of Taos, 29 January 1847. American forces defeated the Taos insurgents before the insurgents' last stand at the Siege of Pueblo de Taos.
- Siege of Pueblo de Taos: Taos, 3–4 February 1847. The insurgent Indians and ranchers finally surrendered to U.S. forces, thus ending the Taos Revolt.

As will immediately be evident, none of these clashes ranks as one of the great battles of world history. The net result is that there are very few artifacts of the war to be found in Santa Fe itself or elsewhere in New Mexico today.

The Butterfield Overland Mail Route

At the peak of his success, Butterfield could marshal 250 Concord stagecoaches; 1,800 head of livestock, i.e., horses and mules; and over 139 stagecoach stations along a route totaling 2,812 miles — from St. Louis to San Francisco. No traces of this route appear to remain in New Mexico today.

Those vestiges that do still exist are all located in other states. To commemorate the 100th anniversary of the Butterfield Overland Mail, a stainless steel pyramid was erected in 1958 on the summit of Guadalupe Peak in Guadalupe Mountains National Park in West Texas. Two stagecoach stations in San Diego County, California (the Oak Grove Butterfield Stage Station and the Warner's Ranch station) were declared to be National Historic Landmarks in 1961.

Another stagecoach stopping point is Elkhorn Tavern, now part of the Pea Ridge National Military Park in Arkansas. One of the few sections of the trail that still exists is the Old Wire Road in Arkansas. The remains of a stagecoach stop can be seen near Franklin, Texas.[5]

The Civil War in New Mexico

As a main route to California, the New Mexico Territory was strategically important to the Union and to the Confederacy alike. Confederate troops from Texas briefly occupied southern New Mexico. The first major battle took place in February of 1862 at Valverde, near Fort Craig (100 miles south of Albuquerque). It was a Confederate victory.

In March 1862, as noted earlier, at the Battle of Glorieta Pass, Union troops burned the Confederate supply wagons. This was the decisive battle of the New Mexico Campaign during the Civil War and is known as the "Gettysburg of the West." The Union victory forced the Southerners to begin withdrawing from New Mexico, leaving it firmly in Union hands through the rest of the war. A visit to Pecos (see above) offers the best opportunity to learn more about the Battle of Glorieta Pass.

The Long Walk of the Navajos

In 1968, Fort Sumner — the U.S. Army post in southeastern New Mexico charged with the internment of Navajos and Mescalero Apaches from 1863 to 1868 at the nearby Indian reservation of Bosque Redondo — was reborn as a New Mexico state monument. In 2005, a modern museum designed by a Navajo architect was opened on this site and named the Bosque Redondo Memorial.

This small museum may not, by itself, be worth the long drive to Fort Sumner. If so, another possibility is for the visitor to learn something about the Navajos in New Mexico today. The best first step here is to consult the website of the New Mexico Tourism Department (www.newmexico.org). It will list forthcoming public events in Indian life — not only for the Navajos but also for many of the other tribes living in the state.

The Goodnight-Loving Trail

The trail itself no longer exists but its memories can be evoked by visiting Roswell, New Mexico. This town took root in the 1860s, when the pioneer cattle drovers Charles Goodnight and Oliver Loving camped near the mouth of the Hondo River during their drives up the trail. Its first structures included an adobe hotel, a house, and cattle pens. The cattlemen John Chisum and Joseph Lea used it as their ranch headquarters in the 1870s. Roswell now offers a tour of its historic district and a good collection at its museum and art center.[6]

The era of long and large cattle drives ended in the 1890s, when the spread of railroads and meatpacking plants and the end of the open range made them obsolete. Today, cattle drives are only small-scale affairs, used to round up cattle within a given ranch and move them from one section to another or to a nearby ranch. Horses are still used where rough terrain or mountains require it, but otherwise cattle are often rounded up by the use of all-terrain vehicles. When cattle are to be moved long distances, they always go by truck.

Steel Trails for the Iron Horse

In the late 1880s, Raton Pass, which lies about 100 miles northeast of Santa Fe, was used by the Atchison, Topeka and Santa Fe (AT&SF) as the railroad's primary route through the Sangre de Cristo Mountains. In the twentieth century it became the route of Interstate 25 between Denver and Albuquerque. Raton Pass was declared a National Historic Landmark in 1960. There is not a great deal to see here, so railroad enthusiasts may wish to visit the Railroad Museum in Las Cruces.

The first AT&SF train arrived in Las Cruces in 1881. Passenger service continued there until 1968; freight service ended twenty years later. The "live" tracks (tracks still in use) located to the west of the depot are owned and operated by the Burlington Northern Santa Fe Railroad Company. The museum interprets the impact of the railroad on the area. Guided tours, field trips and public programs are held throughout the year.

The Southern Trails

As mentioned earlier, a number of lesser-known and now-obscure trails of the Southwest can be loosely lumped together as the southern trails. One of the most interesting of these is the ill-defined network of tracks roughly paralleling the Gila River in southwestern New Mexico.

A good example here is the Gila Lower Box Canyon, located about 20 miles north of Lordsburg, New Mexico. The Bureau of Land Management tells us that this is "a true oasis in the desert." Since 1990, livestock has been prohibited from grazing there; as a result, a lush thicket of cottonwood, willows, and other riparian vegetation has grown up. Today the canyon offers opportunities for bird-watching, canoeing, rafting (during the spring runoff of melting snow), hunting, and year-round hiking, fishing and camping.[7]

A New Mexico County Road leads to Nichol's Canyon, which is on the river itself. Two other access roads stop at the canyon rim; from there it is necessary to follow fishing trails down to the Gila. Off-road vehicle use is prohibited. Because this can be a tough and remote area, travelers should seek local advice before exploring the Gila Lower Box Canyon on foot.

Enduring Significance

In summarizing this book as a whole, we believe that four points are worth remembering:

1. Historic trails, trade, and travels opened up a vast landscape totally unknown to foreigners—that is, to the Spanish, Mexicans, Americans, and others—though of course it was entirely familiar to the Indians themselves. Foreigners, for their part, introduced New Mexico and the rest of the Southwest to the radically different concepts embedded in Western culture—in its politics, economics, military affairs, religion, and social customs. Trails, trade, and travels thus became the pathways of profound and permanent cultural change.

2. The large number of "I-was-there" accounts of historic trails, trade, and travels used in this book are central to our understanding of how contemporary men and women reacted to and understood—or failed to understand—the times they lived in. Their own words give us invaluable insights into their lives and times.

3. As promised in the preface, we have experimented in this book with "literary pointillism." (Pointillism is an artistic technique in which a large number of tiny dots of color are combined to form a single coherent picture.) Our carefully selected dots of historical fact about trails, trade, and travels have, we hope, combined to produce a vibrant portrait of the region.

4. In the end, such dots can have an impact greater than the sum of their parts. As Reid Miller, the Visitor Information Specialist at the Bureau of Land Management's National Historic Trails Interpretative Center in Casper, Wyoming, puts it:

> Trails can take us not only to our destination, but back as well, along a course to our place of departure. For that reason trails are worthy of our understanding and preservation as both physical features on the land, and references in our universal search for a sense of identity as individuals and as cultures.[8]

Appendices

APPENDIX 1: The Oñate Expedition:
Excerpts from *Historia de la Nueva México*
by Gaspar Pérez de Villagrá

In 1598 the Spanish sent an expedition north from Mexico City to colonize New Mexico. This *entrada* was led by Don Juan de Oñate, who would later be recalled to the capital in disgrace for having alienated the local Indians by his cruelty and for wasting government money in his chimerical pursuits of gold and silver.

These excerpts, which have been lightly edited, are taken from a translation into English prose of the epic 34-canto poem written in 1610 by Gaspar Pérez de Villagrá, the official historian of the Oñate expedition, and addressed to King Philip of Spain. In it, as noted earlier, Gaspar Pérez de Villagrá damns Oñate's leadership by revealing the hardships and brutality the expedition experienced in New Mexico.[1]

From Canto XIV:

How the River del Norte [Rio Grande] *was discovered. Of the hardships we endured, and of the other events. How Oñate took possession of the newly discovered land.*

We advanced, and for fifty days we marched, enduring hardships patiently, trusting in God to bring us with safety to the river's shore. At one time it rained unceasingly for seven days. We journeyed on and on until it seemed that we would never find our way out of these unpeopled regions, traversing vast and solitary plains where the foot of Christian had never trod before. Our provisions gave out, and we were forced to subsist on such edible weeds and roots as we found. But we went forward, sometimes through dense thickets which tore our clothes and left us ragged; at other times over rough stony passes where it was almost necessary to drag our tired mounts. Our shoes were worn out, and we suffered terribly from the burning sands, for our horses were scarcely able to drag their tired bodies along and pack our baggage, let alone carry us....

After journeying ... for four days without water, on the morning of the fifth we joyfully viewed in the distance the long sought waters of the Río del Norte. The gaunt horses approached the rolling stream and plunged headlong into it. Two of them drank so much that they burst their sides and died.... Our men, consumed by their burning thirst, their tongues swollen and their throats parched, threw themselves into the water and drank as though the entire river did not carry enough to quench their terrible thirst. Then satisfied, they threw themselves upon the cool sands, like foul wretches stretched upon some tavern floor in a drunken orgy, deformed and swollen and more like toads than men....

From Canto XXXIV:

[After the Spaniards captured the Acoma pueblo, the two Indians, named Tempal and Cotumbo, who had been ringleaders of the rebellious tribesmen, refused to surrender. They asked the Spaniards to give them "two sharp daggers" so they could commit suicide. Oñate refused to do so and instead gave them two ropes, telling them "to hang themselves if they chose to die at their own hands." Gaspar Pérez de Villagrá ends his account as follows]:

The two savages took the ropes and stood in silence for a while. Then they made a noose each and placing them about their necks, came slowly forth. Wending their way to a nearby tree, they climbed to its highest branches. There they knotted the rope to the tree and paused a while. Then one of them spoke:

> Take note, warriors [Spaniards], that here hanging from these branches you will have the miserable spoils of victory which you so desire.... Since such is our fate, gladly do we die, closing the door on this miserable life.... You are secure from harm; for no one ever returned from this journey on which we are about to embark. But, mark well, if it be possible for us to return, a terrible vengeance will be ours!

So saying foaming with rage, they dropped from the branches and there they hung, strangled, their features swollen, their eyes bulging out, their tongues hanging from their mouths. There, on the Golgotha of their choice, they surrendered their immortal souls.

And now, since they are gone, my story is also done.

O worthy king, if it should please your majesty that I should conclude this tale at a future date, I pray you to be patient. [A second part of the *Historia* was never written.] I have served you faithfully with the sword; the pen is a new and strange implement to wield.

APPENDIX 2: "$100,000 Worth of New Goods!" Arrive in Santa Fe

This advertisement appeared in a Santa Fe newspaper, the *Republican*, on July 6, 1848. It was paid for by the trader B.F. Coons, who hired someone to ride into Santa Fe before he arrived and to insert this ad in the local paper.[1] Lightly edited, it reads as follows (the spelling follows the original):

> I would inform the inhabitants of Santa Fe and the surrounding country, that I will arrive in Santa Fe within a few days, with the largest and best assortment of new and fashionable goods ever brought to this market, as I have the advantage of all other merchants in laying in my stock of goods. I am fully confident that I can sell lower than any person bringing out goods this season. My stock consists of the following articles [most of these are different kinds of cloth]:

150 bales Manto	75 Blue do
200 bales Leanso	75 Black do
100 bales Moun.	800 Ps. Pt. Stuffs
75 bales Contenia Blanco	600 Blue Satinett
25 bales Bed Ticking	200 Black do
100 bales Fancy Prints	150 Casimere do
100 Flannel do ["do" stands for "ditto"]	200 Prints do
29 White do	100 Black & Other Colors
200 Ps. Black Muslin	200 Barred Muslin do
200 Red, Green do	100 Boxes Ribbon
100 Black Velvet Cotton do	100 Black Cloth do
25 Silk do	50 Blue do
600 White Cambrick	100 Red Cloth do

TOGETHER WITH

A proportionate lot of Cotton Hose, Silk Hdkfs., Blk. Cravats, Cotton & woolen socks, Cotton woolen and silk shawls, Cintos laces, Red flannel shirts, Linen and Cotton thread, Blankets, Silk Hose, Candle wicking, Elastic suspenders, Jeans vesting, Lawns, Gingham, Muslins and in fact every thing necessary for this or any other trade.

In connection with the above, I have the best, the largest and the most superior lot of

GROCERIES

Ever imported to this country, consisting of Rum, Gin, Peach and Apple Brandy, Irish Whiskey, Port, Madeira, Malaga, and Champaign Wines, Lemon Syrrup, white and brown Sugar, Raisins, Candles, Candies, Pepper, Spice, smoking and chewing Tobacco, Fine Cigars, Soap, Cinamon, Mackerel, Oysters and Sardines, American and Spanish Playing Cards, Indigo, Salaratus, Pipes, bar Lead, Powder, and many other articles too numerous to mention, with a large lot of

HARDWARE & QUEENSWARE

Of all kinds, Axes, Hose, Spades, Nails, brass and iron Tacks, Butts and Screws, cotton Cords, Coffee mills, Locks of all kinds, Saws, pen and pocket knives, also butcher and table Knives, Dirks [daggers], Pistols, Guns [shotguns], Rifles, Rules, Files, Chisels, Gimblets [gimlets, i.e., small tools for boring holes] Augers, Hatchets, Hammers, Rules, Manes [possibly devices used to trim horses' manes], and everything else in this line. Also a large lot of

BOOTS AND SHOES, AND READY MADE CLOTHING

Toys and Fancy Goods, Drugs, Paints, Oil, etc., Tin ware, Hats and Caps, Military cloths and Trimmings and all kinds of Stationary, etc. etc.

I have taken the greatest pains possible in assorting the above stock of goods into different lots amounting to from 8 to 10 thousand dollars so to be able to sell to my old customers at whole sale. A fine and well assorted stock of goods, and at such prices as will suit the times. I would inform my old customers that I will sell as heretofore, on time if necessary.

I merely ask my own friends from the Rio Abajo [the lower Rio Grande, e.g., Albuquerque] and Rio Arriba [the upper Rio Grande, e.g., Santa Fe] that I am coming and want them to await my arrival before they purchase, for I do say I will not be undersold by anyone.

B.F. COONS

APPENDIX 3: "From Fort Smith, Arkansas, to Santa Fe and Albuquerque, New Mexico"

This itinerary is taken from a list of eight detailed itineraries compiled by Colonel Randolph B. Marcy in his excellent guidebook, *The Prairie Traveler*, which was published in 1859. Introducing this list, Marcy promises the traveler that he will accurately describe "the distances between camping-places, the character of the roads, and the facilities for obtaining wood, water, and grass on the principal routes between the Mississippi River and the Pacific Ocean."

This is the most careful and thorough account of the Fort Smith–Santa Fe–Albuquerque trail ever to appear in print. For this reason, it is worth reproducing here, verbatim, in its entirety. Marcy gives distances in miles and in fractions of a mile. His itineraries are not paginated in Marcy's book but follow page 252 of his text.

From Fort Smith, Arkansas, to Santa Fe and Albuquerque, New Mexico. By Captain R.B. Marcy, U.S.A.

Miles

Fort Smith to

15. Strickland's Farm [i.e., it is 15 miles from Fort Smith to Strickland's Farm].—The road crosses the Poteau River at Fort Smith, where there is a ferry; it then follows the Poteau bottom for ten miles. This part of the road is very muddy after heavy rains. At 14 miles it passes the Choctaw Agency, where there are several stores. There is the greatest abundance of wood, water, and grass for all camps for the first 200 miles. Where any of these are wanting it will be specially mentioned. The road passes through the Choctaw settlements for about

150 miles, and corn and supplies can be purchased from these Indians at reasonable rates.

11. Camp Creek.—Road crosses a prairie of three miles in length, then enters a heavy forest. The camp is on a small branch, with grass plenty in a small prairie about 400 yards to the left of the road.

12. Coon Creek.—Road passes through the timber, and is muddy in a rainy season.

12. Sans Bois Creek.—Prairie near; some Choctaw houses at the crossing.

14. Bend of Sans Bois Creek.—Indian farm.

15. South Fork of Canadian, or "Gain's Creek."—Road traverses a very rough and hilly region. There is a ford and a ferry upon the creek. Indian farm on the west bank.

12. First ford of Coal Creek.—Road crosses over a rolling prairie, and at four miles the Fort Washita road turns to the left.

[No mileage given for this entry.] Second ford of Coal Creek.—Indian farm.

4. Little Cedar Mountain.—Very rough, mountainous road.

6. Stony Point.—Very rough, mountainous road.

5. Shawnee Village.—Several Indian houses.

14. Shawnee Town.—Road passes several small prairies. Indian settlement; store on opposite bank of Canadian River, near the camp.

21. Delaware Mountain.—Road passes over a very beautiful country, with small steams of good water frequent, and good camps. It crosses small prairies and groves of timber.

5. Boggy River.—Road passes through a country similar to that mentioned above.

3. Clear Creek.—Road turns to the right near a prominent round mound. Beautiful country, diversified with prairies and timber lands.

7. Branch of Topofki Creek.—Beautiful country and fine roads.

9½. Cane Creek.—Excellent camp.

5. Small Branch.—Road passes about two miles from the old "Camp Arbuckle," built by Captain Marcy in 1853, since occupied by Black Beaver and several Delaware families.

11½. Mustang Creek.—Road runs on the dividing ridge between the waters of the Washita and Canadian, on a high prairie.

17½. Choteau's Creek.—Road passes on the high prairie opposite Choteau's old trading-house, and leaves the outer limits of the Indian settlements. Excellent road, and good camps at short distances.

11¾. Choteau's Creek.—Road runs up the creek; is smooth and good.

12¾. Head of Choteau's Creek.—Road runs up the creek, and is good.

17¼. Branch of Washita River.—Road runs over an elevated prairie country, and passes a small branch at six miles from last camp.

5¾. Branch of "Spring Creek."—Good camp.

16. Head of "Spring Creek."—Road traverses a high prairie country, is smooth and firm.

13. Red Mounds.—Road runs over a rolling prairie country, and is excellent.

5. Branch of Washita River.—Good road.

15¾. Branch of Canadian.—Road continues on the ridge dividing the Washita and Canadian rivers; is smooth and firm.

17¾. Branch of Washita River.—Road continues on the "divide."

18. Branch of Canadian.—Road continues on the divide from one to four miles from the Canadian.

19. On Canadian River.—Good road.

16. Little Washita River.—Good road; timber becoming scarce.

13. Branch of Canadian.—Good road.

17½. Antelope Buttes.—Road runs along the Canadian bottom, and in places is sandy.

14. Rush Lake.—Small pond on the prairie. No wood within half a mile; some buffalo chips; poor water.

16. Branch of Washita River.—Good road on the divide.

10½. Dry River.—Road descends a very long hill, and crosses the dry river near the Canadian. Water can be found by digging a foot in the sand. Good grass on the west bank.

17. Branch of Canadian.—Road winds up a very long and abrupt hill, but is smooth and firm.

22½. Timbered Creek.—Road passes over a very elevated prairie country, and descends by a long hill into the beautiful valley of Timbered Creek.

11½. Spring Branch.—Good camp.

14. Spring Branch.—Good camp.

17¾. Branch of Canadian.—Road passes a small branch 3 1/2 miles from the last camp.

18¾. Branch of Canadian.—Road passes a small branch of the Canadian 8 miles from the last camp.

17⅞. Spring Branch.—Good road.

9½. Branch of Canadian.—Good road and camp.

18½. Branch of the Canadian.—Good road and camp.

10½. Pools of Water.—Good camp.

10. Large Pond.—Good camp.

25. Pools of Water.—No wood; water brackish. The road passes over a very elevated and dry country, without wood or water.

18½. Head of Branch.—At 13½ miles the road crosses a branch of the Canadian.

19¾. Laguna Colorado.—Road here falls into an old Mexican cart-road. Good springs on the left up the creek, with wood and grass abundant.

7. Pools of Water.—Road runs through the cedars.

10⅜. Pajarito Creek.—Grass begins to be rather short in places, but is abundant on the creek.

13½. Gallenas Creek.—Good camp.

15. 2d Gallenas Creek.—Good road.

16½. Pécos River at Anton Chico.—This is the first settlement after leaving Camp Arbuckle. Corn and vegetables can be purchased here. Grass is generally short here. [Anton Chico, New Mexico, is located about 60 miles southeast of Santa Fe.]

15. Pécos River opposite Questa.—Road runs through the cedar, and is firm and good. Camp is in sight of the town of Questa, upon a very elevated bluff.

21¾. Laguna Colorado.—Road passes through a wooded country for a portion of the distance, but leaves it before reaching camp, where there is no wood, but water generally sufficient for trains [wagon trains]. In a very dry season it has been known to fail. The road forks here, the right leading to Santa Fé *via* Galistio (45½ miles), and the left to Albuquerque.

22½. San Antonio.—Good road.

18¾. Albuquerque.—Good road.

Total distance from Fort Smith to Albuquerque, 814¾ miles. Total distance from Fort Smith to Santa Fé, 819 miles. [Although Albuquerque and Santa Fe are in fact about 60 miles apart, the above distances are correct: they reflect trail travels, not the relative locations of these two cities.]

Appendix 4: The Unique Jargon of the Mountain Men

Excerpts from Lewis H. Garrard's *Wah-to-Yah and the Taos Trail*, first published in 1850, have often been used in books about the West. The text used here comes from a University of Oklahoma reprint of 1955.

The scene is a campsite along the Taos Trail, near the valley of Taos. The narrator is the author, Garrard. The speaker is an experienced outdoorsman named John L. ("Long") Hatcher, a Westering mountain man who was born in Virginia, moved to southeastern Colorado, drove sheep from New Mexico to California, and eventually settled in Oregon.[1] The passages below have been broken into short paragraphs for ease of reading. Each is followed by a loose translation, in italics, into standard English. Punctuation is as in the original.

Garrard writes:

> Though the wind was piercingly cold, Hatcher was up early, making a fire, "for," said he, "this hos is no b'ar to stick his nose under cover all the robe season, an' lay round camp like a darned Ned; but," he added in an undertone ... "thar's two or three in this crowd—wagh! [a colloquial exclamation equivalent to "by God!"]—howsomever, the *green is* 'rubbed out' a little."
>
> Translation: *Though the wind was piercingly cold, Hatcher was up early, making a fire, "for," said he, "I'm no bear to hibernate all winter and hang around camp like a darn pork-eating newcomer. But," he added in an undertone, "there are two or three men in this camp who have now managed to learn a very little bit about life on the trail."*
>
> [Hatcher continues] "This child hates an American what hasn't seen Injuns skulped, or doesn't know a Yute from a Khian mok'sin. Sometimes he thinks of makin' tracks for white settlement, but when he gits to Bent's big lodge, on the Arkansa, and sees the bugheways, an' the fellers from the States, how they roll their eyes at an Injun yell, or worse nor if a village of Comanches was on 'em,

and pick up a beaver trap, to ask what it is — just shows whar the niggurs had thar bringin' up — this child says — 'a little bacca, if its a plew a plug, and Dupont and G'lena, a Green River or so,' and he leaves for the Bayou Salade. Darn the white diggins, while thar's buffler in the mountains. Whoopee!" shouted he to us, "are you for Touse? This hos is thar in one sun, wagh!"²

Translation: *"I hate an American who hasn't seen Indians scalped or who can't tell the tribe of an Indian simply by looking at the Indian's footprint on the trail. Sometimes I think about leaving the mountains but when I get to Bent's Fort on the Arkansas River, and see how 'gentlemen' and fellows from the States roll their eyes when they hear an Indian yell — as if they had been attacked by an entire village of Comanches! — and how they pick up a beaver trap* [the most common tool of the mountain man's trade], *to ask what it is — this just shows that these guys were raised in complete ignorance outside the mountains — then I say: all I need is a little tobacco, even if it is so expensive that a pound of tobacco costs one beaver pelt, some gunpowder, lead for bullets, a hunting knife, etc., and I'm off for the Bayou Salade* [literally "Salt Valley," a Rocky Mountain valley teeming with big game because of its salty springs and soil]. *Who cares about settled life while there are buffalo in the mountains? Whoopee!" he shouted to us. "Are you heading for Taos, too? I'll be there in only one day!"*

The conversation now shifts to a dialogue between Louy Simonds (another mountain man) and Hatcher. They are reminiscing about their fights with Indians.

[Simonds says] "[T]his coon has 'raised har' so often sence, he keers fur nothing now. Mind the time we 'took' Pawnee 'topknots' away to the Platte, Hatch?"

Translation: *"I've scalped Indians so often since then* [since an earlier fight Simonds and Hatch were discussing] *that nothing bothers me any more. Do you remember, Hatcher, the time we scalped those Pawnee Indians near the Platte River?"*

[Hatcher replies] "Wagh! Ef we didn't ... and give an ough-ough, longside thar darned screechin, I'm a niggur. This child doesn't let an Injun count a 'coup' on his cavyard always. They come mighty nigh 'rubbing' me 'out,' 'tother side of Spanish Peaks — woke up in the mornin' jist afore day, the devils yellin' like mad. I grabs my knife, 'keels' one, an' made for timber, with four of their cussed arrows in my 'meatbag.' The Paches took my beaver — five packs of the prettiest in the mountain — an' two mules, but my traps was hid in the creek. Sez I, hyars a gone coon ef they keep my gun, so I follers thar trail, an' at night, crawls into camp, an' socks my big knife up to the Green River, first dig. I takes t'other Injun by the har, an' 'makes meat' of him *too. Maybe* thar wasn't coups counted, an' a big dance on hand, ef I was alone. I got old bullthrower, made 'medicine' over him, and no darned niggur kin draw bead with him since."³

Translation: *"Well, and if we didn't hold our own and give the Indians war cry back for war cry, I'll be damned! I never let an Indian steal my band of horses or mules. The Apaches came close to killing me on the other side of the Spanish Peaks — I woke up just before dawn and heard the Indians yelling like devils. I grabbed my knife, killed one Indian and ran off to hide in the forest, despite having four arrows in my belly.* [This last statement is an example of the mountain man's penchant for embellishing his real-life adventures with improbable details.] *The Apaches took my beaver pelts—five packs of the best furs in the mountains—and my two mules, but my beaver traps were hidden in the creek. I said to myself: I'm a dead man if they keep my rifle, so I followed their trail, crawled into their camp at night and on the first strike buried my skinning knife deep into one Indian, all the way to the Green River trademark stamped on the blade near the hilt, and killed him, too. Since I was all alone, there couldn't be a victory celebration in the Indian fashion. Nevertheless, I got my stolen rifle back again and called on the gods to protect it: now no darned Indian will ever be able to use it."*

APPENDIX 5: A Fred Harvey Dinner Menu

This menu, which dates from 1888, was reprinted in L.L. Walters's *Steel Trails to Santa Fe* (p. 273) and has been lightly edited. The dinner was served aboard a Santa Fe railroad car known as the "Redondo."

Little Neck Clams on Shell

Consomme Printaniere Royale

Fillets of Sole, Tartar Sauce, with Sliced Cucumbers and Pommes Persillade

Boiled Westphalia Ham with Spinach

Roast Beef, Spring Lamb with Mint Sauce, or Young Turkey with Cranberry Sauce, accompanied by New Asparagus on Toast or New Green Peas and Mashed Potatoes or New Potatoes in Cream

Fillet of Beef with Mushrooms; Sweetbreads Brazed, Jardiniere; Spanish Puffs with Strawberry Sauce

Punch Benedictine

Boiled Plover on Toast, accompanied by Mayonnaise with Sliced Tomatoes or Chicken Salad with Lettuce, with Apple Pie, Pieplant Pie, and Sago Pudding with Brandy Sauce

Strawberries and Cream, Assorted Cake, Vanilla Ice Cream

Edam and Roquefort Cheese, Bent's Water Crackers, French coffee

APPENDIX 6: Excerpts from Geronimo's Autobiography, *My Life*

One of the very best "I-was-there" accounts of historic trails and travels in the Southwest was dictated by Geronimo, in Apache, to Lawton, Oklahoma, school superintendent S.M. Barrett in 1905 and was published in 1906. The interpreter was an educated Apache named Asa Deklugie. Because Geronimo was a prisoner of war at that time and because Americans had not forgotten the ruthless guerrilla campaign he had waged in the Southwest, Barrett had to get official permission from President Theodore Roosevelt himself to write and publish this book. The way in which the story itself was set down is also unique. Barrett gives us the reasons why:

> Geronimo refused to talk when a stenographer was present, or to wait for corrections or questions when telling the story. Each day he had in mind what he would tell and told it in a very clear, brief manner. He might prefer to talk in his own tepee, at Asa Deklugie's house, in some mountain dell, or as he rode in a swinging gallop across the prairie; wherever his fancy led him, there he told us whatever he wished and no more.
>
> On the day that he first gave any portion of his autobiography he would not be questioned about any details, nor would he add another word, but simply said, "Write what I have spoken," and left us to remember and write the story without one bit of assistance. He would agree, however, to come on another day to my study, or any place designated by me, and listen to the reproduction (in Apache) of what had been told, and at such times would answer all questions or add information whenever he could be convinced that it was necessary.[1]

Geronimo hated Mexican soldiers with an undying passion. He tells us:

> In the summer of 1858, being at peace with the Mexican towns as well as with all the neighboring Indian tribes, we went south into Old Mexico to trade. Our whole tribe ... went through Sonora toward Casa Grande [located in northern Chihuahua about 100 miles south of the New Mexican border], our destination, but just before reaching that place we stopped at another Mexican town called by the Indians "Kas-ki-yeh"....
>
> Late one afternoon when returning from town we were met by a few women and children who told us that Mexican troops from some other town had attacked our camp, killed all the warriors of the guard, captured all our ponies, secured our arms, destroyed our supplies, and killed many of our women and children.... I found that my aged mother, my young wife, and my three small children were among the slain.[2]

Geronimo and his fellow warriors from two other Apache tribes wanted to take revenge and decided to go on the warpath. Geronimo said:

> It was in summer of 1859, almost a year from the date of the massacre of Kaskiyeh, that these three tribes were assembled on the Mexican border to go upon the warpath.... When all were ready the chieftains gave command to go forward. None of us were mounted and each warrior wore moccasins and also a cloth wrapped about his loins. This cloth could be spread over him when he slept, and when on the march would be ample protection as clothing. In battle, if the fight was hard, we did not wish much clothing. Each warrior carried three

days' rations, but as we often killed game while on the march, we were seldom without food....

We usually marched about fourteen hours per day, making three stops for food, and traveling forty to forty-five miles a day. I acted as guide into Mexico, and we followed the river courses and mountain ranges because we could better thereby keep our movements concealed. We entered Sonora and went southward past Quitaco, Nacozari, and many smaller settlements.

When we were almost at Arispe [Arizpe is a small town located about 100 miles southwest of where the borders of Sonora, Arizona, and New Mexico meet] we camped, and eight men rode out of the city to parley with us. These we captured, killed, and scalped. This was just to draw the troops from the city, and the next day they came....

As we had anticipated, about ten o'clock in the morning the whole Mexican force came out. There were two companies of cavalry and two of infantry. I recognized the cavalry as the soldiers who had killed my people at Kaskiyeh. This I told to the chieftains, and they said that I might direct the battle.[3]

During this ferocious battle, Geronimo so distinguished himself in hand-to-hand combat that he won the admiration of all his fellows. At the end of the battle, he says,

Still covered with the blood of my enemies, still holding my conquering weapon [a spear], still hot with the joy of battle, victory, and vengeance, I was surrounded by Apache braves and made war chief of all the Apaches. Then I gave orders for scalping the slain. I could not call back my loved ones, I could not bring back the dead Apaches [many warriors had been killed in this battle], but I could rejoice in this revenge. The Apaches had avenged the massacre of "Kas-ki-yeh."[4]

Geronimo makes it clear that it was not only Apache men who were capable of great endurance and great deeds: Apache women were quite remarkable, too. This is what Geronimo reports about four Apache women who were captured by the Mexicans during a battle and were taken to Sonora, where they were forced to work for some years. Finally, they escaped, fled into the mountains, and set out to find their tribe:

They had knives which they had stolen from the Mexicans but they had no other weapons. They had no blankets; so at night they would make a little tepee by cutting brush with their knives, and setting [the brush] up for the walls. The top was covered over with brush. In this temporary tepee they would all sleep. One night when their camp fire was low they heard growling just outside the tepee. Francisco, the youngest woman of the party (about seventeen years of age), started to build up the fire, when a mountain lion crashed through the tepee and attacked her. The suddenness of the attack made her drop her knife, but she fought as best she could with her hand. She was no match for the lion, however; her left shoulder was crushed and partly torn away.

The lion kept trying to catch her by the throat; this she prevented with her hands for a long time. He dragged her for about 300 yards, then she found her strength was failing her from loss of blood, and she called to the other women for help. The lion had been dragging her by one foot, and she had been catching hold of his legs, and of the rock and underbrush, to delay him. Finally he stopped and stood over her. She again called to her companions and they attacked him with their knives and killed him. Then they dressed her wounds and nursed her in the mountains for about a month. When she was again able to walk they resumed their journey and reached our tribe in safety.[5]

Geronimo and his tribe traveled so extensively on both sides of the border between the United States and Mexico that in the interests of brevity we will cite only one further example here:

Early the next summer (1866) I [Geronimo] took thirty mounted warriors and invaded Mexican territory. We went south through Chihuahua as far as Santa Cruz, Sonora, then crossed over the Sierra Madre Mountains, following the river course at the south end of the range. We kept on westward from the Sierra Madre Mountains to the Sierra de Sahuripa Mountains, and followed that range northward. We collected all the horses, mules, and cattle we wanted, and drove them northward through Sonora into Arizona.

Mexicans saw us at many times and in many places, but they did not attack us at any time, nor did any troops attempt to follow us. When we arrived at our homes we gave presents to all, and the tribe feasted and danced. During this raid we had killed about fifty Mexicans.[6]

Chronology

c. 850–1250 CE: Anasazi Indians build a prehistoric culture which is centered on the Four Corners area and extends into New Mexico, Colorado, Utah, and Arizona. Chaco Canyon becomes a major urban center of pueblo life. Its roads have a religious and symbolic value in addition to their practical importance.

c. 1100s–1200s: Archeological studies show that Indians are living in adobe and rock villages in the Upper Pecos Valley.

c. 1450: Pecos Indians build a large, multistoried, rectangular pueblo on the Pecos mesa.

1517: Álvarez Alonso de Pineda is the first person to explore the Gulf Coast by sea.

1536: Cabeza de Vaca and his "four ragged castaways" survive eight years of wandering on foot through the deserts of the Southwest.

1539: Fray Marcos de Niza sets off from Culiacán to find the golden "Seven Cities of Cíbola." His sun-dazzled eyes will see the mica-flecked adobe walls of Háwikuh, a pueblo in western New Mexico, as being one of these mythical cities.

1540–1542: The great expedition of Francisco Vásquez de Coronado is a great failure.

1540: First Spanish contact with Pecos: the Pecos Indians visit Coronado at Zuni.

1581: Fray Agustín Rodríguez and Captain Francisco Sánchez Chamuscado set out from Santa Bárbara, leading a small expedition to New Mexico.

1582: Antonio de Espejo, accompanied by Fray Bernaldino Beltrán, leaves San Bartolomé en route to Texas and New Mexico.

1590: Pioneering the first cart-route into New Mexico, Gaspar Castaño de Sosa reaches the Rio Grande River.

1590–1591: Gaspar Castaño de Sosa leaves us the most detailed contemporary description of Pecos.

1593: Francisco Leyva de Bonilla and António Gutiérrez de Humaña mount a freelance, illegal expedition into New Mexico.

1598: Juan de Oñate, "the last conquistador," leads the first group of settlers into New Mexico. The trail he follows will become El Camino Real de Tierra Adentro and will be used until 1882.

1610: Governor Pedro de Peralta founds Santa Fe.

1610: Gaspar Pérez de Villagrá writes a long poem describing some of the hardships suffered by the Oñate expedition.

1617: The first mission church is built at Pecos. It will be replaced and remodeled over the years.

1629–1632: Juan de Salas, Diego López, Ascencio de Zárte, and Pedro de Ortega, inspired by a mysterious "Lady in Blue," try to convert the Jumano Indians.

1650: Hernando Martín and Diego del Castillo are sent out from Santa Fe to look for freshwater pearls.

1654: Diego de Guadalajara leads an expedition to harvest freshwater pearls.

1680: Pueblo Revolt: this great rebellion, unique in the annals of Indian-European relations in North America, forces the Spanish out of New Mexico for 12 years.

1684: Juan Domínguez de Mendoza and Fray Nicolás López seek the Caddo-speaking Indians' mythical "Kingdom of the Tejas."

1693: The Spanish reconquer New Mexico after the Pueblo Revolt.

1724–1766: Pedro de Rivera and the Marqués de Rubí inspect the northern frontier of New Spain. They recommend numerous measures to strengthen it but little is done because of the high cost.

1773: Juan Bautista de Anza receives permission from the Viceroy of New Spain to pioneer a 1,200-mile long trail from Sonora, Mexico, to northern California.

1776: Fray Francisco Anastasio Domínguez and Fray Silvestre Vélez de Escalante leave Santa Fe to blaze a trail west to Monterey, California. Heavy snows force them to abort their trip and return to New Mexico.

1776: Acting on orders from the governor of New Mexico, Juan María de Rivera sets out on a prospecting and exploring trip from Abiquiú. This is the first recorded expedition to use the eastern end of the Old Spanish Trial.

1787–1788: Fearing an unwanted growth of French influence, the governor of New Mexico sends José Mares to blaze a new trail between Santa Fe and Bexar (San Antonio).

1792–1793: In successive summers, Pedro Vial, the last of the great Spanish explorers of the Southwest, makes a round-trip between Santa Fe and St. Louis estimated at 2,279 miles.

Early 1800s: Many Pecoseños leave the Pecos mesa and settle in the Pecos valley.

1808: In a belated effort by Spain to strengthen its ties with Santa Fe and to protect its territory against American expansion, Francisco Amangual leads an expedition from El Paso to San Antonio, then to Santa Fe, and, finally, back to El Paso.

1809–1868: The eventful, colorful, and well-documented life of Kit Carson.

1821: Mexico wins its independence from Spain; William Becknell is the first trader to use the Santa Fe Trail; as the last campsite before Santa Fe, Pecos becomes a popular rest stop for travelers along the Santa Fe Trail.

1829: Antonio Armijo leads a group of traders from Abiquiú to Santa Barbara, California.

1830–1831: William Wolfskill, George C. Yount, and other trappers explore the entire route of the Old Spanish Trail.

1831: Mexican-American trade now flows over both El Camino Real de Tierra Adentro and the Santa Fe Trail; Jedediah Strong Smith is killed by Comanche warriors on the Cimarron Route of the Santa Fe Trail; James O. Pattie writes about the challenges he encountered on the Gila River Trail.

1839: Dr. F. Adolph Wislizenus chronicles his experiences in the Rocky Mountains and, later (in 1848), in northern New Mexico.

1841: Many of the horses and mules from California which were driven east to New Mexico were stolen in California. Rufus B. Sage writes about a party of men engaged in this illegal trade; the *New York Tribune* describes Santa Fe through the eyes of an unidentified traveler from Indiana.

1843: María Gertrudis Barceló is in her prime as the most expert monte dealer in Santa Fe.

1844: Publication of Josiah Gregg's definitive two-volume work, *Commerce of the Prairies*.

1846–1848: Mexican–American War.

1846: Lieutenant William Hemsley Emory produces the first reliable map of the Gila River Trail.

1846–1847: Colonel James W. Abert records his varied experiences in New Mexico; Susan Shelby Magoffin describes her life in New Mexico and in northern Mexico during the early days of the Mexican–American War; Lewis H. Garrard writes about frontier life in New Mexico. His transcriptions of the unique jargon of the mountain men are of unique historical value; George Frederick Ruxton travels extensively in Mexico and the Rocky Mountains. His "I-was-there" accounts still make excellent reading.

1848: Treaty of Guadalupe Hidalgo ends the Mexican–American War; Lieutenant George Douglas Brewerton rides with Kit Carson along the Old Spanish Trail and records their adventures; the diary of Orville C. Pratt is the only surviving document with entries for each day spent on the Old Spanish Trail; in a record-breaking feat, Francis Xavier Aubry rides from Santa Fe to St. Louis, Missouri, in under six days; a newspaper advertisement by the businessman B.F. Coons lists $100,000 worth of goods he is offering for sale in Santa Fe.

1849: Edward Griffin Beckwith lists the difficulties of pathfinding along the Zuni Trail; former Texas Ranger J.C. Hays follows the Apache Trail and eventually travels to California, where he becomes sheriff of San Francisco; Thomas B. Eastland complains of the slowness of travel over the Lower Emigrant Trail.

1849 or 1850: James Frederick Thibault describes the frightening section of the Southern Trail leading out of Guadalupe Pass.

1850 to 1872: Extensive cessions of public land are made to states and to railroad companies to promote railroad construction.

1850: Territory of New Mexico becomes an organized territory of the U.S.

1851: Daniel W. Jones describes how the slave trade was conducted by New Mexican traders along the Old Spanish Trail.

1854: United States and Mexico negotiate the Gadsden Purchase.

Mid-1850s: Horse thieves, slavers, and U.S. government expeditions are the last to use the Old Spanish Trail.

1858–1861: Butterfield Overland Mail follows a southern route.

1859: Colonel Randolph B. Marcy's classic guidebook, *The Prairie Traveler*, provides excellent advice to travelers heading for the trans–Mississippi West. His "List of Itineraries, showing the distances between camping places, the character of the roads, and the facilities for obtaining wood, water, and grass on the principal routes between the Mississippi River and the Pacific Ocean" was especially valuable; Cyrus K. Holliday founds the Atchison & Topeka Railroad Company. In 1863 it will be renamed the Atchison, Topeka & Santa Fe Railway Company.

1861: Lieutenant George Bascom is sent out to capture Cochise but instead prompts a long series of Apache attacks.
1861–1862: Civil War campaigns in New Mexico.
1862: Battle of Glorieta Pass; Brigadier General James H. Carleton's troops battle Apache warriors at Apache Pass.
1863: Construction of the third and final Fort Union is begun.
1863–1868: The Long Walk of the Navajos.
1865: Businessmen in San Francisco found the Southern Pacific Railroad.
1866: "Uncle Dick" Wootton hires a tribe of Ute Indians to build a toll road over Raton Pass. This toll road will later become the route followed by the Santa Fe railroad into New Mexico.
1866–1880s: Goodnight-Loving Trail.
1869: Central Pacific and Union Pacific trains meet at Promontory Summit, Utah, thus establishing the first transcontinental railroad.
1876: Fred Harvey opens a restaurant at the Atchison, Topeka & Santa Fe's depot in Topeka. By the late 1880s there will be a Fred Harvey dining facility every 100 miles along the Santa Fe's tracks.
1878: As a result of "the first railroad war," the Santa Fe wins control of Raton Pass.
1879: After sharp fighting during the "second railroad war," the Denver and Rio Grande Railroad wins control of the Royal Gorge — a deep canyon on the Arkansas River near Cañon City, Colorado.
1880: The first train puffs into Santa Fe. The coming of the Iron Horse brings the usefulness of the Santa Fe Trail to an end.
1881: The second transcontinental railroad is completed when the Southern Pacific's tracks from Los Angeles meet the Galveston, Harrisburg and San Antonio Railway's tracks in Texas, just north of the Pecos River.
1882: In his *Log of a Cowboy* (published in 1903), Andy Adams gives a fictionalized but historically accurate account of the hardships of life on the cattle trails in 1882; the advent of the railroad ends the usefulness of El Camino Real de Tierra Adentro.
1886: Final surrender of Geronimo marks the high point of Fort Bowie's existence.
1893: Completion of numerous railway lines in the trans–Mississippi West leads a contemporary newspaper to conclude that "the prairie schooner has passed away and is replaced by the railway coach."
1915–1927: Alfred K. Kidder excavates Pecos and develops a chronology for the ancient Southwest, a modified version of which is still in use today.
1960: Fort Bowie is declared a National Historical Landmark.
1965: Pecos is designated as a national monument.
1987: Congress establishes the Santa Fe National Historic Trail.
2000: The 404-mile-long section of El Camino de Tierra Adentro that lies within the U.S. is added to the U.S. National Trails System as a National Historic Trail.
2002: The Bureau of Land Management and the National Park Service officially recognize the Old Spanish Trail as a National Historic Trail.

Chapter Notes

Preface

1. Private communication of 4 August 2007 from Dr. Marc Simmons.
2. "New Mexico Territory," http://en.wikipedia.org/wiki/New_Mexico_Territory
3. Hunt Janin, *Claiming the American Wilderness: International Rivalry in the Trans-Mississippi West, 1528–1803* (Jefferson, NC: McFarland, 2006), 11.
4. Spanish explorations have been discussed in many books. For a concise summary of their adventures, see Janin, *Claiming the American Wilderness*, chapter 2, "The Spaniards: Children of the Sun," 48–95.

Introduction

1. John L. Kessell, *Kiva, Cross, and Crown: The Pecos Indians and New Mexico, 1540–1840* (Albuquerque: University of New Mexico Press, 1990), xi, quoting Bolton, *Coronado*.
2. "New Mexico Pueblos," GeoNative. "New Mexico Pueblos," http://www.geocities.com/Athens/9479/pueblo.html?200817 (accessed 17 April 2008), 1–8.
3. Albert H. Schroeder and Dan S. Matson, *A Colony on the Move: Gaspar Castaño de Sosa's Journal, 1590–1591* (Santa Fe: School of American Research, 1965), 81.
4. The best overall history of Pecos itself is still Kessell's detailed study, *Kiva, Cross, and Crown: The Pecos Indians and New Mexico, 1540–1840* (second printing, 1990).
5. Schroeder, "Pecos Pueblo," 430.
6. *Ibid.*
7. Sanchez, *Explorers, Traders, and Slavers*, 19.
8. Brooks, *Captives*, 47.
9. Quoted by Kessell, in *Kiva*, 406.
10. Swagerty, "Indian Trade," 352.
11. Schroeder and Matson, *Colony*, 81.
12. Quoted by Calloway, *Count*, 161.
13. John, *Storms*, 31–32.
14. Quoted by National Park Service, "Pecos," 1.
15. Abert, *Abert's New Mexico Report*, 110.
16. This section is drawn from private communications with archeologist Thomas Windes.
17. Sanchez, *Explorers, Traders, and Slavers*, 19.
18. John, *Storms*, 235–237.
19. Quoted by Janin, *Wilderness*, 228.
20. John, *Storms*, 321–322.
21. Gregg, *Commerce*, 182–183.
22. Magoffin, *Down the Santa Fe Trail*, 99–101.
23. Quoted by Etter, *To California on the Southern Route*, 29.
24. Abert, *Abert's New Mexico Report*, 42.
25. Quoted by National Park Service, "Kidder," 1.
26. National Park Service, "Kidder," 1.
27. Fagan, *Chaco Canyon*, 37–38.

Chapter I

1. Calloway, *Count*, 83, 460 (note 69).
2. Diamond, *Collapse*, 144.
3. Fagan, *Chaco Canyon*, 172.
4. National Park Service, "Chaco Culture: The Road System," 2–3.
5. National Park Service, "Chaco Culture: The Center of Chacoan Culture," 2.
6. Fagan, *Chaco Canyon*, 167, 173.
7. Dubin, *History of Beads*, 289.
8. Fagan, *Chaco Canyon*, 167.

9. Gabriel, *Roads to Center Place*, 184–185.
10. National Park Service, "A Brief History of Chaco Culture," National Historical Park, 1.
11. Fagan, *Chaco Canyon*, 151–152.
12. Fagan, *Chaco Canyon*, 153–154.
13. Diamond, *Collapse*, 151–153.
14. Ford, "Inter-Indian Exchange," 719; Swagerty, "History of Indian-White Relations," 354.
15. Ford, "Inter-Indian Exchange," 715.
16. Ford, "Inter-Indian Exchange," 720–721.

Chapter II

1. For an edited version of a *Requerimiento*, see Janin, *Wilderness*, 233–234.
2. Janin, *Wilderness*, 50.
3. Janin, *Wilderness*, 49–50.
4. Cabeza de Vaca, *Chronicle*, ix.
5. Cabeza de Vaca, *Chronicle*, 40–41.
6. Cabeza de Vaca, *Chronicle*, 87.
7. *Handbook of Texas Online*, "Cabeza de Vaca," 2.
8. Some of this information was drawn from a private communication of 25 January 2008 from Nancy Coggeshall.
9. Cabeza de Vaca, *Chronicle*, 73.
10. Cabeza de Vaca, *Chronicle*, 80, 81.
11. Cabeza de Vaca, *Chronicle*, 86.
12. Cabeza de Vaca, *Chronicle*, 86–87 (emphasis added).
13. Cabeza de Vaca, *Chronicle*, 95.
14. Golay and Bowman, *North American Exploration*, 96–97.
15. Pedro de Castañeda, *Narrative of the Coronado Expedition*, 27–28.
16. Castañeda, *Narrative of the Coronado Expedition*, 37.
17. Marcos de Niza, "A Relation of the Estevánico Reverend Father Fray," 2.
18. Quoted by Golay and Bowman, *North American Exploration*, 101.
19. Some of this account is drawn from Janin, *Wilderness*, 55–58.
20. Quoted by Golay and Bowman, *North American Exploration*, 75.
21. Quoted by Kessell, *Kiva*, 8–9.
22. Castañeda, *Narrative of the Coronado Expedition*, 135.
23. Castañeda, *Narrative of the Coronado Expedition*, 297, 381.
24. Castañeda, *Narrative of the Coronado Expedition*, 219.
25. PBS, "Coronado's Report to the King of Spain," 3
26. Simmons, "History of Pueblo-Spanish Relations," 178.
27. Other reasons for the hiatus in Spanish explorations included a local conflict in Nueva Galicia; the discovery of silver in Zacatecas; Spanish expansion into other parts of Mexico; and preoccupation with European threats. See Jones, "Spanish Penetrations," 41–42.
28. Texas Almanac, "Franciscan Missionaries," 2.
29. National Park Service, "Jumanos," 1.
30. This account follows Southwest Crossroads, "The Chamuscado-Rodriguez Expedition," 1–2, and Janin, *Wilderness*, 60.
31. A copy of the map can be found in Simmons, "Pueblo-Spanish Relations," 188.
32. *Handbook of Texas Online*, "El Paso del Norte."
33. Quoted by Calloway, *Count*, 143.
34. Kessell, *Kiva*, 39.
35. A contemporary saying quoted by Calloway, *Count*, 143.
36. *Handbook of Texas Online*, "Espejo-Beltrán Expedition," 1.
37. American Journeys, "Espejo," 2.
38. New Mexico Office of the State Historian, "Espejo Expedition," 3.
39. Golay and Bowman, *North American Exploration*, 87.
40. Quoted by Kessell, *Kiva*, 42.
41. Quoted by Kessell, *Spain in the Southwest*, 57.
42. Quoted by Kessell, *Kiva*, 43.
43. Jones, "Spanish Penetrations," 44.
44. This section is drawn both from John, *Storms*, 33–36, and from Schroeder and Matson, *Colony*, 9, 25.
45. Quoted by John, *Storm*, 33.
46. This section is drawn from Schroeder and Matson, *Colony*, 11–12; *Handbook of Texas Online*, "Castaño de Sosa," 1; and Janin, *Wilderness*, 60–61.
47. Quoted by Schroeder and Matson, *Colony*, 50.
48. Schroeder and Matson, *Colony*, 55.
49. Jones, "Spanish Penetrations," 44–45.
50. Quoted by John, *Storms*, 35.
51. Quoted by Schroeder and Matson, *Colony*, 8.
52. Jones, *Spanish Penetrations*, 45.
53. Cited by Kessell, *Kiva*, 406.
54. This section is drawn from Jones, *Spanish Penetrations*, 45; Kessell, *Kiva*, 87; *Handbook of Texas Online*, "Bonilla," 1; Golay

and Bowman, *North American Exploration*, 92–93; John, *Storms*, 36–37; and Calloway, *Count*, 145.

55. This section is drawn from Janin, *Wilderness*, 63–65; Golay and Bowman, *North American Exploration*, 107–109.

56. Quoted by Simmons, *Last Conquistador*, 65.

57. Simmons, *Last Conquistador*, 65–67.

58. Quoted by Kessell, *Spain in the Southwest*, 79–80.

59. Quoted by Kessell, *Spain in the Southwest*, 80.

60. Weber, *Spanish Frontier*, 82.

61. Quoted by Kessell, *Spain in the Southwest*, 71.

62. Janin, *Wilderness*, 64–65.

63. Texas Almanac, "Franciscan Missionaries," 2.

64. This section is drawn from Golay and Bowman, *North American Exploration*, 225.

65. Golay and Bowman, *North American Exploration*, 217–218, and *Handbook of Texas Online*, "Exploration," 1.

66. Weber, *Spanish Frontier*, 153.

67. *Handbook of Texas Online*, "Domínguez de Mendoza," 1.

68. For a detailed discussion of such international rivalry, see Janin, *Claiming the American Wilderness: International Rivalry in the Trans-Mississippi West*.

69. Murphy, "Journey of Pedro de Rivera," 4.

70. Janin, *Wilderness*, 71.

71. Quoted in Loomis and Nasatir, *Pedro Vial*, 19.

72. *Handbook of Texas Online*, "Apache Indians," 2.

73. John, *Storms*, 439.

74. These and the following details of Rubí's inspection are from Janin, *Wilderness*, 72–73.

75. Loomis and Nasatir, *Pedro Vial*, 9.

76. Only the foundations of the presidio at Tubac remain today. It was probably quite difficult for the authorities to find men willing to serve at this remote post. Today a small museum displays this contemporary notice, translated from Spanish: "Soldiers Needed at the Presidio de San Ignatius de Tubac/Qualifications:/- tall in stature [5' 2" minimum]/- of good disposition/- robust and agile/for frontier duty/- Roman Catholic/- free from notable facial defects/- free from immorality/Will be issued:/- uniform [short jacket, breeches, cape, hat, two shirts, long stockings, shoes]/- leather body armor and shield/- saddle, bridle, other tack/- 6 good horses/- arms: long lance, broad sword, musket [all of the above to be paid for out of the first year's salary]/Pay:/- 290 pesos per year [mostly in products] plus 2 reales per day in coin/- 10 acres for housing and farming/- medical attention/- pension upon retirement/- spoils of war."

77. This section is drawn from Center for Advanced Technology in Education, "Historical Context," 1–2.

78. See Janin, *Wilderness*, 48–95.

79. DesertUSA, "Juan Bautista de Anza," 2.

80. During the years when they were relied on as an essential means of transportation, there was nothing at all romantic about mule trains. In the modern era, however, they have become invested with a certain glamour. Beginning in 1949, for example, Frankie Laine, Bing Crosby, Tennessee Ernie Ford, Vaughn Monroe, and other noted singers recorded "Mule Train." This was a very popular novelty song, supposedly sung by a wagon driver in the Southwest to spur his mules on and thus make better time. In the song, he regales the listener with a list of the goods he is carrying, including "a plug of chaw tobaccy [chewing tobacco] for a rancher in Corolla"; "a guitar for a cowboy way out in Arizona"; "a dress of calico for a pretty Navajo"; "cotton thread and needles for the folks way out yonder"; "a shovel for a miner who left his home to wander"; "a letter full of sadness and it's black around the border" [such a letter announced a death]; and "a pair of boots for someone who had them made to order." In the bibliography, see Wikipedia, "Mule Train," and "Frankie Laine, Mule Train Lyrics."

81. While doing research in southwestern New Mexico, the authors of this book had a unique and memorable meeting with a modern muleteer in the wilderness along the Gila River. This man was riding one mule and was leading two others. These latter were barely broken and needed his constant attention. All three mules were heavily laden with supplies and equipment destined for a ranch 50 miles away. When we asked him how he could expect any help in the wilderness if he became ill or injured, he told us that on an earlier mule trip he had been thrown by a mule he was riding and had broken his back. He had no way to get help but he did have a brilliant idea that undoubtedly saved his life: he lit a fire near where he lay. Forest rangers soon saw

the smoke, came to investigate its source, and rescued him. We noticed that this muleteer, in the best traditions of the Old West, was well armed and could defend himself against any human or animal assailant. In a holster on his right hip, he carried a .45 caliber single action revolver; in a scabbard on his left hip, he carried a big Bowie knife.

82. Sidney, *The Book of the Horse*, 285, 286. See, in the bibliography, Wikipedia, "Mule Train," and CowboyLyrics.com, "Frankie Laine, Mule Train Lyrics."

83. Private communication of 28 November 2007 from Ken Bevins of Single Tree Farm.

84. Nordhoff, *Flame*, 56.

85. Gregg, *Commerce*, 248–249.

86. As used in this book (and, indeed, in virtually all other modern reference works), the term "American West" refers to the trans-Mississippi West. Historically, however, this was never the "first" West. The American frontier gradually moved westward in the decades after the settlement of the first non–Indian immigrants along the eastern coast of what would later become the United States. The crest of the Appalachian Mountains was initially seen by American and other colonists as constituting the farthest limit of their frontier. The vast lands west of the Appalachians were little known; indeed, easterners feared them as the likely abode of ferocious Indians and dangerous beasts. Between the Appalachians and the eastern shore of the Mississippi River lay a confusing hodgepodge of territories. In 1789, when the Northwest Territory (also known as the "old Northwest") was organized, these included (counting from north to south): (1) the Northwest Territory itself, which would eventually be carved into the states of Ohio, Indiana, Illinois, Michigan, Wisconsin, and the northeast part of Minnesota; (2) the western reaches of Virginia; (3) an unorganized territory west of North Carolina; (4) Georgia, which extended all the way to the Mississippi River; (5) a region of disputed sovereignty, claimed by both the United States and by the Spanish colony of West Florida; and (6) West Florida itself. To round out the continental picture in 1789, we can add that west of the Mississippi River lay two vast Spanish colonies (the Colony of Louisiana, and the Viceroyalty of New Spain), one British possession (part of Rupert's Land), and an unclaimed territory in the Pacific Northwest (Oregon).

87. "Bancroft's History of Utah," 1.

88. Janin, *Wilderness*, 7–8.

89. McDonald, "Derrotero y Diario," 1, and Jones, "Spanish Penetrations," 49–50.

90. See *The Domínguez-Escalante Journal*. The notes and maps in the edition used here are especially useful.

91. McDonald, "Derrotero y Diario, 2.

92. Quoted in Warner, *Domínguez-Escalante Journal*, 84–85.

93. Quoted in Warner, *Domínguez-Escalante Journal*, 89.

94. Quoted in Warner, *Domínguez-Escalante Journal*, 90.

95. Quoted in Warner, *Domínguez-Escalante Journal*, 119–120.

96. Jones, "Spanish Penetrations," 50.

97. Weber, *Spanish Frontier*, 255.

98. Calloway, *Count*, 391–392.

99. Sources used here include Tyson, "Vial," 1, and *Handbook of Texas Online*, "Vial," 1.

100. Quoted by Kavanagh, *Comanche Political History*, 102.

101. Quoted by Kavanagh, *Comanche Political History*, 103.

102. Quoted by Loomis and Nasatir, *Pedro Vial*, 276.

103. Boyle, *Los Capitalistas*, 4–5.

104. This account is drawn from Loomis and Nasatir, *Pedro Vial*, 288–315.

105. Quoted by Loomis and Nasatir, *Pedro Vial*, 304.

106. Quoted by Loomis and Nasatir, *Pedro Vial*, 463.

107. Quoted by Loomis and Nasatir, *Pedro Vial*, 482.

108. Quoted by Loomis and Nasatir, *Pedro Vial*, 505.

109. Quoted by Loomis and Nasatir, *Pedro Vial*, 520.

110. Loomis and Nasatir, *Pedro Vial*, 534.

Chapter III

1. Moorhead, *New Mexico's Royal Road*, 4.

2. Moorhead, *New Mexico's Royal Road*, 3–4.

3. For an excellent description of Oñate's 1598 expedition, see Moorhead, *New Mexico's Royal Road*, 7–27.

4. Kessell, *Spain in the Southwest*, 75–76.

5. Riley, *Rio del Norte*, 247.

6. Moorhead, *New Mexico's Royal Road*, 5.

7. Details on the supply caravan are taken from Moorhead, *New Mexico's Royal Road*, 32–36.
8. Quoted by Moorhead, *New Mexico's Royal Road*, 33.
9. Moorhead, *New Mexico's Royal Road*, 33.
10. Moorhead, *New Mexico's Royal Road*, 34.
11. Moorhead, *New Mexico's Royal Road*, 35.
12. Moorhead, *New Mexico's Royal Road*, 36.
13. Moorhead, *New Mexico's Royal Road*, 36–37.
14. Marcy, *Prairie Traveler*, 52.
15. The following details of the lawsuit are drawn from Moorhead, *New Mexico's Royal Road*, 41–42.
16. Moorhead, *New Mexico's Royal Road*, 45.
17. Murphy, "Journey of Pedro de Rivera," 3.
18. Moorhead, *New Mexico's Royal Road*, 50–52.
19. Moorhead, *New Mexico's Royal Road*, 51.
20. Boyle, *Los Capitalistas*, 31.
21. Gregg, *Commerce*, 121.
22. Boyle, *Los Capitalistas*, 18.
23. Abert, *Abert's New Mexico Report*, 126.

Chapter IV

1. "History of the Old Spanish Trail," 1.
2. Old Spanish Trail Association, "Welcome," 2.
3. Sanchez, *Explorers, Traders, and Slavers*, ix.
4. Quoted by Sanchez, *Explorers, Traders, and Slavers*, 8.
5. Hafen and Hafen, *Old Spanish Trail*, 19.
6. Hafen and Hafen, *Old Spanish Trail*, 57.
7. Hafen and Hafen, *Old Spanish Trail*, 52.
8. "Old Spanish Trail: Mojave Desert Roads & Trails," 1.
9. Quoted by Hafen and Hafen, *Old Spanish Trail*, 74–75.
10. Quoted by Hafen and Hafen, *Old Spanish Trail*, 78–79.
11. Hafen and Hafen, *Old Spanish Trail*, 83.
12. Quoted by Hafen and Hafen, *Old Spanish Trail*, 156–158.
13. Hafen and Hafen, *Old Spanish Trail*, 165–166.
14. Quoted by Hafen and Hafen, *Old Spanish Trail*, 156–158.
15. This section is drawn from Hafen and Hafen, *Old Spanish Trail*, 139–154.
16. National Park Service, "Santa Fe National Historic Trail: Special History Study," chapter 4, p. 1.
17. Quoted by Hafen and Hafen, *Old Spanish Trail*, 146–147.
18. Hafen and Hafen, *Old Spanish Trail*, 154.
19. This section is drawn from Hafen and Hafen, *Old Spanish Trail*, 179–181.
20. Quoted by Hafen and Hafen, *Old Spanish Trail*, 180–181.
21. Quoted by Hafen and Hafen, *Old Spanish Trail*, 241 (citing Rufus B. Sage, *Scenes in the Rocky Mountains* (Philadelphia, 1846)), 51.
22. Quoted by Hafen and Hafen, *Old Spanish Trail*, 187.
23. Hafen and Hafen, *Old Spanish Trail*, 191–192.
24. This account is drawn from Wikipedia, "Kit Carson," 1–14, and from Sides' book, *Blood and Thunder*, in its entirety.
25. Quoted by Russell, *Guns on the Early Frontiers*, 87, citing Parker, *Journal*, 79.
26. "Bent's Fort" refers to two different forts. The first, known as Bent's Old Fort, was located eight miles northeast of La Junta, Colorado. It was in business from 1833 to 1849. The second fort, named Bent's New Fort, was located about 60 miles to the east. Bent operated it until 1860, when he leased it to the U.S. Army. See Dary, *The Santa Fe Trail*, 313–314.
27. Quoted by Quaife, *Kit Carson's Autobiography*, 133–134.
28. Quoted by Quaife, *Kit Carson's Autobiography*, 135.
29. Quoted by Thompson, *The Army and the Navajo*, 122.
30. Trafzer, *Kit Carson Campaign*, 58.
31. Quoted in "Early Forts of New Mexico," 1.
32. Quoted by Wikipedia, "Kit Carson," 10.
33. Quoted by Wikipedia, "Kit Carson," 10, citing Harvey L. Carter, *Dear Old Kit* (Norman: University of Oklahoma Press, 1968), 210.
34. Trafzer, *Kit Carson Campaign*, 59, 73.

35. Brewerton, *Overland with Kit Carson*, 56–59.
36. Quoted by Hafen and Hafen, *Old Spanish Trail*, 357.
37. Quoted by Hafen and Hafen, *Old Spanish Trail*, 268, citing D.W. Jones, *Forty Years Among the Indians* (Salt Lake City, 1890), 49–50.

Chapter V

1. These estimates of the length of the Santa Fe Trail come from Moorhead, *New Mexico's Royal Road*, 96–98, 102.
2. We are much indebted to Frank Norris, historian at the National Trails System Office in Santa Fe, for a personal communication of 13 April 2009, which gave us some of the figures used in these two paragraphs.
3. Moorhead, *New Mexico's Royal Road*, 102.
4. Marcy, *Prairie Traveler*, 18–19.
5. Etter, *To California*, 25.
6. National Park Service, "Santa Fe Trail," 1.
7. Weber, *Taos Trappers*, 50.
8. Janin, *Wilderness*, 121–122.
9. This account of Becknell is drawn from Time-Life, *Expressmen*, 21–22, and *Handbook of Texas*, "Becknell," 1.
10. *Handbook of Texas Online*. "Santa Fe Trail," 1.
11. Dary, *The Santa Fe Trail*, 317.
12. Boyle, *Los Capitalistas*, 112.
13. Gregg, *Commerce of the Prairies*, 55.
14. Morgan, *Jedediah Smith*, 7.
15. Morgan, *Jedediah Smith*, 329–330.
16. European double rifles, i.e., rifles which had two barrels and therefore held two shots, were available at that time but they were much more expensive than single-short rifles and were not as accurate at long range. For this reason they were very rarely seen in the trans-Mississippi West. Of the few frontiersmen known to have carried a double rifle there was George Frederick Ruxton, described elsewhere in this book. See also Rounds, *Mountain Men*, 89.
17. Quoted by Morgan, *Jedediah Smith*, 362–363.
18. Quoted by Morgan, *Jedediah Smith*, 364.
19. Marcy, *Prairie Traveler*, 211–212.
20. Gregg, *Commerce of the Prairies*, 37–38.
21. The following account of life on the Santa Fe Trail is drawn from National Park Service, "Santa Fe National Historic Trail," 3.
22. Quoted by National Park Service, "Santa Fe Trail," 4.
23. Quoted by National Park Service, "Santa Fe National Historic Trail," 4.
24. Ruxton, *Wild Life*, 74.
25. Boyle, *Los Capitalistas*, xi–xiii.
26. Wislizenus, *Journey to the Rocky Mountains*, 28–31.
27. Wislizenus, *Memoir of a Tour to Northern Mexico*, 12–13.
28. Quoted in Dary, *Santa Fe Trail*, 169–170. This account has been lightly edited.
29. Gregg, *Commerce*, 72–73.
30. Abert, *Abert's New Mexico Report*, 57.
31. American Gaming Association, "Responsible Gaming," 1.
32. "Spanish Monte," 1–2.
33. In placing La Tules in Taos, the Mexican-American war correspondent Richard Smith Elliott wrote in 1847 that Gregg was mistaken. Elliott believed that Gregg had confused La Tules with her sister-in-law, Dolores Barceló. See Elliott, *The Mexican War Correspondence of Richard Smith Elliott*, 165.
34. Gregg, *Commerce*, 160–161.
35. Magoffin, *Diary*, 120–121.
36. Magoffin, *Diary*, 145.
37. Cook, *Doña Tules*, 25–26.
38. Cook, *Doña Tules*, 26.
39. Cook, *Doña Tules*, 35.
40. Cook, *Doña Tules*, 55.
41. Cook, *Dona Tules*, 33.
42. González, "Borderlands," 1.
43. Alfredo, "A Trip to New Mexico," 2.
44. American Women, "La Tules," 1.
45. Garrard, *Wah-to-Yah*, xii.
46. Garrard, *Wah-to-Yah*, 13.
47. Garrard, *Wah-to-Yah*," 47.
48. Garrard, *Wah-to-Yah*, 78–79.
49. Spartacus Educational, "George Ruxton," 1.
50. Ruxton, *Wild Life*, 8–9.
51. Ruxton, *Wild Life*, 19.
52. Private communication of 5 June 2008 from Holly Snowden, Conference Center Coordinator, Town of Red River, New Mexico.
53. Ruxton, *Wild Life*, 31.
54. *Ibid.*
55. *Ibid.*
56. Dobie, "Aubry's Great Ride," 375–378.
57. Dary, *Santa Fe Trail*, 227.
58. Davis, *El Gringo*, 49, 51.

59. Quoted by National Park Service, "Fort Union: Administrative History," 3.
60. Quoted by National Park Service, "Fort Union," 2.
61. Moorhead, *New Mexico's Royal Road*, 199.
62. National Park Service, "Fort Union: Administrative History," 1.

Chapter VI

1. Wikipedia. "Mexican-American War," 1–18.
2. "The Mexican War: Campaigns in the American West," 1.
3. National Park Service. "Fort Scott National Historic Site: Mexican War," 2.
4. Couchman, *Cooke's Peak*, 32.
5. "The Mexican War: Campaigns in the American West," 2.
6. Abert, *Abert's New Mexico Report*, 118.
7. Abert, *Abert's New Mexico Report*, 34–35.
8. New Mexico Office of the State Historian, "Susan Shelby Magoffin," 1–6.
9. Magoffin, *Down the Santa Fe Trail*, 2, 4.
10. Magoffin, *Down the Santa Fe Trail*, 68.
11. Magoffin, *Down the Santa Fe Trail*, 96.
12. Magoffin, *Down the Santa Fe Trail*, 102–103, 105.
13. Magoffin, *Down the Santa Fe Trail*, 107.
14. Magoffin, *Down the Santa Fe Trail*, 110.
15. Magoffin, *Down the Santa Fe Trail*, 156. This citation has been very lightly edited.
16. Magoffin, *Down the Santa Fe Trail*, 193–194.
17. Magoffin, *Down the Santa Fe Trail*, 259–260.
18. New Mexico Office of the State Historian, "Susan Shelby Magoffin," 5–6.

Chapter VII

1. Some of the information in the first pages of this chapter comes from "Butterfield Stage," 1–2.
2. Quoted by Time-Life, *The Expressmen*, 31.
3. Ormsby, *Butterfield Overland Mail*, viii.
4. The Concord coach was manufactured by Abbot, Downing and Company in Concord, New Hampshire, beginning in about 1827. Because of the high quality of its design and construction, it can properly be thought of as the Rolls Royce of stagecoaches. The carriage of this coach was made of carefully chosen, well-seasoned basswood, elm, oak and hickory. It was not suspended on springs but was supported instead by two long, thick pieces of leather known as thoroughbraces. These imparted such a gentle, rocking motion to the coach that Mark Twain described riding in it as being in "a cradle on wheels." A fine Concord coach is now on permanent display at the Wells Fargo headquarters in San Francisco and is worth a visit. See also "The Ultimate Stagecoach" in Janin, *Fort Bridger*, 84–86.
5. Cited, respectively, by "Nothing Must Stop the Mail!" 2; Underwood, "Butterfield Overland Stage Route," 3; Sharp, "Butterfield's Grand Adventure," 4; and Time-Life, *The Expressmen*, 33.
6. Quoted by Hafen in *The Overland Mail*, 302.
7. Passengers were eventually allowed to carry up to 40 pounds of baggage without extra cost. One common question from prospective passengers was "What shall I bring?" In reply, a San Diego newspaper recommended the following equipment (spelling as in the original): "One Sharp's rifle and a hundred cartridges; a Colts navy revolver and two pounds of balls; a knife and sheath; a pair of boots and woolen pants; a half dozen pairs of thick woolen socks; six undershirts; three woolen overshirts; a wide-awake [broad-brimmed] hat; a cheap sack coat; a soldier's overcoat; one pair of blankets in summer and two in winter; a piece of India rubber [waterproof] cloth for blankets; a pair of gauntlets, a small bag of needles, pins, a sponge, hair brush, comb, soap, etc., in an oil silk bag; two pairs of thick drawers, and three or four towels." Quoted by Hafen in *The Overland Mail*, 98.
8. Twain, *Roughing It*, 54, 55, 66, 71, 72.
9. Ormsby, *Butterfield Overland Mail*, 79–80.
10. Ormsby, *Butterfield Overland Mail*, 82–83.
11. Quoted by California State Parks, "Butterfield Overland Mail," 2.
12. Quoted by Hafen in *The Overland Mail*, 99.
13. Quoted in "Butterfield Stage," 2.
14. "Butterfield State,"3.

Chapter VIII

1. Much of the strategic and tactical information in this chapter is drawn from Bennett, "The Civil War in New Mexico," 1–8.
2. Quoted by Bennett, "The Civil War in New Mexico," 3.
3. The American military presence in New Mexico began with the Mexican-American war of 1846–1848, i.e., with General Stephen Watts Kearny's Army of the West. Over the next half-century, the U.S. Army built about 60 military posts in New Mexico. By 1900 most of them had been abandoned. Fort Craig was founded in 1854 to protect travelers along the Jornada del Muerto route linking northern and southern New Mexico. It was closed in 1885.
4. Quoted by Bennett, "The Civil War in Mexico," 5.
5. Quoted by Northeast New Mexico Regional Board in "Civil War in New Mexico," 2.
6. *Ibid.*
7. *Ibid.*
8. *Ibid.*

Chapter IX

1. Most of the following account is adapted from Sides, *Blood and Thunder*, 419–497.
2. Quoted by Thompson, *The Army and the Navajo*, 1.
3. Quoted by Sides, *Blood and Thunder*, 403–404.
4. Quoted by Thompson, *The Army and the Navajo*, 10.
5. Quoted by Sides, *Blood and Thunder*, 404–405.
6. Quoted by Sides, *Blood and Thunder*, 409.
7. Quoted by Sides, *Blood and Thunder*, 410.
8. Questia Media America, 1.
9. Quoted by Thompson, *The Army and the Navajo*, 158.
10. Quoted by Sides, *Blood and Thunder*, 419.
11. Quoted by Sides, *Blood and Thunder*, 420.
12. The following information is drawn from Trafzer, *Kit Carson Campaign*, 75–76, 85.
13. Quoted by Lindgren, "Diary of Kit Carson's Navajo Campaign," 232–233.
14. Quoted by Sides, *Blood and Thunder*, 422.
15. Quoted by Sides, *Blood and Thunder*, 424.
16. The name "Chelly" is a Spanish borrowing, transliterated first into French and then into English, of the Navajo word "Tséyi" (canyon).
17. Quoted by McNitt in *Navajo Wars*, 431.
18. Fort Defiance was evacuated by the U.S. Army in April 1861 but when the deserted buildings fell into Navajo hands, the army reoccupied the fort and in July 1863 renamed it Fort Canby. See McNitt, *Navajo Wars*, 417. Although this was its new official name, it appears that the old name, Fort Defiance, continued to be used too. See McNitt, *Navajo Wars*, 417.
19. After Thompson, *The Army and the Navajo*, map of "New Mexico Territory in the 1860s," facing 1.
20. Quoted by Thompson, *The Army and the Navajo*, 46 (italics in original).
21. Quoted by Sides, *Blood and Thunder*, 477.
22. Quoted by Thompson, *The Army and the Navajo*, 84.
23. Quoted by Thompson, *The Army and the Navajo*, 100.
24. Quoted by Thompson, *The Army and the Navajo*, 140.
25. *Ibid.*

Chapter X

1. Janin, *Fort Bridger*, 114.
2. Some of the following account is drawn from "Texas Longhorns," 1–4.
3. *Handbook of Texas Online*, "Cattle Trailing," 1.
4. Life-Time, *The Cowboys*, map entitled "Highways for the Herds," 145.
5. The Texas historian J. Frank Dobie noted that herds from Texas had been trailed out of Texas before the Civil War, e.g., to New Orleans (1836), Missouri and Louisiana (1840s), New York (c. 1850), and California (1850s). See "Texas Longhorns," 2–4.
6. The information on Goodnight used in this chapter comes in part from *Texas Almanac*, "Cattle Drives," 1–6.
7. Some of these facts on Goodnight are drawn from PBS, "Charles Goodnight," 1–2.
8. This quotation has been edited and adapted from Time-Life, *The Cowboys*, 49–57, 145.

9. Quoted in Harding County, "Goodnight-Loving Trail," 2.
10. Quoted by Sharp in "Goodnight on the Pecos," 3.
11. Quoted by Sharp, "Goodnight on the Pecos," 8.
12. Harding County, "Goodnight-Loving Trail," 3, quoting J. Evetts Haley's *Charles Goodnight, Cowman and Plainsman* (1936).
13. *Texas Almanac*, "Cattle Drives," 4–5.
14. Old Colorado City Historical Society, "Routes to Colorado and Wyoming from Texas," 1.
15. Quoted in "Texas Longhorns," 3.
16. Sharp, "Goodnight on the Pecos," 8.
17. Quoted in Time-Life, *The Cowboys*, 136, 141.
18. "S.O.B. Stew," 1.
19. Quoted in "Texas History/Texas Trail Drives," 17–18, 19, 20 (italics added).

Chapter XI

1. These estimates of railway mileage are taken from Draffan, "Chronology," 1–11.
2. Myrick, *New Mexico's Railroads*, xiv.
3. *National Atlas*, 1.
4. *Along Your Way*, 4–5.
5. U.S. Department of State, "Gadsden Purchase," 1.
6. Quoted by Waters, *Steel Trails to Santa Fe*, 21.
7. Quoted by Ward, "Cyrus K. Holliday," 1.
8. Gleed, "The Atchison Topeka & Santa Fe," 9.
9. Quoted in "Richard Lacy 'Uncle Dick' Wootton," 2.
10. Waters, *Steel Trails*, 98.
11. The legend of the Harvey Girls inspired a 1946 film, *The Harvey Girls*, starring Judy Garland. It popularized a catchy tune — "On the Atchison, Topeka and the Santa Fe" — which won an Academy Award for Best Original Song. The opening stanza, which we quote here from distant memory and not from a printed score, sets the scene thus: "Do you hear that whistle comin' down the line?/I reckon that it's engine number forty-nine./ She's the only one that sounds that way/On the Atchison, Topeka and the Santa Fe."
12. Myrick, *New Mexico's Railroads*, 2.
13. Waters, *Steel Trails*, 100.
14. Wikipedia, "Railroad Wars," 1.
15. After Myrick, *New Mexico's Railroads*, 15.
16. Couchman, *Cooke's Peak*, 203.
17. *Ibid*.
18. Myrick, *New Mexico's Railroads*, 5–15.
19. Quoted by Moody, "The Railroad Builders," 3.
20. Gómez, *Manifest Destinies*, 85.
21. Wikipedia, "Drill, Ye Tarriers, Drill," 1 (lightly edited).
22. Not all Americans were in favor of the railroad. The naturalist and philosopher Henry David Thoreau (1817–1862) had this to say about the railroad's "sleepers" in his lapidary work, *Walden*: "We do not ride on the railroad; it rides upon us. Did you ever think what those sleepers are that underlie the railroad? Each one is a man, an Irish-man, or a Yankee man. The rails are laid on them, and they are covered with sand, and the cars run smoothly over them. They are sound sleepers, I assure you. And every few years a new lot is laid down and run over.... I am glad to know that it takes a gang of men for every five miles to keep the sleepers down and level in their beds as it is, for this is a sign that they may sometime get up again" (Thoreau, *Walden*, chapter 2: "Where I Lived and What I Lived For").
23. Wikipedia, "Gandy dancer," 1.
24. Gleed, "The Atchison Topeka & Santa Fe," 1, 4.
25. Tice, *Early Railroad Days*, 11–12.
26. Gleed, "Atchison, Topeka and Santa Fe," 10.
27. Quoted by Janin, *Fort Bridger*, 94.

Chapter XII

1. Etter, *To California on the Southern Route*, 8.
2. Etter, *To California on the Southern Route*, 51.
3. Quoted by Etter, *To California on the Southern Route*, 53, 54.
4. Quoted by Etter, *To California on the Southern Route*, frontispiece (italics in original).
5. Quoted by Etter, *To California on the Southern Route*, 54.
6. Quoted by Etter, *To California on the Southern Route*, 55.
7. Quoted by Etter, *To California on the Southern Route*, 62.
8. Hague, *Road to California*, 11.
9. Etter, *To California on the Southern Route*, 86, 100.
10. Walker and Bufkin, *Historical Atlas of Arizona*, 18.

11. Hague, *Road to California*, 264.
12. Quoted by Hague, *Road to California*, 265.
13. "Anglo-American Trails," 1.
14. Pattie, *Personal Narrative*, 79–80.
15. Quoted by Jenkinson, *Land of Clear Light*, 172.
16. Jenkinson, *Land of Clear Light*, 172–173.
17. Emory, quoted by Hague, *Road to California*, 224–225.
18. Emory, *Lieutenant Emory Reports*, 173.
19. Utley, *Life Wild and Perilous*, 252–254.
20. Time-Life, *Trailblazers*, 174–181.
21. Etter, *To California on the Southern Route*, 38–39.
22. Cooking with a bean pot, a type of camp cookery still used today, involves digging a hole about 2½ feet deep; lining the hole with rocks to absorb heat; building a fire in the hole; burying a cast iron pot filled with beans, water, meat, vegetables, etc., in the embers; filling up the hole with dirt and tamping it down, thus in effect creating an oven; and, finally, waiting several hours — or even overnight — for the slow process of cooking to be finished. On camping trips, both authors of this book have used variations of this method of cooking. Ursula Carlson made a pineapple upside down cake in the high desert of Nevada. In the coastal mountains of California, Hunt Janin cooked a pork tenderloin so tasty that, at night, a mountain lion came into his camp to eat the leftovers.
23. Jenkinson, *Land of Clear Light*, 185.
24. Quoted by Janin, *Fort Bridger*, 131.
25. Etter, *To California on the Southern Route*, 73, 84.
26. Quoted by Etter, *To California on the Southern Route*, 56.
27. This section is drawn in part from Sharp, "Cochise and the Bascom Affair," 1–11; Wikipedia, "Cochise," 1–4; and Wikipedia, "Geronimo," 1–7.
28. Quoted by Roberts, *Once They Moved Like the Wind*, 38.
29. Quoted by Dawson, *New Mexico in 1876–1877*, 58.
30. "Geronimo's surrender," 4–5.
31. Quoted by Etter, *To California by the Southern Route*, 103–104.
32. Quoted by Etter, *To California by the Southern Route*, 32–33, 135.

Epilogue

1. National Park Service, "Coronado National Memorial: Mission and Significance," 1.
2. National Park Service, "Coronado National Memorial: Your Safety," 1.
3. National Park Service, "Santa Fe National Historic Trail: Things To Know Before You Come," 1.
4. Adapted from Wikipedia, "Battles of the Mexican-American War," 1–4.
5. After Wikipedia, "Butterfield Overland Mail," 1–3.
6. Sharp, "Goodnight on the Pecos," 10.
7. Bureau of Land Management, "Gila Lower Box Canyon," 1.
8. Private communication of 18 December 2008 from Reid Miller, Visitor Information Specialist at the Bureau of Land Management's Historic Trails Interpretive Center.

Appendix 1

1. This translation had been adapted from a text on the Website of the National Humanities Center (see bibliography).

Appendix 2

1. The text of this advertisement appears in Dary, *Santa Fe Trail*, 202–203.

Appendix 4

1. Janin, *Fort Bridger*, 47.
2. Garrard, *Wah-to-Yah*, 161–162.
3. Garrard, *Wah-to-Yah*, 163.

Appendix 6

1. *Geronimo: My Life*, xvi.
2. *Geronimo: My Life*, 27.
3. *Geronimo: My Life*, 30–33.
4. *Geronimo: My Life*, 33–34.
5. *Geronimo: My Life*, 39–40.
6. *Geronimo: My Life*, 49, 51.

Bibliography

Abert, James W. *Abert's New Mexico Report 1846–1847*. Albuquerque: Horn and Wallace, 1962.
Adams, Andy. *Log of a Cowboy: A Narrative of the Old Trail Days*. Liskeard, Cornwall: Diggory Press, 2008.
Albuquerque Museum. "The Founding of Albuquerque." Albuquerque: n.d.
Alfredo, Don. "A Trip to New Mexico." http:www.htg.net/~artpike/farwest2.htm (accessed 27 May 2008).
"Along Your Way: Facts about stations and scenes on the Santa Fe 1946." http://titchenal.com/atsf/ayw1946/paths.html (accessed 4 November 2008).
Allen, John Logan. "Exploration and Explorers." http://www.americanforeignrelations.com/En-Fl/Exploration-and-Explorers.html (accessed 10 June 2008).
_____, ed. *North American Exploration*. Vol. 2, *A Continent Defined*. Lincoln: University of Nebraska Press, 1997.
_____. *North American Exploration*. Vol. 3, *A Continent Comprehended*. Lincoln: University of Nebraska Press, 1997.
American Gaming Association. "Responsible Gaming." http://www.americangaming.org/programs/responsiblegaming/guide_to_odds.cfm (accessed 2 May 2008).
American Journeys. "Espejo, Antonio de." http://www.americanjourneys.org/aj-008/summary/index.asp (accessed 24 February 2008).
American Women. "'La Tules' [Gertrudis Barceló] Dealing Monte in Her Santa Fe Gambling House." http://lcweb2.loc.gov/ammem/awhhtml/awas12/d10.html (accessed 2 May 2008).
"Anasazi." http://www.mnsu.edu/emuseum/cultural/northamerica/anasazi.html (accessed 5 December 2008).
"Ancient Pueblo Peoples." http://en.wikipedia.org (accessed 5 December 2008).
"Anglo-American Trails through Southeast Arizona." http://www.discoverseaz.com/History/Anglo.html (accessed 29 December 2007).
Bancroft, Hubert Howe. "*Bancroft's History of Utah 1540–1886.*" http://www.utlm.org/onlinebooks/bancroftshistoryofutah_chapter1.htm (accessed 31 March 2008).
"Battles of the Mexican-American War." http://en.wikipedia.org (accessed 10 August 2008).
Beebe, Rose Marie, and Robert M. Senkewicz. *Lands of Promise and Despair: Chronicles of Early California, 1535–1846*. Berkeley: Heyday, 2001.
Bennett, Charles. "The Civil War in New Mexico:1861–1862." http://www.nmculturenet.org/heritage/civil_war/essays/1.html (accessed 20 August 2008).
Bolton, Herbert E. "The Spanish Occupation of Texas, 1519–1690." http:www/tashaon

line.org/publications/journals/shq/online/v16/n1/article_3.html (accessed 3 March 2008).

Boyle, Susan Calafate. *Los Capitalistas: Hispano Merchants and the Santa Fe Trade.* Albuquerque: University of New Mexico Press, 1997.

Brewerton, George Douglas. *Overland with Kit Carson: A Narrative of the Old Spanish Trail in '48.* Lincoln: University of Nebraska Press, 1993.

Brooks, James F. *Captives and Cousins: Slavery, Kinship, and Community in the Southwest Borderlands.* Chapel Hill: University of North Carolina Press, 2002.

Bureau of Land Management. "Gila Lower Box Canyon." http://www.blm.gov/nm/st/en/prog/recreation/las_cruces/gila_lower_box.html (accessed 18 December 2008).

"Butterfield Overland Mail." http//en.wikipedia.org/w/index.php?title=Butterfield_Overland_Mail&printable=yes (accessed 23 August 2008).

"Butterfield Stage." http:www.discoverseaz.com/History/Butterfield.html (accessed 30 December 2007).

Cabeza de Vaca, Alvar Núñez. *Chronicle of the Narváez Expedition.* New York: Penguin, 2002.

———. "The Journey of Alvar Núñez Cabeza de Vaca (1542)." Translated by Fanny Bandelier, 1905. http://www.pbs.org/weta/thewest/resources/archives/one/cabeza.htm (accessed 27 February 2008).

California State Parks. "Butterfield Overland Mail." http://www.parks.ca.gov/?page_id=25444 (accessed 23 August 2008).

Calloway, Colin G. *One Vast Winter Count: The Native American West Before Lewis and Clark.* Lincoln: University of Nebraska Press, 2003.

Castañeda, Pedro de. *Narrative of the Coronado Expedition.* Edited by John Miller Morris. Chicago: Lakeside Press, 2002.

Catlin, George. *North American Indians.* New York: Penguin, 2004.

Center for Advanced Technology in Education, University of Oregon. "Historical Context." http://anza.uoregon.edu/intro/historical.html (accessed 4 March 2008).

"Chaco Culture National Historic Park." *http://en.wikipedia.org/w/index.php?title=Chaco_Culture_National_Historical-Park* (accessed 11 December 2008).

Cline, Gloria Griffen. *Exploring the Great Basin.* Reno: University of Nevada Press, 1988.

"Cochise." http://en.wikipedia.org/w/index.php?title=Cochise&printable=yes (accessed 21 August 2008).

Cook, Mary J. Straw. *Doña Tules: Santa Fe's Courtesan and Gambler.* Albuquerque: University of New Mexico Press, 2007.

Couchman, Donald Howard. *Cooke's Peak — Pasaron Por Aqui: A Focus on United States History in Southwestern New Mexico.* Las Cruces: BLM, Cultural Resources, No. 7, 1990.

Dary, David. *The Santa Fe Trail: Its History, Legends, and Lore.* New York: Penguin, 2000.

Davis, William H. *El Gringo, or New Mexico and Her People.* http://southwest.library.arizona.edu/elgr/ (accessed 6 June 2008).

Dawson, William D. *New Mexico in 1876–1877, A Newspaperman's View: The Travels and Reports of William D. Dawson.* Edited by Robert J. Tórrez. Los Ranchos de Albuquerque: Rio Grande Books, 2007.

DesertUSA. "Juan Bautista de Anza: Blazed the Anza Trail." http://www.desertusa.com/magjan98/janpap/du anza.html (accessed 10 March 2009).

DeVoto, Bernard. *The Course of Empire.* New York: Houghton Mifflin, 1998.

———. *The Year of Decision: 1846.* New York: St. Martin's Griffin, 2000.

Diamond, Jared. *Collapse: How Societies Choose to Fail or Succeed.* New York: Penguin, 2005.

Dobie, J. Frank. "Aubry's Great Ride." In *The Best of the West: An Anthology of Classic Writing from the American West,* by Tony Hillerman, 375–378. New York: HarperPerennial, 1991.

Draffan, George. "Chronology of the Northern Pacific & Related Land Grant Railroads." http://www.landgrant.org/history.html (accessed 2 November 2008).

"Drill, Ye Tarriers, Drill." http://en.wikipedia/org/w/index.php?title=Drill,_Ye_Tarriers,_Drill&printable=yes (accessed 15 November 2008).

Dubin, Lois Sherr. *The History of Beads from 30,000 B.C. to the Present.* London: Thames and Hudson, 1987.

"Early Forts of New Mexico." http://www.htg.net/~artpike/fort7.htm (accessed 14 October 2008).

Elliott, Richard Smith. *The Mexican War Correspondence of Richard Smith Elliott.* Norman: University of Oklahoma Press, 1997.

Emory, William Hemsley. *Lieutenant Emory Reports.* Albuquerque: University of New Mexico Press, 1951.

Etter, Patricia A. *To California on the Southern Route, 1849: A History and Annotated Bibliography.* Spokane: Clark, 1998.

Fagan, Brian. *Chaco Canyon: Archaeologists Explore the Lives of an Ancient Society.* New York: Oxford University Press, 2005.

Faulk, Odie B. *Destiny Road: The Gila Trail and the Opening of the Southwest.* New York: Oxford University Press, 1973.

Fehrenbach, T.R. *Comanches: The History of a People.* New York: Anchor, 2003.

Ford, Richard I. "Inter-Indian Exchange in the Southwest." In *Handbook of North American Indians: Southwest,* by Alfonso Ortiz, 711–722. Vol. 10. Washington, D.C.: Smithsonian Institution, 1983.

Foster, Edward Halsey. *Josiah Gregg and Lewis H. Garrard.* Boise: Boise State University, 1977.

"Frankie Laine, Mule Train Lyrics." http://www.cowboylyrics.com/lyrics/laine-frankie/mule-train-12552.html (accessed 23 February 2009).

Gabriel, Kathryn. *Roads to Center Place: A Cultural Atlas of Chaco Canyon and the Anasazi.* Boulder, CO: John Books, 1991.

_____. "Gandy dancer." http://en.wikipedia.org/w/index.php?title=Gandy_dancer&printable=yes (accessed 15 November 2008).

Garrard, Lewis H. *Wah-to-yah and the Taos Trail.* Norman: University of Oklahoma Press, 1955.

GeoNative. "New Mexico Pueblos." http://www.geocities.com/Athens/9479/pueblo.html?200817 (accessed 17 April 2008).

"Geronimo." http://en.wikipedia.org/w/index.php?title=Geronimo&printable=yes (accessed 22 August 2008).

Geronimo. *Geronimo: My Life.* Edited by S.M. Barrett. Mineola: Dover, 2005.

"Geronimo's surrender — Skeleton Canyon, 1886." http://www.southernnewmexico.com/Articles/People/Geronimossurrender-Skelet.html (accessed 30 November 2008).

"Geronimo Trail National Scenic Byway." http://www.geronimotrail.com/tour.html (accessed 27 November 2008).

Gleed, Charles S. "The Atchison Topeka & Santa Fe." *Cosmopolitan* (February 1893). http://www.catskillarchive.com/rrestra/statsf.html (accessed 2 November 2008).

Golay, Michael, and John S. Bowman. *North American Exploration.* Hoboken: Wiley, 2003.

Gómez, Laura. *Manifest Destiny: The Making of the Mexican American People.* New York: New York University Press, 2008.

González, Deena. "The Borderlands — The Travail of War: Women and Children in the Years after the U.S.-Mexican War." http://www.pbs.org/kera/usmexicanwar/travail_of_war.html (accessed 27 May 2008).

Gregg, Josiah. *Commerce of the Prairies: Life on the Great Plains in the 1830's and 1840's.* Santa Barbara: Narrative, 2001.

Gustafson, Sarah. *Pecos National Historical Park*. Tucson: Southwest Parks and Monuments Association, 1997.
Hafen, LeRoy R. *The Overland Mail, 1849–1869*. Norman: University of Oklahoma Press, 2004.
Hafen, LeRoy R., and Ann W. Hafen. *Old Spanish Trail: Santa Fé to Los Angeles: With Extracts from Contemporary Records and Including the Diaries of Antonio Armijo and Orville Pratt*. Lincoln: University of Nebraska Press, 1993.
Hague, Harlan. *Road to California: The Search for a Southern Overland Route, 1540–1848*. Lincoln: Authors Choice, 2001.
Handbook of Texas Online. "Amangual, Francisco." http://tashaonline.org/handbook/online/articles/AA/fam_1print.html (accessed 27 November 2008).
_____. "Apache Indians." http://www.tashaonline.org/handbook/online/articles/AA/bma 33_print.html (accessed 16 April 2008).
_____. "Becknell, William." http://www.tashaonlinia.org/handbook/online/articles/BB/fbe17_html (accessed 22 May 2008).
_____. "Bonilla, Francisco Leyva de." http://www.tashaonline.org/handbook/online/articles/BB/fbo16_print.html (accessed 28 February 2008).
_____. "Cabeza de Vaca, Ávar Núñez." http:www.tshaonline.org.handbook/online/articles/CC/fca6_print.html (accessed 25 January 2008).
_____. "Castaño de Sosa, Gaspar." http://www.tshaonline.org/handbook/online/articles/CC/fca87_print.html (accessed 17 February 2008).
_____. "Cattle Trailing." http://www.tashaonline.org/handbook/online/articles/CC/ayc1.html (accessed 26 October 2008).
_____. "Domínguez de Mendoza, Juan." http://www.tashaonline.org/handbook/online/articles/DD/fdo52_print.html (accessed 4 March 2008).
_____. "El Paso del Norte." http://www.tashaonling.org/handbook/online/articles/EE/hdelu_print.html (accessed 9 April 2009).
_____. "Espejo-Beltrán Expedition." http://www.tashaonline.org/handbook/online/articles/EE/upe2_print.html (accessed 24 February 2008).
_____. "Exploration." http://www.tashaoline.org/handbok/online/articles/EE/uzeuj.html (accessed 2 March 2008).
_____. "Goodnight-Loving Trail." http://www.tsha.utexas.edu/handbook/online/articles/GG/ayg2_print.html (accessed 26 August 2007).
_____. "Gregg, Josiah." http://www.tsha.utexas.edu/handbook/online/articles/FF/fgr51_print.html (accessed 28 December 2007).
_____. "Horsehead Crossing." http://www.tashaonline.org/handbook/online/articles/HH/rih1_print.html (accessed 30 October 2008).
_____. "Loving, Oliver." http://www.tshaonline.org/handbook/online/articles/LL/flo38.html (accessed 22 October 2008).
_____. "Posada, Alonso de." http://www.tshaonline.org/handbook/online/articles/PP/fpo25_print.html (accessed 23 August 2008).
_____. "Rivera y Vallalón, Pedro de." http://www.tashaonline.org/handbook/online/articles/RR/fri27_print.html (accessed 13 April 2008).
_____. "Rodríguez-Sánchez Expedition." http://www.tashaonline.org/handbook/online/articles/RR/uprl_print.html (accessed 22 February 2008).
_____. "Rivera y Vallalón, Pedro de." http://www.tashaonline.org/handbook/online/articles/RR/fri27_print.html (accessed 13 April 2008).
_____. "Santa Fe Trail." http://www.tsha.utexas.edu/handbook/online/articles/SS/exs3.html (accessed 7 December 2007).
_____. "Vial, Pedro (?–1814)." http:www.shaonline.org/handbook/online/articles/VV/fvl_print.html (accessed 9 March 2008).

Harding County. "The Story of Oliver Loving and the Goodnight-Loving Trail." http://www.hardingcounty.org/People/Oliver_Loving.htm (accessed 25 October 2008).

Hillerman, Tony, ed. *The Best of the West: An Anthology of Classic Writing from the American West*. New York: HarperCollins, 1991.

"History of Railroads and Maps — Part 1." http://nationalatlas.gov/articles/history/a_railroads-p1.html (accessed 2 November 2008).

"History of the Old Spanish Trail." http://www.museumtrail.org/OldSpanishTrail.asp (accessed 17 June 2008).

Holling, Clancy Holling. *Tree in the Trail*. Boston: Houghton Mifflin, 1970.

Inman, Colonel Henry. *The Old Santa Fé Trail: The Story of a Great Highway*. 1981 reprint by Time-Life (Classics of the Old West) of the original edition published in New York by Macmillan in 1897.

Jackson, Hal. *Following the Royal Road: A Guide to the Historic Camino Real de Tierra Adentro*. Albuquerque: University of New Mexico Press, 2006.

Janin, Hunt. *Claiming the American Wilderness: International Rivalry in the Trans-Mississippi West, 1528–1803*. Jefferson, NC: McFarland, 2006.

_____. *Fort Bridger, Wyoming: Trading Post for Indians, Mountain Men and Westward Migrants*. Jefferson, NC: McFarland, 2001.

Jenkinson, Michael. *Land of Clear Light*. New York: Dutton, 1977.

John, Elizabeth A.H. *Storms Brewed in Other Men's Words: The Confrontation of Indians, Spanish, and French in the Southwest, 1540–1795*. 2nd ed. Norman: University of Oklahoma Press, 1996.

Jones, Oakah L., Jr. "Spanish Penetrations to the North of New Spain." In *North American Exploration*. Edited by John Logan Allen. Vol. 2, *A Continent Defined*, 9–64. Lincoln: University of Nebraska, 1997.

Kavanagh, Thomas W. *Comanche Political History: An Ethnohistorical Perspective, 1706–1875*. Lincoln: University of Nebraska Press, 1996.

Kessell, John L. *Kiva, Cross, and Crown: The Pecos Indians and New Mexico, 1540–1840*. Albuquerque: University of New Mexico Press, 1990.

_____. *Spain in the Southwest: A Narrative History of Colonial New Mexico, Arizona, Texas, and California*. Norman: University of Oklahoma, 2002.

Kincaid, Chris, ed. *Chaco Roads Project Phase I: A Reappraisal of Prehistoric Roads in the San Juan Basin*. U.S. Department of the Interior and Bureau of Land Management. New Mexico State Office: Albuquerque District Office, 1983.

"Kit Carson." http://en.wikipedia.org/w/index.php?title=Kit_Carson&printable=yes (accessed 20 October 2007).

Linegren, Raymond E., ed. "A Diary of Kit Carson's Navajo Campaign 1863–1864." In *New Mexico Historical Review* 21 (1946): 226–247.

Loomis, Noel M., and Abraham P. Nasatir. *Pedro Vial and the Roads to Santa Fe*. Norman: University of Oklahoma Press, 1967.

Magoffin, Susan Shelby. *Down the Santa Fe Trail and into Mexico: The Diary of Susan Shelby Magoffin, 1846–1847*. Edited by John Logan Allen. Lincoln: University of Nebraska Press, 1982.

Maguire, James H., Peter Wild, and Donald A. Barclay. *A Rendezvous Reader: Tall, Tangled, and True Tales of the Mountain Men, 1805–1850*. Salt Lake City: University of Utah Press, 1997.

Marcos de Niza (Fray). "A Relation of the Reverend Father Fray [sic]." http://etext.lib.virginia.edu/subjects/eaw/essays/nizatext.html (accessed 12 February 2008).

Marcy, Randolph B. *The Prairie Traveler*. Old Saybrook: Globe Pequot, 1969.

Marshall, James. *Santa Fe: The Railroad that Built an Empire*. New York: Random House, 1945.

McDonald, Jarom. "Derrotero y Diario: The Diary and Itinerary of Fathers Domínguez and Escalante." http:www.mith2.umd.udu/eada/gateway/diario/intro.html (accessed 6 March 2008).

McKeehan, Wallace L. "The Rivera Expedition 1727." http://www.tamu.edu/ccbn/dewitt/alarconex3.html (accessed 13 April 2008).

McNitt, Frank. *Navajo Wars: Military Campaigns, Slave Raids and Reprisals*. Albuquerque: University of New Mexico Press, 1972.

"Mexican-American War." http://en.wikipedia.org/wiki/Mexican-American_War (accessed 10 August 2008).

"Mexican War: Campaigns in the American West." http://www.lone-star.net/mall/texas info/mexicow.htm (accessed 17 June 2008).

Moody, John. *The Railroad Builders: A Chronicle of the Welding of the States*. New Haven: Yale University Press, 1919.

Moorhead, Max. *New Mexico's Royal Road: Trade and Travel on the Chihuahua Trail*. Norman: University of Oklahoma Press, 1958.

Morgan, Dale. *Jedediah Smith and the Opening of the West*. Lincoln: University of Nebraska Press, 1967.

"Mule Train." http://en.wikipedia.org/w/index.php?title=Mule_Train&printable=yes (accessed 23 February 2009).

Murphy, Retta. "Journey of Pedro de Rivera, 1724–1728." *Southwestern Historical Quarterly* (Online) 41, no. 2 (October 1937). http://www.tsha.utexas/edu/publications/journals/shq/online/v041/n2/contrib_D (accessed 13 April 2008).

Myers, Joan, and Mark Simmons. *Along the Santa Fe Trail*. Albuquerque: University of New Mexico Press, 1986.

Myrick, David F. *New Mexico's Railroads: A Historical Survey*. Revised edition. Albuquerque: University of New Mexico Press, 1990.

National Atlas of the United States. "History of Railroads and Maps — Part 1." http://nationalatlas.gov/articles/history/a_railroads-p1.html (accessed 2 November 2008).

National Park Service. "Chaco Culture National Historical Park: A Brief History of Chaco Culture National Historical Park." http://www.nps.gov/archive/chcu/briefhis.htm (accessed 3 February 2008).

_____. "Chaco Culture National Historical Park: The Center of Chacoan Culture." http://www.nps.gov/archive/chucu/chacoan.html (accessed 3 February 2008).

_____. "Chaco Culture National Historical Park: The Road System." http://www.nps.gov/archive/chcu/roads.html (accessed 3 February 2008).

_____. "Coronado National Memorial: Mission and Significance." http://www.nps.gov/coro/history/culture/parkmission.htm (accessed 12 December 2008).

_____. "Coronado National Memorial: Your Safety." http://www.nps.gov/coro/planyourvisit/yoursafety.htm (accessed 12 December 2008).

_____. "Fort Scott National Historic Site: Mexican War." http://www.nps.gov/archive/fosc/mexican.htm (accessed 9 August 2008).

_____. "Fort Union." Washington, D.C.: Government Printing Office No. 320 369/00467, reprint 2002.

_____. "Fort Union: Administrative History." http://www.nps.gov/archive/foun/adhi/adhiO.htm (accessed 20 January 2008).

_____. "Jumanos." http://www.nps.gov/archive/foda/Fort_Davis_WEB_PAGE/About_the_Fort/Jumanos.htm (accessed 5 March 2008).

_____. "Pecos." Washington, D.C.: GPO:2006-320-369/00547, 2006.

_____. "Pecos: The Battle of Glorieta Pass March 26–28, 1862." National Park Service brochure with no place or date of publication.

_____. "Pecos National Historical Park: Alfred Vincent Kidder." http//www.nps.gov/pecos/historyculture/alfred-vincent-kidder.html (accessed 4 February 2008).

_____. "Pecos National Historical Park: People of Pecos." http://www.nps.gov/pecos/historyculture/people-of-pecos.htm (accessed 4 February 2008).
_____. "Santa Fe National Historic Trail: A Brief Interpretive History." http://www.nps.gov/archive/safe/fnl-sft/broch/newbro.htm (accessed 16 April 2008).
_____. "Santa Fe National Historic Trail: Special History Study (chapter 4)." http://www.nps.gov/history/history/online_books/safe/shs4.htm (accessed 14 December 2008).
_____. "Santa Fe National Historic Trail: Things to Know Before You Come." http://www.nps.gov/safe/planyourvisit/things2know.htm (accessed 13 December 2008).
_____. "Santa Fe Trail." Washington, D.C.: Government Printing Office no. 417-48/60135, 1997.
New Mexico Office of the State Historian. "1582 — Espejo Expedition." http://www.newmexicohistory.org/filedetails.php?fileID=467 (accessed 24 February 2008).
_____. "Susan Shelby Magoffin (1827–1855)." http://www.newmexicohistory.org/filedetails. php?fileID=4835 (accessed 1 May 2008).
"New Mexico Pueblos." http://www.geocities.com/Athens/9479/pueblo.html?200817 (accessed 17 April 2008).
"New Mexico Territory." http://en.wikipedia.org/w/index.php?title=New_Mexico_Territory&printable=yes (accessed 5 October 2008).
"New Spain." http://www.americanforeignrelations.com/Mu-Ne/New-Spain.html (accessed 3 April 2008).
Noble, David Grant, ed. *Pecos Ruins: Geology, Archaeology, History, and Prehistory*. Santa Fe: Ancient City, 1993.
Nordhoff, Walter. *The Journey of the Flame*. Santa Clara: Heyday, 2002.
Northeast New Mexico Regional Board. "Civil War in New Mexico 1861–1862." No place or date of publication is given on this brochure itself but it cites http://www.Nenewmexico.com/civilwar.
"Nothing Must Stop the Mail!" http//www.over-land.com/mail.html (accessed 23 August 2008).
Old Colorado Historical Society. "Routes to Colorado and Wyoming from Texas." http://history.oldcolo.com/oldtown/maps/cattle.html (accessed 21 October 2008).
"Old Spanish Trail: Mojave Desert Roads & Trails." http://digital-desert.com/old-spanish-trail (accessed 27 December 2008).
Old Spanish Trail Association. "Welcome to the Old Spanish Trail Association." http://www.olspanishtrail.org (accessed 28 July 2007).
Ormsby, Waterman L. *The Butterfield Overland Mail*. Edited by Lyle H. Wright and Josephine M. Bynum. San Marino: Huntington Library, 2007.
Parkman, Francis. *The Oregon Trail*. New York: Airmont, 1964.
"Paths of Empire." http://www.tichenal.com/atsf/ayw1946/paths.html (accessed 28 July 2007).
Pattie, James O. *The Personal Narrative of James O. Pattie of Kentucky*. Santa Barbara: Narrative, 2001.
PBS. "Charles Goodnight." http://www.pbs.org/weta/thewest/people/d_h/goodnight.htm (accessed 28 August 2007).
_____. "Coronado's Report to the King of Spain Sent from Tiguex on October 20, 1541." http://www.pbs.org/weta/resources/archives/one/corona9.htm (accessed 27 February 2008).
Preston, Douglas, Christine Preston, and José Antonio Esquibel. *The Royal Road: El Camino Real from Mexico City to Santa Fe*. Albuquerque: University of New Mexico Press, 1998.
Quaife, Milo Milton, ed. *Kit Carson's Autobiography*. Lincoln: University of Nebraska Press, 1935.
Questia Media America. "William F.M. Arny." http:www.questia.com/reader/action/open/20584370 (accessed 19 October 2008).

"Railroad Wars." http://en.wikipedia.org/w/index.php?title=Railroad_Wars&printable=yes (accessed 17 April 2009).

"Richard Lacy 'Uncle Dick' Wootton." http://www.sangres.com/history/uncledick.htm (accessed 14 November 2008).

Riley, Carroll L. *Rio del Norte: People of the Upper Rio Grande from Earliest Times to the Pueblo Revolt.* Salt Lake: University of Utah Press, 1995.

Roberts, David. *Once They Moved Like the Wind: Cochise, Geronimo, and the Apache Wars.* New York: Simon & Schuster, 1994.

Rounds, Glen ed. *Mountain Men: George Frederick Ruxton's Firsthand Accounts of Fur Trappers and Indians in the Rockies.* New York: Holiday House, 1996.

Russell, Carl P. *Guns on the Early Frontiers: A History of Firearms from Colonial Times through the Years of the Western Fur Trade.* Lincoln: University of Nebraska Press, 1957.

Russell, Peter. "Gila Cliff Dwellings National Monument: An Administrative History." http://www.nps.gov/archive/gicl/adhi/adhi.htm (accessed 28 January 2008).

Ruxton, George F. *Wild Life in the Rocky Mountains.* New York: Macmillan, 1916. Reproduced in digital format at http://www.xmission.com/~drudy/mtman/html/ruxton.html (accessed 28 May 2008).

Sanchez, Joseph P. *Explorers, Traders, and Slavers: Forging the Old Spanish Trail, 1678–1850.* Salt Lake City: University of Utah Press, 1997.

Schroeder, Albert H. "Pecos Pueblo." In *Handbook of North American Indians,* 420–437. Vol. 9. Edited by Alfonso Ortiz. Washington, DC: Smithsonian Institution, 1979.

Schroeder, Albert H., and Dan S. Matson *A Colony on the Move: Gaspar Castaño de Sosa's Journal, 1590–1591.* Santa Fe: School of American Research, 1965.

Senate Documents. First Session, 30th Congress, Vol. III, 1847–48. Lt. Emory, William H. "Notes of a Military Reconnaissance, from Fort Leavenworth, in Missouri, to San Diego, in California, including part of the Arkansas, Del Norte, and Gila Rivers."

Sharp, Jay W. "Butterfield's Grand Adventure." http://www.desertusa.com/mag00/may/stories/butter.html (accessed 23 August 2008).

———. "Cochise and the Bascom Affair." http:www.desertusa.com/ind1/Cochise.html (accessed 23 April 2009).

———. "Goodnight on the Pecos." http:www.desertusa.com/mag04/july/goodnight.html (accessed 28 October 2008).

Sides, Hampton. *Blood and Thunder: The Epic Story of Kit Carson and the Conquest of the American West.* New York: Anchor, 2006.

Sidney, S. *The Book of the Horse.* London: Cassell Petter & Galpin, n.d. [1875?].

Simmons, Marc. "History of Pueblo-Spanish Relations to 1821." In *Handbook of North American Indians.* Edited by Alfonso Ortiz. Vol. 9, 178–193. Washington, DC: Smithsonian Institution, 1979.

———. *The Last Conquistador: Juan de Oñate and the Settling of the Far Southwest.* Norman: University of Oklahoma Press, 1991.

———. *The Old Trail to Santa Fe: Collected Essays.* Albuquerque: University of New Mexico Press, 1996.

Singletary, Otis A. *The Mexican War.* Chicago: University of Chicago Press, 1960.

"S.O.B. Stew." http://www.popeye-x.com/antippx7/0000005a.htm (accessed 26 October 2008).

Southwest Crossroads. "The Chamuscado-Rodriguez Expedition of 1581–1582." http://southwestcrossroads.org/record/php?num=918&hl=chamuscado (accessed 25 May 2008).

"Spanish Monte." http://www.lahacal.org/gentleman/monte.html (accessed 21 May 2008).

Spartacus Educational. "George Ruxton." http://www.spartacus.schoolnet.co.uk/Wwruxton.htm (accessed 28 May 2008).

_____. "Santa Fe Trail." http://www.spartacus.schoolnet.co.uk/WWWsantefe.htm (accessed 1 June 2007).
"States and Territories of the United States of America, August 7, 1789 to May 26, 1790." http://en.wikipedia.org/wiki/File:United States 1789-08-1790.png (accessed 2 April 2009).
Swagerty, William R. "Indian Trade in the Trans-Mississippi West to 1870." In *Handbook of North American Indians: History of Indian-White Relations.* Edited by Wilcomb E. Washburn. Vol. 4, 351–390. Washington, D.C.: Smithsonian Institution, 1988.
Texas Almanac. "Cattle Drives." http://www.texasalmanac.com/history/highlights/cattle (accessed 26 October 2008).
_____. "Franciscan Missionaries in Texas before 1690." http://www.texasalmanac.com/history/highlights/franciscan/ (accessed 1 March 2008).
"Texas History/Texas Trail Drives/Chisholm & Goodnight-Loving Trails." http://forttumbleweed.net/cattledrives.html (accessed 21 October 2008).
"Texas Longhorns: A history of longhorn cattle and guide to viewing the State of Texas' longhorn herd." http://www.dfwnetmall.com/e-mag/longhorn.html (accessed 26 October 2008).
Thompson, Gerald. *The Army and the Navajo.* Tucson: University of Arizona Press, 1976.
Thoreau, Henry David. "Thoreau's Walden." http://xroads/virginia.edu/~Hyper/WALDEN/hdto2.html (accessed 17 November 2008).
Tice, Henry Allen. *Early Railroad Days in New Mexico, 1880.* Santa Fe: Stagecoach, n.d., reprint of original 1932 edition.
Time-Life Books. *The Cowboys.* Alexandria: Time-Life, 1973.
_____. *The Expressmen.* Alexandria: Time-Life, 1974.
_____. *The Indians.* Alexandria: Time-Life, 1973.
_____. *The Great Chiefs.* Alexandria: Time-Life, 1977.
_____. *The Trailblazers.* New York: Time-Life, 1973.
Torres, Robert J. "A Cuarto Centennial History of New Mexico: Chapter Seven: The Quest for Statehood." http://www.nmgs.org/artciar7/htm (accessed 30 November 2008).
Trafzer, Clifford E. *The Kit Carson Campaign: The Last Great Navajo War.* Norman: University of Oklahoma Press, 1982.
Twain, Mark. *Roughing It.* New York: Penguin, 1985.
Tyson, Carl. "Vial, Pedro (ca.1750?-1814)." http://digital.library.okstate.edu/encyclopedia/entries/V/VI001.html (accessed 9 March 2008).
Underwood, Todd. *Butterfield Overland Stage Route.* http:www.frontiertrails.com/oldwest/butterfield.htm (accessed 23 August 2008).
U.S. Department of State. "Gadsden Purchase, 1853–1854." http://www.state.gov/r/pa/ho/time/dwe/87721.html (accessed 26 April 2008).
Utley, Robert M. *The Indian Frontier of the American West, 1846–1890.* Albuquerque: University of New Mexico Press, 1984.
_____. *A Life Wild and Perilous: Mountain Men and the Paths to the Pacific.* New York: Holt, 1997.
Vestal, Stanley. *The Old Santa Fe Trail.* Lincoln: University of Nebraska Press, 1996.
de Villagrá, Gaspar Pérez. "*Historia de la Nueva México.*" National Humanities Center. www.nationalhumanitiescenter.org/pds/amerbegin/exploration/text1/villagra.pdf (accessed 14 April 2008).
Walker, Henry P., and Don Bufkin. *Historical Atlas of Arizona.* Norman: University of Oklahoma Press, 1986.
Ward, Tom and Carolyn. "Cyrus K. Holliday." http://skyways.lib.ks.us/genweb/archives/1918ks/bioh/hollidck.html (accessed 27 February 2009).
Warner, Ted J., ed. *The Domínguez-Escalante Journal: Their Expedition through Colorado,*

Utah, Arizona, and New Mexico in 1776. Translated by Fray Angelico Chavez. Salt Lake City: University of Utah Press, 1995.

Waters, L.L. *Steel Trails to Santa Fe.* Lawrence: University of Kansas Press, 1950.

Weber, David J. *The Taos Trappers: The Fur Trade in the Far Southwest, 1540–1846.* Norman: University of Oklahoma Press, 1982.

_____. *The Spanish Frontier in North America.* New Haven: Yale University Press, 1992.

_____. *What Caused the Pueblo Revolt of 1680?* Boston: St. Martin's, 1999.

Wislizenus, F.A. *A Journey to the Rocky Mountains in the Year 1839.* New York: Cosimo, 2005.

_____. *Memoir of a Tour to Northern Mexico Connected with Col. Doniphan's Expedition in 1846 and 1847.* Albuquerque: Calvin Horn, 1969.

Woodbury, Richard B. *60 Years of Southwestern Archeology: A History of the Pecos Conference.* Albuquerque: University of New Mexico Press, 1993.

Index

Abert, James W. 10, 14, 70, 102, 115, 116
Abiquiú 73, 75, 77, 92
Acoma pueblo 36, 37, 42, 43, 44, 186
Adams, Andy 148
Ágreda, María de Jesús of (also known as "Lady in Blue") 45
Amangual, Francisco 59–60
Anasazi Indians 1, 17, 18, 20
Anza, Juan Bautista de 49–52
Apache Indians 1, 7, 9, 11, 12, 21, 37, 41, 42, 45, 46, 48, 49, 51, 52, 57, 65, 71, 80, 83, 84, 108, 111, 125, 129, 135, 138, 139, 144, 152, 157, 163, 166, 168, 170, 171, 172, 173, 174, 175, 181, 192, 193, 194, 195
Apache Pass Trail 163, 170–175
Argonauts (gold seekers) 163, 164
Armijo, Manuel 104, 105, 114, 118, 119, 179
Atchison, Topeka and Santa Fe Railroad (abbreviated Santa Fe or AT&SF) 70, 112, 152–153, 154, 155, 156, 157, 158, 160, 161, 182, 193
Aubry, Francis Xavier 109–111, 151–152

Barceló, María Gertrudis v, 103–105
Battle of Glorieta Pass 112, 130–131, 181
Becknell, William 92–93
Bent's Fort 85, 105, 114, 118, 154, 192
Bigotes (Pecos Indian war captain) 8, 32
Bosque Redondo 132, 134–135, 137, 138, 139–140, 181
Brewerton, George Douglas 80, 85–86
Butterfield Overland Mail and John Butterfield 121–126, 144, 175, 180, 210

Cabeza de Vaca 23–26, 27, 28, 29, 34
El Camino ... *see under* El
Canby, Edward R.S. 84, 128–129, 131
Canyon de Chelly 137–138
Carleton, James H. 84, 85, 132, 133–136, 137, 139, 172, 173

Carson, Christopher "Kit" 2, 3, 80–85, 86, 115, 128, 134, 136, 137, 138
Castañeda, Pedro de 8, 28, 30, 31
Castaño de Sosa, Gaspar 9, 10, 38–40
Castillo, Diego del 45–46
Central Pacific Railway 154
Chaco Canyon 17–20, 177
Chamuscado, Francisco Sánchez 33, 34, 35, 36, 38, 40
Cheyenne Indians 80, 81, 84, 92
Chihuahua Trail 61
Chronicle of the Narváez Expedition 24; *see also* Cabeza de Vaca
Cíbola 8, 27, 28, 29, 30
Ciboleros (Mexican buffalo hunters) 100–101
Civil War 5, 11, 84, 85, 112, 121, 126, 127–131, 141, 143, 176, 181
Cochise (Apache chief) 172–173
Comanche Indians 7, 12–13, 41, 48, 49, 51–52, 57, 58, 59, 84, 94, 95, 111, 145, 171, 191, 192
Comanchería (region of the Great Plains) 57
Comancheros (low-income Spaniards) 52, 95
Commerce of the Prairies 13, 102, 106; *see also* Gregg, Josiah
Concho pearls 45–46
Cooke, Philip St. George 166–167
Coronado, Francisco Vásquez de 8, 29–33, 35, 43, 122, 177
Coronado National Monument 177–178
Council of the Indies 40, 42, 50

Denver and Rio Grande Railroad (abbreviated D&RG) 112, 155–156
Domínguez, Anastasio 7, 52–54, 56, 75
Domínguez, Juan de Mondoza 46–47
Domínguez-Escalante expedition 52–56, 75
"Drill, ye tarriers, drill" (folksong) 158–159

Index

El Camino Real de Tierra Adentro (Royal Road to the Interior Land) 34, 44, 61–70, 91, 105, 107, 117, 119, 164, 178

El Paso del Norte (Pass of the North; later renamed Juarez) 34–35, 36, 40, 47, 59, 61, 63, 65, 66, 67, 68, 70, 122, 128, 163, 175, 178

El Turco ("the Turk") 31, 32

Emory, William Hemsley 168–169

Entradas (Spanish expeditions) 9, 22, 23, 26, 29, 30, 32, 34, 35, 36, 38, 39, 40, 43, 44, 46, 50, 53, 55, 56, 63, 102, 177, 185

Espejo, Antonio de 9, 10, 36–38, 40

Estevánico (also known as Estevan) 23, 27, 28

Fort Smith–Santa Fe trail 91, 188–191

Fort Union 91, 111–112, 127–128, 129, 131

Frémont, John C. 81–82

Gadsden Purchase 2, 127, 152

Garcés, Francisco 73–75

Garrard, Lewis H. 106–107, 191–193, 206, 210

Geronimo (Apache chief) 1, 163, 173–175, 193, 194, 195–196, 210

Gila River 24–25, 30, 50, 72, 74, 80, 82, 92, 115, 135, 163, 165–166, 167, 168, 169, 171, 182

Gila River Trail 72, 115, 163, 165–170, 182–183, 193

Gila Wilderness 163, 168, 170

Gleed, Charles S. 153, 160, 161

Gold, God, and glory 10, 22, 33, 46

Goodnight, Charles 143–147, 146, 147, 181

Goodnight-Loving Trail 141–148, 181–182

Gregg, Josiah 13, 52, 69, 91, 94, 96–97, 102, 103, 106; see also *Commerce of the Prairies*

Guadalajara, Diego de 46

Gutiérrez, Antonio 40–41, 42

Harvey, Fred 154–155, 193

Hatcher, John L. ("Long") 165, 191, 192–193

"Hidalgo-mania" 41–42

Hopi Indians 20, 37, 52

Imaginary coins 68–69

Indian trade routes and trade 17, 18, 20–21

"Iron Horse" 91, 149, 150, 151, 152, 153, 154, 155, 156, 157, 158, 159, 160–161, 179, 182; see also Railroads

Jornada del Muerto (Day's Journey of the Dead Man) 65, 66, 89, 107–108

Juan Bautista de Anza National Historic Trail 51

Jumano Indians 33–34, 45, 46–47

Kearny, Stephen Watts 9, 82, 99, 114–115, 118, 119, 166, 179

Kidder, Alfred K. 15

Kivas 6, 11, 18, 30, 37

Leyva, Francisco 40–41, 42

Long Walk of the Navajos 84, 132, 133, 135–139, 181

López, Diego 45

López, Nicolás 46–47

Loving, Oliver 143, 144, 145, 181

Magoffin, Susan Shelby 13–14, 70, 103, 104, 114, 117–120

Manifest Destiny, concept of 113, 135

Marcy, Randolph B. 66, 91, 96, 110, 175, 188–189, 191

Mares, José 58–59

Martín, Hernando 45–46

Mexican-American War 2, 35, 79, 81, 82, 100, 104, 113–120, 127, 113–131, 152, 166, 168, 179–180

Miera y Pacheco, Bernardo 19, 53, 54, 55

Mojave Indians 74, 77, 94

Mormon Road 88

Mountain Men 76, 78–79, 80–81, 85, 87, 94, 96, 106–107, 154, 165, 191–193

Mules, advantages 50–51

Navajo Indians 17, 19, 20, 80, 84, 85, 87, 132–140, 144, 181

New Spain 3, 9, 26, 29, 37, 38, 42, 44, 47, 48, 50, 68, 73

Niza, Marcos de 27–29, 30

Northern Mystery 53

Old Spanish Trail 56, 71–88; trade 75–76, 77–80, 85–86, 178–179

Oñate, Juan de 10, 38, 40–44, 62–63, 71, 185–186

Ormsby, Waterman L. 125–126

Ortega, Pedro de 45

Pawnee Indians 47, 192

Pecos Pueblo 5–15, 30–31, 32, 39, 42, 58, 59, 176–177, 181

Pecos River 8, 10, 39, 45, 47, 130, 132, 134, 144–145, 154, 156, 190

Pecos Wilderness 176–177

Pima Indians 21, 52, 164, 165, 166, 167

Pineda, Álvarez Alonso de 22–23

Pratt, Orville C. 86–87

Provincias Internas (Interior Provinces) 50

Index

Pueblo Bonito 17–18, 19
Pueblo Indians 65, 71, 135, 158
Pueblo Revolt 11, 34, 65

Quivera 31, 32, 41, 43

Railroads 91, 112, 116, 123, 126, 141, 146, 149–162, 182
Raton Pass 89, 116, 145, 146, 154, 155, 156, 182
Rio Grande River 2, 5, 8, 10, 20, 24, 26, 33, 34, 35, 36, 39, 40, 42, 47, 51, 63, 65, 66, 71, 84, 108, 111, 112, 115, 120, 128, 129, 130, 138, 156, 157, 160, 185, 186, 188
Rivera, Pedro de 47–49, 68
Rodríguez, Agustín 33–37
Rodríguez-Chamuscado expedition 33–36
Rubí, Marqués de 47–49
Ruxton, George F. 98, 107–109

Salas, Juan de 45
Santa Fe 2, 5, 11, 12, 13, 14, 15, 17, 20, 39, 41, 45, 46, 47, 48, 49, 52, 53, 54, 55, 56, 57, 58, 59, 61, 63, 64, 68, 69, 70, 71, 72, 73, 75, 76, 77, 79, 80, 82, 84, 86, 89, 91, 92, 93, 95, 99, 100, 101–102, 103, 104, 105, 108, 110, 111, 112, 114, 115, 118, 119, 120, 129, 131, 135, 136, 138, 139, 151, 156, 157, 161, 163, 178, 179, 180, 186, 187, 188, 191, 193, 202, 203
Santa Fe trade 14, 56, 58, 69–70, 83, 86, 91, 92, 93, 94, 95, 98, 99, 109–110, 117; freight wagons 93; international aspects of the trade 93
Santa Fe Trail 2, 6, 13, 14, 58, 69, 70, 76, 83, 86, 89–112, 114, 116, 117, 128, 129, 130, 149, 151, 153, 156, 160, 176, 179
Sibley, Henry Hopkins 127–129, 131
Silver and silver mines 9, 20, 26, 29, 31, 32, 33, 34, 35, 36, 37, 41, 42, 43, 61, 63, 64, 73, 127, 156, 185

Slave trade 2, 7, 12, 22, 23, 25, 26, 27, 33, 38, 40, 56, 87–88, 113
Smith, Jedediah Strong 94–96
Southern Pacific Railroad (abbreviated SP) 151, 153–154
Southern Trail 163, 164–165, 171
Spanish monte (card game) 102–103, 105

Taos Trail 105–106, 191
Taovaya Indians 56, 57, 58, 59
Teguas Indians 14
Teja [Teya] Indians 8–9, 46, 47
Trappers 29, 47, 76, 81, 92, 98, 105, 108, 163; *see also* Mountain Men
Treaty of Guadalupe Hidalgo 2, 35, 113, 169
Trinity (code name) 66–67
El Turco 31, 32
Twain, Mark 124–125

Union Pacific Railway 144, 154
Upper and Lower Emigrant Trails 163, 171, 175
Ute (or Yuta) Indians 51, 71, 80, 87, 111, 135, 154, 191

Vargas, Diego de 11
Vélez de Escalante, Silvestre 52–56, 75
Vial, Pedro 56–58
Villagraá, Gaspar Pérez de 44, 185–186
Villasur, Pedro de 47

Wislizenus, F. Adolph 99–101
Wolfskill, William 76–77
Wootton, Richard Lacy ("Uncle Dick") 146, 154

Yount, George C. 76, 77
Yuma Indians 74

Zárate, Ascencio de 45
Zuni Trail 163, 165

www.ingramcontent.com/pod-product-compliance
Lightning Source LLC
Chambersburg PA
CBHW032052300426
44116CB00007B/704